CONTENDING THEORIES ON DEVELOPMENT AID

Contending Theories on Development Aid
Post-Cold War evidence from Africa

LESLIE O. OMORUYI
East Carolina University

LONDON AND NEW YORK

First published 2001 by Ashgate Publishing

Reissued 2018 by Routledge
2 Park Square, Milton Park, Abingdon, Oxon OX14 4RN
711 Third Avenue, New York, NY 10017, USA

Routledge is an imprint of the Taylor & Francis Group, an informa business

Copyright © Leslie O. Omoruyi 2001

The author has asserted his moral right under the Copyright, Designs and Patents Act, 1988, to be identified as the author of this work.

All rights reserved. No part of this book may be reprinted or reproduced or utilised in any form or by any electronic, mechanical, or other means, now known or hereafter invented, including photocopying and recording, or in any information storage or retrieval system, without permission in writing from the publishers.

Notice:
Product or corporate names may be trademarks or registered trademarks, and are used only for identification and explanation without intent to infringe.

Publisher's Note
The publisher has gone to great lengths to ensure the quality of this reprint but points out that some imperfections in the original copies may be apparent.

Disclaimer
The publisher has made every effort to trace copyright holders and welcomes correspondence from those they have been unable to contact.

A Library of Congress record exists under LC control number: 2001093267

ISBN 13: 978-1-138-70136-6 (hbk)
ISBN 13: 978-0-415-79297-4 (pbk)
ISBN 13: 978-1-315-21004-9 (ebk)

Table of Contents

List of Figures   vi

List of Tables   vii

Acknowledgements   viii

PART ONE

1 Introduction   1

2 Scholarship on the Motivation Question: Pieces of a Similar Puzzle   11

3 Variables, Hypotheses and Methodology   38

4 The Findings: Realist Lore and Liberal Principles: Another Case for Muted Optimism   48

PART TWO (THE STUDY OF FOUR CASES)

5 France: The Enduring Salience of *Besoin de Rayonnement*   87

6 Japan: A Rear Entry into Great Power Rank   106

7 Norway: The Inexorable Influence of National Role Conception?   129

8 USA: Simultaneous Tides of Retrenchment and Recommitment   145

9 Rethinking Aid to Sub-Saharan Africa in the New Millennium: Enduring Threats and Opportunities for a New Partnership   160

Appendices   191

Bibliography   202

Index   218

List of Figures

5.1   France's Gross Bilateral ODA Allocation (1998) by Income Group   99

5.2   France's Gross Bilateral ODA Allocation (1998) by Region   99

5.3   Scattergram Showing the Favorite Recipients of France's Bilateral ODA (1990-1997)   103

6.1   Scattergram Showing the Favorite Recipients of Japan's Bilateral ODA (1990-1997)   114

6.2   Japan's Gross Bilateral ODA Allocation (1998) by Income Group   119

6.3   Japan's Gross Bilateral ODA Allocation (1998) by Region   119

7.1   Scattergram Showing the Favorite Recipients of Norway's Bilateral ODA (1990-1997)   132

7.2   Norway's Gross Bilateral ODA Allocation (1998) by Income Group   142

7.3   Norway's Gross Bilateral ODA Allocation (1998) by Region   142

8.1   Scattergram Showing the Favorite Recipients of USA's Bilateral ODA (1990-1997)   153

8.2   USA's Gross Bilateral ODA Allocation (1998) by Income Group   156

8.3   USA's Gross Bilateral ODA Allocation (1998) by Region   156

List of Tables

2.1	Parallel Theoretical Perspectives on Aid to Sub-Saharan Africa	32
4.1	Results of Pooled Time-Series Regression for Bilateral ODA and Independent Variables (1990-1997)	51
5.1	Top Ten Recipients of France's Global ODA in 1998	97
5.2	Comparison of Favorite Recipients of France's ODA to Sub-Saharan Africa (Cold War Years v Post-Cold War Period)	100
5.3	Dimensions of France's ODA (1991-1997)	102
6.1	Dimensions of Japan's ODA (1991-1997)	117
6.2	Top Ten Recipients of Japan's Global ODA (1998)	118
7.1	Dimensions of Norway's ODA (1991-1997)	134
7.2	Comparison of Favorite Recipients of Norway's ODA to Sub-Saharan Africa (Cold War Years v Post-Cold War Period)	137
7.3	Top Ten Recipients of Norway's Global ODA (1998)	140
8.1	Dimensions of US ODA (1991-1997)	151
8.2	Comparison of Favorite Recipients of US ODA to Sub-Saharan Africa (Cold War Years v Post-Cold War Period)	152
8.3	Top Ten Recipients of US Global ODA (1998)	155
9.1	Geographic Distribution of Financial Flows (Total ODA net) from DAC Donors by Region (1960-1997)	165
9.2	Results from a Sample of Scholarly Studies Measuring the Effectiveness of Aid	169
9.3	Geographic Distribution of Financial Flows (Direct Investment) from DAC Donors by Region (1960-1997)	173

Acknowledgements

The pleasurable devoir of acknowledging the efforts of the people whose intellectual, material and moral support over the years have contributed in one form or the other to the completion of this book is somewhat analogous to attempting to re-erect the scaffold of a completed building. No matter how diligent one might be one could never quite recall the exact contributions of all the people whose labors have yielded the emergent product. For me, the charge is rendered doubly challenging because of the temporal gap between the completion of my undergraduate studies at the University of Jos, Nigeria; my relocation to the United States; my commencement and completion of graduate studies at University of Connecticut, Storrs; and my acceptance of a teaching appointment at East Carolina University. A list of all those who may properly claim to find prints of their influence on my thoughts and world-view is, therefore, quite long, hence I must restrict myself to that which even a faded memory can readily recall.

I owe my earliest intellectual development and interest in the dialectical method of inquiry to my father. Although lacking formal education, his steepness in the rich oral and cultural history of the Edo speaking people of mid-western Nigeria provided the opportunity for my earliest encounter with the techniques of inquiry. The oral-traditional method of inquiry of the Edo speaking people imbues parables, proverbs and rhetoric with architectonic elements, which then serve to further and clarify earnest and intelligent discourse. The contagion of my father's passion for this tradition kindled in me the zeal to explore the unfamiliar more deeply, and scrutinize the orthodox with fresh skepticism.

My mom remains my primary source of inspiration, comfort and joy. Absent her understanding, faith in my dreams and support for my goals, this project would have been a non-starter. Other members of my immediate and extended family have, over the years, demonstrated their love and affection for me in countless ways. To them I express my profound gratitude.

At the University of Jos, Aaron Gana, Ali Mazrui, and Omafume Onoge were the first teachers to stoke my interest in scholarly endeavor. That interest was reinforced at the University of Connecticut where I benefited from the support and criticisms of many teachers including, Larry Bowman, John Rourke, Gary Clifford, Fred Turner, Fred Burke, Rich Hiskes, Jeffrey Lefebvre, Lucy Creevy, Henry Krisch, Carmen Cirricioni, Martha Gibson, and Robert Gilmore. I owe a more intangible and general debt to Mark Boyer, Rich Vengroff, and Betty Hanson for their contributions to my intellectual development. Mark

Boyer's scholarly interests, insights, and devotion to the teaching of international relations provided a point of departure for my own foray into the subject of foreign aid. As the major advisor on my doctoral dissertation committee, he patiently read numerous drafts of this book while it was still in its formative dissertation stage, and provided invaluable direction, criticisms, and encouragement along the way. Rich Vengroff generously availed me his expertise on Africa, read many drafts of my dissertation and offered many suggestions that have contributed to this book. As much as his intellectual inspiration and guidance, the example of his kindness and understanding has reinforced my faith in the common bond that binds us all. Betty Hanson's encouragement and well-meaning criticisms sharpened my intellectual reflexes and compelled me to reexamine the claims tendered by the realist/neorealist paradigm about the nature of international relations. While I retain a healthy admiration for the analytical insights offered by the giants of that paradigm, I have become richly skeptical about the accuracy of many of their claims. Remarkably, just as the affection that David Walker has shown towards me has been comforting, so have his wisdom and guidance been inspiring. I am immensely grateful to him.

My thanks also go to Penn Handwerker of the Anthropology Department at University of Connecticut who was my major resource person on the methodological issues relating to this book. He helped me navigate the arcane contours of time-series analysis, and enriched my understanding of quantitative methods in the process.

Here at East Carolina University, I have enjoyed the friendship of many colleagues especially Festus Eribo, and Nancy Spalding who read and offered suggestions on strengthening the chapter on Japan. Rick Kearney offered me a teaching opportunity here in the Department of Political Science, and provided me with material support for the completion of this book. In the course of coming to know him, his wife Kathy, and their son Joel, I have been blessed by their kindness and friendship. As the chairman of the Political Science department, my mentor, colleague, and friend, Rick has been a trusted guide, an insightful critic, and a good friend.

In reading and criticizing portions of the thoughts and ideas that metamorphosed into this book, Jami Leibowitz rescued me from the many errors one tends to make when one thinks alone for too long. I gratefully acknowledge her support over the years. The conversion of this book from thoughts to printed material was facilitated by the cooperation and hard work of Christy Sims and Pamela Cox. I am grateful to them for their patience and diligence. I am also grateful to Sarah Horsley of Ashgate Publishing Company for her invaluable editorial assistance. I alone bear the responsibility for the criticisms of this book.

Leslie Omoruyi
Greenville, North Carolina

Part One

Part One

1 Introduction

Setting and Purpose

Although the affairs of humanity do not occur in neat temporal packages, few events of the 20th century rival in their historic significance, dramatic symbolism, and confounding coincidence, the fateful events of December 25, 1991. On that day, Mikhail Gorbachev, then president of the Union of the Soviet Socialist Republic (USSR), marking his final hours in office, telephoned his American counterpart, President George Bush, to bid him good-bye. A few hours later, the red flag bearing the hammer and sickle emblem of the USSR was lowered for the last time, and a new flag of a Russia with curtailed ambitions was hoisted in its place. Like the epochal events of the preceding two years – the fall of the Berlin Wall in 1989, the unification of Germany in 1990, and the break away of the Baltic republics of Estonia, Latvia and Lithuania from the USSR in 1991 – this event was a symbolic testimony to the end of the Cold War. In its aftermath, the theoretical edifice of realism as the dominant paradigm in the study of international relations has come under vigorous attack. Whereas it was once considered heretical in the discipline to question the assumptions of realism and its variants, it is now deemed necessary to "revise, reconstruct or more boldly, reject its theoretical postulates" (Kegley, 1995:3). This peeling of the prophylactic that once sheltered realism is attributable to the triumph of neo-liberal ideas.

One of the many areas in the discipline where the realist - liberal divide has been sharpest is in studies of the motivations for the flow of foreign aid from advanced-industrial countries (AICs) to African states. Although many realists claim that African states, and indeed the whole of the Third World lack *intrinsic* strategic significance to the West, throughout much of the Cold War period, the realist justification for the allocation of foreign aid to African states was the strategic imperative inherent in the containment of communism.[1]

---

[1] Within the realist school of thought, there exists an inferred unanimity on the peripheral nature of sub-Saharan African states to the core interests of the West. This consensus is, perhaps, attributable to the tendency of many realists to hierarchically divide issues of international relations into high and low politics. There is, however, ambiguity among realists about whether particular states in sub-Saharan Africa are of intrinsic, extrinsic, or zero strategic significance to AICs. For a discussion of the intra-paradigm disagreement on the relevance of the Third World in realist theory, see Desch 1996. Remarkably, Desch

Some liberal theorists, on the other hand, posit that during this period, "developed countries provided aid [to the Third World] mainly because of their belief that they had a humane responsibility to do so" (Lumsdaine 1993:283).[2] Lumsdaine's arguments notwithstanding, a review of the literature on foreign aid reveals that a majority of scholars support the realist position that the containment of communism played a significant role in the allocation of aid to developing countries, especially for a donor such as the United States.[3] Now that the Cold War has ended, it is unclear what motivations undergird the aid policies of the key members of the Development Assistance Committee (DAC). Equally puzzling are the reasons why these donors should continue to coordinate their aid efforts, as suggested by Boyer (1993), in the absence of a potent security threat to the Western alliance. Moreover, initial review of the record of the aid allocation pattern of DAC member-states in the post Cold War period appears to contradict the propositions of realism and liberalism on the motivation question. For if the realist explanation that donors use aid to serve their disparate national interest is correct, it is not clear why a county like Malawi should attract so much aid from a donor like Germany with no clear national interest in a region like sub-Saharan Africa. The suggestion by liberal theory that donors provide aid to developing countries for humanitarian reasons and the promotion of democracy around the world is equally problematic. For if that is the case, why has bilateral aid from all DAC member states to sub-Saharan Africa not disproportionately gone to the poorest countries, or to those with more impressive records on democratization? It is also puzzling that despite the euphoria generated by the transformation of the international system from a bipolar to an increasingly multipolar one, and the great expectations about increased North-South cooperation stimulated by the triumph of liberal ideas, the prosperity gap between rich and poor countries in general continues to widen. And more specifically, countries in sub-Saharan Africa continue to experience intense marginalization in the international system.

---

argues elsewhere that with respect to the United States, certain parts of the Third World have extrinsic value to its strategic interests. He identified these areas (which did not include sub-Saharan Africa) as the Caribbean, the Indian Ocean littoral and the Western Pacific (Desch, 1989: 113). For a more elaborate argument about the irrelevance of the Third World, especially to US strategic interests, see Van Evera (1990). For a counter argument to Desch and Evera's positions, see David (1989) and (1992).

[2] Other liberal scholars, for example, Pearson (1969), Brandt (1980), Keohane (1977), (1984), and Stokke (1996) argue the case for foreign aid on the grounds that it promotes free trade, democracy and good governance.

[3] Examples of works, which make such arguments, include Pincus (1967), Nelson (1968), Wittkopf (1972), Organski (1990), Mansour (1994), and Schraeder (1995).

If therefore, the propositions of both realist and liberal theories are lacking in their resolution of these puzzles, what then are the motivations for the allocation of aid to sub-Saharan Africa in the post-Cold War period? How much has the transformation of the international system influenced these motivations? What are the implications of these motivations for sub-Saharan Africa in particular, and the larger international system in general? These are the questions, which animated this study. My primary objective has been to assess the adequacy of realist and liberal theories on the motivation question. In a sense, such a focus is problematic since the complexity of the motivations behind each donor's foreign aid policy is inexplicable by any single factor or set of factors. The argument which I present, however, is that despite the multiplicity of issues pushing and pulling foreign policy in, sometimes, unpredictable directions, the flow of development assistance to sub-Saharan Africa has recurrent patterns, which could be better understood by comparing the primary propositions of the dominant theories of international relations on why states behave the way they do. An adequate theoretical framework should be able to account for the broad similarities and differences in the factors motivating different donor countries to disburse aid to sub-Saharan African states. All donor countries are sovereign entities that, though encumbered by the constraints of anarchy as realists contend, do have ample latitude to define and pursue their interests as they see fit. An important observation of this study is that in the post-Cold War era, neither the assumptions of traditional realism about an unchanging world where military might will always be the most effective determinant of international relations, nor liberal theory's expectation of the emergence of a more humane, just and benevolent order where the states in the international system will have a harmony of interest, adequately explain the motivations which translate donors interests into foreign aid allocations.

Relevance of the Study

This study is relevant for several reasons. First, while considerable descriptive and analytic work has been produced on the effects of the end of the Cold War on international relations in general, there is a dearth of works that measure the effects of this system transformation on the allocation of aid to a resource needy region like sub-Saharan Africa. This is despite the impressive scope of the foreign aid literature in general.[4] Given that the Cold War ended about a decade ago, this is, perhaps, understandable.

---
[4] Stating the case for the alleged dearth of 'critical analysis' on the motivation for aid in the foreign aid literature, Schraeder, Hook and Taylor (1998), opined: "...except for the pioneering work of McKinlay and the recent analysis of Hook, there has been a dearth of systematic

Second, even though foreign policy decisions are seldom amenable to the often mutually exclusive categories suggested by the realist – liberal divide, it is of some heuristic relevance to ascertain whether on balance, foreign aid allocations to sub-Saharan African states reflect the theoretical propositions of realism, or the postulation of liberalism. Bearing in mind the influence which dominant paradigms tend to exert on the foreign policies of advanced-industrial states (especially the United States), the results from this type of research could call such theoretical assertions into question. Moreover, as Kegley (1993:142) reminds us:

> The realist-idealist dialogue can be informed by the insights generated through scientific investigation without requiring acceptance of the logical positivists' most extreme claims about the possibility of an objective science. Scholars can creatively build new theories and refine old ones on the basis of concrete evidence and deduction.

A third way in which this study is useful is that, an understanding of the motivations undergirding the allocation of aid to sub-Saharan Africa by the members of the DAC, and the adequacy of the propositions of theories of international relations on the subject, could supply valuable insights into the behavior of aid-donor states in relation to adjacent fields like foreign investment and trade policies. Besides, the current era in international relations - the end of the Cold War coupled with systemic turbulence[5] - presents ample opportunities for one to peek into broader intra-disciplinary debates such as the propositions of liberal theory about the "democratic peace" and the arguments of realist theory with respect to the notion of relative gains. The

---

and critical analysis of the donor side of the equation." It is certainly true that McKinlay's 1979 work and his series of studies with R.D. Little (1977, 1978a, 1978b, and 1979) have enhanced our understanding of the determinants of foreign aid. And while it is equally true that Schraeder, Hook and Taylor's recent work has contributed to the body of knowledge on foreign aid, a review of the literature reveals that their assessment is not quite accurate. To be sure, a careful review of the foreign aid literature reveals that, not only is there an impressively dense body of work on "the donor side of the equation", but also scholarly investigations of the motivation question have, for the most part, proceeded along a cumulative part whereby different scholars, building on previous efforts sought to refine their methodologies in furtherance of a more coherent understanding of the foreign aid puzzle. Examples of these are: Davenport (1970), Henderson (1971), Wittkopf (1972), Maizels and Nissanke (1984), Mosley (1985), (1987), McGillivray (1989), Rultan (1989), Stokke (1989a), (1989b), (1991), Brown (1990), Robinson, (1993), Boyer (1993), Lumsdaine (1993), Bobrow and Boyer (1995), (1996), Cassen (1994), Tisch and Wallace (1994), and Patterson (1997).

[5] Systemic turbulence is used here to denote what Rosenau (1990), refers to as the simultaneous existence of change and continuity.

proposition that democratic states do not go to war with one another has emerged as the new orthodoxy in studies of international relations. For some scholars, this proposition is so persuasive that it is "as close as anything we have to an empirical law in international relations" (Levy, 1989:270). Yet, as Mueller (1989), Layne (1996), Caprioli (1998) and numerous other scholars have pointed out, the propositions of democratic peace are flawed in several ways. In particular, incidents of war, the premise upon which arguments for the democratic peace have been most frequently tested are such historically rare events that a statistically significant finding of zero war among democratic states in the international system, which boasted few democratic states until recently, is statistically insignificant (Spiro, 1996). An examination of the foreign aid policies of Western donors to sub-Saharan African states in the post-Cold War era, therefore, could serve as additional relevant test of the democratic peace proposition. If the democratic peace theory is correct, one should find greater degrees of peaceful cooperation between AICs and democratizing states in developing countries. With respect to sub-Saharan Africa, such cooperation should translate into more aid disbursements to states with relatively more impressive records on democratization.

A focus on the motivation for foreign aid allocation could also supply additional, even if tentative, insights into the veracity of the neorealist argument about the salience of relative gains in cooperation among states, especially now that the Cold War is over. Neorealists, such as Layne (1992), Waltz (1993), and Measheimer (1990, 1995a, 1995b), for examples, contend that with the end of the Cold War, the international system is undergoing transition from a bipolar structure to a multipolar one. Reasoning along the same lines, other realists, like Grieco (1991), assert that because states are relative-gains maximizers, such structural shifts would reinforce the salience of the relative gains problem in international cooperation. An examination of the motivation for the allocation of foreign aid to sub-Saharan African states, therefore, promises valuable insights into the veracity of such positions.

Furthermore, just as traditional realists have argued that a state's intentions are shaped by its capabilities (Morgenthau, 1973:5), neorealists have reiterated that when a state climbs to the highest rungs of the international ladder, as Japan has done in recent years, it will "try to expand its economic, political, and territorial control; it will try to change the international system in accordance with its own interests" (Gilpin, 1987:94-95). An examination of the behavior of seemingly ambitious states such as Japan and Germany in sub-Saharan Africa, therefore, could contribute valuable strokes to the intellectual sketches of the emerging structure of the international system.

This study is relevant for a sixth, and perhaps, even more important reason: of the many issues competing for scholarly attention since the end of the Cold War - nuclear proliferation, resurgent nationalism, the expansion of NATO, the European Union, and the intensification of global economic competition - arguably, none presents a more realistic and immediate external threat to sub-Saharan African states as much as the fate of foreign aid. Pertinently, as a review of global financial flows from 1960-1997 shows, during the Cold War era, despite the low levels of financial transfers from advance industrialized states to sub-Saharan Africa, compared to other regions, such transactions represented the largest financial transfers to the sub-continent.[6] Since the global economy began to attain greater degrees of integration in the 1970s, the future of sub-Saharan African states has increasingly depended on the willingness of AICs and international organizations to provide the region with finance for development, because of the reluctance of private lenders to fund development projects whose viability are not readily measured by their short term profitability. In essence, given the high dependency rates of some sub-Saharan African states on foreign aid, an examination of the donors' motivations for aid allocation may yield findings which could help generate policy relevant suggestions for such dependent states on how they could better attract other forms of development assistance and manage their scarce resources. The contradictory tendencies which one observes in the features of the contemporary global economy - the triumph of liberal ideas and an increasing economic marginalization of sub-Saharan African states, evident in the inability of a majority of the sub-continent's peoples to afford the most basic needs of adequate food and shelter - lend even greater credence to the urgency of policy relevant studies.

The Argument

Results from this study provide ample support for several propositions. First, the discarding of the Cold War mask brings us face to face with an unsettling reality: despite the divergence of motivations behind the allocation of aid to sub-Saharan Africa by the prominent donors whose aid policies are investigated in this study, the results from this study speak with a single voice about the continuous marginalization of sub-Saharan Africa in the emerging structure of the international system. Just as the low levels of statistical correlation between ODA and the independent variables derived from the propositions of realist and liberal theories in this study, indicate the difficulty of applying mainstream IR thinking to the study of sub-Saharan Africa (*marginalization 1*), so has there been, in the post-Cold War period, a pattern of diversion of aid

---

[6] See *Geographic Distribution of Financial Flows to Aid Recipients, 1960-1997.* (CD-ROM). Paris, OECD (1998).

resources by hitherto generous donors away from the sub-continent to regions such as the newly independent states in the former Soviet Union and Eastern Europe (*marginalization 2*). These observations evince the peripheralization of sub-Saharan Africa at a time when the people of the sub-continent appear to have embraced the liberal ideas of democracy and capitalism, and advances in the technologies of communication, food production and storage have condensed the world into the now fabled global village.

Second, the original goal of poverty alleviation, the avowed objective of ODA in several DAC documents, has been a prominent feature in the pattern of aid allocation to sub-Saharan Africa in the post-Cold War period. Judged by the relative poverty of the recipient states, the grant element of ODA and the inverse correlation between aid and the values of the gross domestic product (GDP) of the recipient states, bilateral aid allocations to the region reveal strong humanitarian motives. This finding is at odds with the realist proposition about the parochial national interest motivation behind foreign aid. Among DAC members, however, there have been notable differences in the priority accorded this goal. The Scandinavian countries, more than France and Italy tended to disburse substantial portions of their bilateral aid, oftentimes 100 percent, as grants. This evidence provides support for the assertion by liberal scholars like Lumsdaine (1993:29) that foreign aid cannot be explained on the basis of the donors' economic and political interest alone.

Third, in the post-Cold War era, the pattern of bilateral aid allocation from the key members of the DAC to sub-Saharan Africa reveals a strong correlation with trade. With the exception of Japan and the United States, all other key donors whose aid policies were examined in this study tended to disburse aid, preferentially, to the sub-Saharan African countries, which imported greater amounts of goods from them. This finding provides tentative support for the neorealist's position about the self-interested motivation behind the flow of aid. Although, in comparison to their commercial interests in other parts of the world - for instance, the emerging markets in Asia and Latin America - most donors covered in this study have low levels of trade ties to sub-Saharan Africa. Arguably too, the profits that they receive from their existing trade ties with the region are marginal. Still, it is curious that within the interstices of such expected marginal returns, aid has dovetailed trade. A corollary neorealist proposition that aid recipient states naturally endowed with strategic minerals would attract more aid is not, however, statistically confirmed by the results of this study for most donors. With respect to sub-Saharan African states, "those who have what others want or badly need" (Waltz, 1979:147), have not been favored recipients of aid by most members of the DAC.

Fourth, whereas in the Cold War era, the allocation of aid to sub-Saharan

African states was unmindful of the type of political regimes in these states, the pattern of aid allocation to the region in the post-Cold War era, indicates a shift in favor of countries with relatively more impressive records on democratization for donors like Japan and Denmark. While being welcome this finding, nonetheless, falls short of a deep support for liberal values which the alleged triumph of liberal ideas occasioned by the demise of the Cold War would lead one to expect. For the majority of the donors covered in this study, the application of the democratization metric was not evident in their pattern of aid allocation to sub-Saharan Africa.

Finally, in the realm of theorizing about the nature and study of international relations, the neorealist's position, which asserts that structuralism exerts an inexorable influence on the behavior of states, pushing and shoving them into self-interest calculations, presents a partially useful perspective for understanding the pattern of aid allocation by countries such as Japan, France and Canada. It is, however, inadequate and flawed in several particulars for deciphering the motivations undergirding aid allocations even for a hegemonic power such as the United States. Neorealist theory is even more flawed as a normative standard for effecting positive change in the future of international relations. On the other hand, liberal theory, while being less coherent and parsimonious than its rival, offers in its embracement of the possibilities of positive and purposeful human action, more promise for the development of a mutually rewarding partnership between the DAC and sub-Saharan African states.

Subsequent Chapters: A Road Map

The following is a preview of the subsequent chapters in this study. In chapter two, I provide a review of the literature on the motivation question and point out how this study differs from pervious efforts. Synthesizing these divergent bodies of scholarship enables me to locate this study within the theoretical framework of the dominant theories of international relations and derive testable propositions, which then serve as my basis for (1) evaluating the motivations behind the allocation of aid, and (2) assessing the explanatory and predictive power of the two theories under investigation. I conclude chapter two by providing a brief discussion of the challenges of evaluating the explanatory power of rival theories of international relations. Doing this is valuable for two reasons: first, because reason, as Immanuel Kant exhorts us, "must approach nature not in the character of a pupil who must listen to all his master chooses to tell him, but in that of a judge who compels the witness to reply to all those questions which he himself thinks fit to propose" (Kant, 1990); the difficulties inherent in the evaluation of rival theories of international relations is worth underscoring so that the faltering of either theory in accounting for some of the questions it has been summoned to answer is not mistaken for its falsification. Second, I seek to call attention to an important, but little studied area of our discipline. Many of the propositions of realist and liberal theories are so opposite, and yet with the exception of Vasquez (1997), no systematic effort has been made to evaluate the comparative utility of some of the cardinal propositions tendered by both theories. Granted that such ventures must contend with some problematic issues, the stakes involved are too high for such task to remain *under-attempted*.[7]

In chapter three, I provide a detailed discussion of the methodology and variables I adopted for the study. The method by which I arrived at the mathematical calculation of the strategic mineral index (SMI), one of the original contributions of this study is also raised in this chapter and discussed in detail in Appendix I.

In chapter four I provide a table showing the results of the pooled time series regression calculation and then discuss these results. These results provide ample support for the assertion that, although the aid donors examined in this study appear to have incorporated the values of democratization, poverty reduction, and good governance as conditionalities for their aid recipients in sub-Saharan Africa, the diversion of aid resources away from the sub continent to other regions where aid is deemed more "rewarding" mutes optimism about the triumph of liberal ideas in the post-Cold War era.

Chapters five, six, seven, and eight are case studies of the patterns of French, Japanese, Denmark, Norway and Sweden, and the US ODA to sub-Saharan Africa in the post-Cold War period. The selection of these cases is based on multiple and important considerations which allow one to better understand the salience, or diminishing value of the propositions offered by realist/neorealist and liberal theories on the motivation question. The reason for the selection of France is straightforward. In addition to having a rich history of involvement in sub-Saharan Africa, France has, unquestionably, become the single highest donor of foreign aid to the sub continent in terms of absolute volume. A focus on the pattern of France's post-Cold War aid allocation to the region therefore, offers valuable insights into the influence, which historic and cultural ties tend to exert on foreign aid.

The rationale for selecting Japan is based on a consideration of the size of its global aid effort. Measured in absolute volume, Japan is currently the

---

[7] As Vasquez (1997:900), accurately observes "individual decisions about where scholars are willing to place their research bets as well as collective decisions as to which research programs deserve continued funding, publication and so forth" depend on perceptions about which of the rival theories has greater explanatory power.

highest foreign aid donor in the world. In recent years, it has begun a concerted effort to engage Africa in a new development partnership. It has sponsored international conferences intended to rekindle intellectual debates and the interest of the international community on the most productive approach to tackling the developmental challenges confronting African states. The Japanese government has also begun to actively encourage Japanese firms to invest in the region. Moreover, given the consideration that Japan's emergence as the largest aid donor in the world (in absolute volume), places her at an advantageous position to make her bid for great power status, evidence from Africa could provide valuable insights into Japan's behavior in the emerging structure of the international system.

As for the Scandinavian countries of Denmark, Norway, and Sweden, their widely acknowledged reputations as the most generous aid donors in the DAC (measured by the GNP/ODA ratio), coupled with their unique approach to development assistance present another perspective from which to understand the many faces of foreign aid in sub-Saharan Africa.

With respect to the United States, despite the unprecedented scale of retrenchment in its global aid programs in recent years, the fact that it remains, by many important indicators - economic muscle, military power, technological advancement, and intellectual capital - the most powerful nation-state in the international system, recommends that one examine the pattern of its post-Cold War aid allocation to sub-Saharan Africa in more detail. Besides, the contemporary evolution of development assistance has its roots in the United States. And even though in the post-Cold War period the US has only been the third largest bilateral aid donor to the sub continent (in absolute volume), the amount of its aid effort has been quite substantial. Any study of foreign aid, which omits a consideration of the United States would be patently incomplete.

Chapter nine synthesizes the discussions and findings of the study. This chapter also explores the opportunities for a stronger, mutually beneficial partnership between the DAC and sub-Saharan Africa on issues of development. In particular, I examine some of the reasons for the reductions in the volume of aid to the sub-continent. I also weigh in on the debate about whether this phenomenon is attributable to the allegation that aid to the region has been grossly ineffective.

Finally, because "thinking for thinking sake is as abnormal and barren as the miser's accumulation of money for its own sake" (Carr, 1946:3), in a concluding section to chapter nine, I offer policy relevant suggestions for promoting a new partnership between the members of the DAC and sub-Saharan Africa.

2 Scholarship on the Motivation Question: Pieces of a Similar Puzzle

By and large, the trajectory of scholarship on the motivation question has traversed the course of cumulative knowledge. This bears a striking resemblance to the development of *normal science* whereby succeeding generations of scholars seek to build on the efforts of their intellectual forebears by replicating and adjusting their propositions.[8] Even though the bulk of previous efforts on the motivation behind the foreign aid policies of members of the DAC have not expressly focused on the empirical evaluation of the dominant theories of international relations, it is possible to glean from these works, lines of inquiry and arguments approximating the theoretical propositions of realist and liberal theories.

One of the earliest efforts to investigate the motivations for the allocation of aid by the member states of the Organization of Economic Cooperation and Development (OECD) to developing countries was undertaken by Davenport in 1970. Using four independent variables - the level of real income as measured by per capita gross national product (GNP), the inflow of private capital as a percentage of GNP, foreign reserve assets as a percentage of imports, and the size of the recipient states' population - he observed that the foreign reserve ratio of the recipient state was the most significant predictor of aid allocated by the donor countries in his study. He also reported that there was no significant relationship between the amount of aid received by the recipient states and their GNP. This finding, he noted, suggested that since aid was not preferentially allocated to the poorer states, humanitarian concern was not the motivation behind the aid policies of the advanced industrial states.

In 1971, P. D. Henderson undertook a similar inquiry. While Davenport's study had focused on a universe of 34 developing countries in the period of 1962-64, Henderson's research broadened this universe to include 84

---

[8] For a discussion of the route and nature of normal science in the physical and natural sciences, see Kuhn (1970:10-35).

developing countries many having attained independence between 1958 and 1962. The independent variables he used were population, per capita GNP, and per capita GNP growth rates. He reported that, of these three variables, only the size of the recipient states' population had a significant correlation with the amount of aid disbursed to them by the donors. This relationship, however, was contrary to his predicted result because per capita aid from donor countries tended to decrease with the size of the recipient states' population.

I should note that this present study benefited a lot from Davenport and Henderson's insights. There are, however, significant differences between their pioneering study and my work. The most obvious difference is that this present study encompasses a different and broader time period – the post-Cold War era and an eight-year period respectively. The other difference is that, while Davenport adopted the three-year average aid allocation by the donors in his study as his dependent variable, I use the raw annual figures of the aid allocations by donors for the eight years covered by this study as my dependent variable. Davenport had defended his use of the average aid figures on the grounds that he needed to avoid some of the major distortions "in the normal patterns of aid caused by catastrophes such as the Chilean earthquake" of 1960 (p.27). His point is cogent and well taken. It underscores the necessity of controlling for the effects of episodic events on fluctuations in the normal patterns of aid given by donors to recipient states. I have borne this point in mind in my interpretation of the regression results for aid to countries such as Somalia, Burundi and Rwanda during the crises years in those countries. For the sake of delineating an accurate pattern of the flow of aid from donors to the recipient states in this study, however, it was necessary for me to use the actual values of the amount disbursed by donors as my dependent variable. Equally important is that, the use of the actual values of the disbursed amounts allows me to assess the predictive power of realism and liberalism by juxtaposing their propositions against the statistically significant independent variables which tend to pull and push the foreign aid policies of donor states toward, sometimes, unpredictable directions.

Another respect in which this present study differs from Davenport's pioneering work is that it goes beyond the exclusive economic independent variables that he used in his study. Recall that the four independent variables in his study were levels of real income, inflow of private capital, foreign reserve assets, and population. The restriction of the variables used to tap into the motivation question to only economic ones is problematic because it does not take into account the political nature of foreign aid. This point appeared not to have been lost on Davenport, because by his admission, "to try to explain the patterns of aid allocation on economic criteria [alone] is a hopeless task" (p.36). Yet his study neglected to factor in the impact of such variables. Bearing this in mind, I have adopted a somewhat comprehensive mixture of economic and political variables to try and tap into the motivation question.

Some of the above observations about Davenport's study are also applicable to how my study differs from Henderson's (1971) study. Although Henderson improved upon Davenport's study by broadening his focus to include eighty-four countries, his study was limited to a two-year period. Since two time points do not constitute a pattern, one is unable to track how the motivation factors change, if at all, from year to year for different donors. Furthermore, with respect to the geographic focus of his study, although Henderson again improved upon Davenport's study by dividing the recipient states in his study into distinct regions, his study is best characterized as a good description of the distribution of aid by sources and recipients. In essence, his findings are very useful in answering the "what" and, perhaps, the "how" questions, but they are inadequate in probing the "why" questions. Let me illustrate. In reference to the regional variation in the volume of aid disbursed by the donors in his study, for instance, Henderson reported that there "was an overall worsening of the terms of ODA commitments; the grant element of these was 76 percent in 1967 and 69 percent in 1968" (p.7). He even identified the region, which suffered the worst fate in this decline (South Asia), but he did not offer any explanation for this observation. The result of this omission is that one is left wondering why south Asia suffered a worse fate than other regions. In this study, I guard against such pitfalls by providing cogent analysis of my findings, and taking care to underscore why particular donors favor some recipient countries. It is not sufficient to know the "what" and "how" questions. Answers to the "why" questions, even if tentative, could supply useful insights to the foreign aid puzzle. In venturing to provide such answers, theoretical propositions prove to be indispensable guides; hence the focus of this study on a comparative evaluation of the propositions of realist and liberal theories.

In addition to Davenport and Henderson's studies, the early 1970s witnessed the publication of another study that adopted a research methodology more germane to this present effort. This was the study undertaken by Eugene Wittkopf. In his 1972 book, *Western Bilateral Aid Allocation: A Comparative Study of Recipient State Attributes,* Wittkopf developed eleven independent variables, and he grouped them into four clusters to examine the motivation for the allocation of aid by the United States, France, German Federal Republic, and the United Kingdom to 48 developing countries. These four variable clusters were: (1) the political importance of the recipient to the donor; (2) the Cold War, which he measured as: (i) recipient's border on a communist state, (ii) percentage of recipient's total trade with Soviet bloc states, and (iii) receipt by recipient state of a commitment for bilateral economic assistance from the Soviet bloc; (3) the recipient's need and performance; and (4) the availability of alternative sources of assistance.

Wittkopf's study covered the years 1961, 1964, and 1967. He reported that the motivation for the allocation of aid varied among the four countries he investigated. Even though per capita income and trade balances were significant determinants of British, French and German aid allocations, he found this to be more prevalent with respect to France and Britain. The United State's aid allocation, he noted, was significantly premised on Cold War considerations. Without a doubt, the study by Wittkopf, despite the limitations of its three time points provides a more comprehensive picture of the motivations behind the allocation of foreign aid than the, (nonetheless, commendable) efforts of Davenport and Henderson.

Building on the works of Pincus (1967) and Nelson (1968), Wittkopf broadened the independent variables in his study to include a mixture of economic and political variables. More importantly, Wittkopf's study moved beyond the descriptive focus of earlier efforts to provide a persuasive analysis of the factors undergirding the aid policies of the donor countries in his study. His efforts are indeed commendable. It is from the intellectual insights of his study that this present study makes its own departure. Since 1972, when Wittkopf's work was published, however, other than the obvious transformation which the international system has undergone, there have been other significant changes in the scope and volume of aid allocation that now allow one to conduct a more comparative study of the aid policies of different donors. For example, for the periods covered by Wittkopf's study, the number of aid recipients varied greatly by donor. A testament to this point is that in 1964, the United States extended aid to seventy-two developing countries, while France, the second largest donor, allocated aid to twenty-six countries. In contrast, the ten donor states whose aid policies are investigated in this present study all provide aid to many of the thirty-six recipient states included in this study. This is one way in which this study differs from that of Wittkopf. Another difference relates to the aforementioned longitudinal approach of this present study. Despite these differences, however, Wittkopf's goal some twenty-eight years ago remains proximate to my objective, and that is, to bring empirical evidence to bear on generalizations and subjective knowledge about the motivations for the allocation of foreign aid to developing countries.

In the late 1970s, R.D. Mckinlay, initially alone, then later in a series of collaborative effort with R. Little, were among the first scholars to approach the foreign aid puzzle from a longitudinal perspective. In their studies, they reexamined the aid allocation practices of the four major donors identified by Wittkopf (R.D. Mckinlay 1977, and R.D. Mckinlay and R. Little 1977, 1978a, 1978b, 1979). Their studies were remarkable in at least two respects: First, they introduced a new level of sophistication into the examination of the determinants of aid allocation by developing a two-model (recipient need model and donor interest model) method of analysis. While the recipient need model hypothesized that the economic and welfare needs of the recipients would determine aid allocation, the donor-interest model hypothesized that foreign aid allocation would reflect the interests of the donors. Equally significant was that their studies adopted a much wider array of predictor variables than was utilized by either Davenport or Henderson. In addition, more than any previous work, their study spanned a longer time period, 1960-1970. This enabled them to sketch a more accurate pattern for the motivations behind the foreign aid policies of the donor countries in their studies.

With respect to the aid policies of France, they reported that apart from manifesting a strong concentration on its formal colonies, French aid allocation also reflected France's tendency to summon aid to the service of her political and economic interests. The US aid allocation pattern on the other hand, while sharing some similarities with France's pattern, differed in that it spanned a broader scope. According to Mckinlay and Little, this reflected the global tendencies of the United State's power-political and security interests. As for Britain and Germany, they reported a mixed finding. Even though the patterns of British and German aid allocation failed to reflect the needs of the recipient states in a consistent manner, they contained, nonetheless, elements of a quasi-humanitarian concern.

Given the breadth of Mckinlay and Little's studies, and the sophisticated level of their research methods, how does this present study differ from their study? This present study differs from Mckinlay and Little's studies in two significant ways. The first difference relates to methodological issues. In measuring the effect of their chosen independent variables on aid allocation, for example, Mckinlay and Little ran separate regression analyses for each of the donor states, and for each of the ten years in their study. This research method is problematic because it renders the accuracy of their "statistically significant" findings suspect. Running separate regressions for multiple donors over a time series is analogous to doing separate zero-order correlation coefficients. There are at least two difficulties with such method: First, one capitalizes on chance to find low probabilities in the correlation coefficients. Second and more importantly, such method does not adequately control for other potential influences. It is as if one has decided to run a series of t-tests in the absence of a prior F-test that should tell one if there is a real difference between the results from one's regression and the results that one would obtain by random chance alone. The validity of the results from such analyses therefore becomes suspect.[9] By contrast, this present study adopts a time-series regression analysis to probe the effects of the independent variables on changes in aid allocation (see chapter three for a comprehensive discussion of the methodology and variables used in this study).

The other difference between this study and that of Mckinlay and Little is that they did not locate their study within any theoretical framework. Their juxtaposition of the "donor-interest model" with the "recipient-need model" at best evinces traces of a concern for theory, but not a concrete articulation of any theoretical framework. This is not a trivial omission. Nor is the point an argument for theory for its own sake. The point rather is that the quest for significant association between variables is more meaningful if, where possible, one allows theory to guide inquiry. Kenneth Waltz articulated this point tersely when he observed:

> To proceed by looking for associations without at least some glimmering of theory is like shooting a gun in the general direction of an invisible target. Not only would much ammunition be used up, but also, if the bull's eye were hit, no one would know it (Waltz, 1979:8).

In the above regard, Richard Vengroff's 1982 study fills an important gap in the foreign aid literature. Apart from being one of the few studies to primarily focus on sub-Saharan Africa, Vengroff (1982) derived the hypotheses in his study from the stated goals of American policy on food aid as outlined in US Public Law 480. He then compared these goals with the alternative propositions offered by dependency theory. He reported, *interalia* that two of his adopted variables – economic and political dependence – were found to be systematically associated with food aid. The direction of this association, however, was opposite to theoretical expectations because "more dependence was associated with more food aid" (Vengroff, 1982:43). Vengroff also observed that if the Francophone and Anglophone nations were examined separately, the pattern of US aid allocation revealed that food aid to the former group was consistent with their need for aid and US desire to maintain access to their markets. On the other hand, US aid allocation to the Anglophone nations correlated positively with their size and the accessibility of their markets to the US, and negatively with their need. Vengroff then concluded that the search for raw materials and markets appeared to be the dominant element in the explanation of American food aid to sub-Saharan Africa.

---

[9] I am grateful to Prof. Penn Handweker for this observation.

Remarkably, this present study draws some of the inspiration for its theoretical focus from Vengroff's insights. Still, there are important differences between the two studies. For one, although the regional focus of the two studies are the same, this present study encompasses a broader array of donor states, and arguably, sheds more comparative light on motivations for foreign aid. In essence, while one of the advantages of Vengroff's study is that it helps one to understand the motivations for the allocation of a specific type of aid (food aid) for a particular donor (the United States), it is limited in its comparative utility with respect to probing the policies of different donors. Furthermore, while the theoretical propositions of dependency represented his alternative explanation for the food assistance provided by the US, the theoretical concerns of this present study are the propositions of realism and liberalism. The reasons for making such shift in theoretical focus will be discussed later in this chapter.

Other scholars who have made notable contributions to the motivations for the allocation of aid include, Maizels and Nissanke (1984), Tsousoplides (1991) Lumsdaine (1993) and Schraeder, Hook and Taylor (1998). In their 1984 study, Alfred Maizels and Machiko Nissanke, using McKinlay and Little's two-model method of investigation, set out to re-examine the motivation behind the foreign aid policies of OECD member states. Their study covered 84 developing countries in the 1969-70 and 1978-80 time periods. Whereas the dependent variable in the Mckinlay and Little studies was bilateral aid, Maizels and Nissanke incorporated multilateral aid flows into their study. In addition to other findings, their study yielded the following results:

1. The recipient-need model (which assumed that aid was given to compensate for short falls in the domestic resources of the recipient states) provides a reasonable explanation for the allocation of multilateral aid.
2. The donor interest model (which assumed that all aid was allocated to serve donors' interests such as political, security, investment and trade interests), while being adequate in the explanation of bilateral aid, revealed a poor fit with multilateral aid flows.

True, these are interesting and significant findings. Equally notable is that Maizels and Nissanke (1984) introduced into the foreign aid literature an important way of measuring donor's trade interests by examining aid flows to countries exporting strategic minerals. They reported positive coefficients for this variable for the two periods covered by their study (1969-70 and 1979-80). Neither of the coefficients were, however, statistically significant.

One significant difference between this present study and Maizels and

Nissanke's (1984) study relates to my exclusive focus on sub-Saharan Africa. Focusing specifically on sub-Saharan Africa, one of the poorest regions in the world, allows me to scrutinize the data on foreign aid from a closer range and see observations possibly missed by Maizels and Nissanke because of the aggregate nature of their data. This point is cogent and merits elaboration. For example, Maizels and Nissanke (1984), reported in their study that their recipient-need model was of poor explanatory power in understanding the motivation behind the aid allocation of the donors in their study. This finding is supported by their data. Due to the aggregate nature of their data, however, there is the possibility that their study might have yielded opposite results had they disaggregated their data and exclusively focused on any of the poorest regions in the world. As they admit themselves, because their study covered 84 developing countries with significant income disparities, the possibility exist that the recipient-need model, which in some respect approximates the proposition of liberal theory, "might yield a good explanation of aid distribution to low income countries" (see their footnote #10).

Next, in 1991, Constantine Tsoutsoplides, also utilizing the two-model method, undertook a similar investigation into the determinants of the European Community's (EC) aid to 62 Less Developing Countries (LDCs) from 1975-1980. His findings largely confirmed Maizels and Nissanke's 1984 results. He reported that the EC's multilateral aid was motivated by the needs of the recipient states in terms of the status of their current account balance of payments and their state of basic human needs. His examination of the bilateral side of the aid ledger, however, revealed that the export interest of the donors was the most frequent determinant of their aid allocation. Also, like Maizels and Nissanke (1984), Tsousoplides (1991) adopted the presence of strategic minerals in recipient states as a variable to measure donors' interest in those states. He, however, broadened the number of strategic minerals in his study from the original nine, (minus rubber) in Maizels and Nissanke's 1984 study to fourteen.[10] In this regard, this present study is similar to the above studies. The inventory of strategic minerals included in this study is, however, more comprehensive than the ones in previous studies. I have also attempted to introduce a more sophisticated way of measuring this variable by developing a strategic mineral index for this study.

Between the publication of McKinlay and Little's first study in 1977 and Tsoutsoplides article in 1991, there appeared to be an emerging consensus

---

[10] The nine strategic minerals selected by Maizels and Nissanke (1984) were bauxite, cobalt, copper, nickel, petroleum, rubber, tin, tungsten, and uranium. They measured this by assigning the value of 1 for countries exporting more than 1% of the world exports and zero for others. Tsousoplides (1991) expanded this list, minus rubber, to include iron-ore, phosphates, zinc, lead, manganese, and uranium.

in the scholarly community that bilateral aid was used to promote the foreign policy interests of donor states. Despite the apparent humanitarian basis of aid allocations by the Nordic states (especially Norway, Denmark and Sweden), many scholars frequently interpreted the results of quantitative studies on bilateral aid flows to developing countries in a way that was supportive of the theoretical assumptions of realist theory. The publication of Lumsdaine's work in 1993, however, seriously questioned such a position.

In his 1993 book, *Moral Visions in International Politics: The Foreign Aid Regime, 1949-1989,* Lumsdaine launched a spirited assault on the position of the realist school of thought. Whereas realists like Robert Gilpin advocate the separation of morality from international politics on the assumption that "morality functions best *within* and not *among* groups" (Gilpin, 1996:9), Lumsdaine directly challenged this assumption. He argued instead:

> Foreign aid is a paradigm case of the influence of crucial moral principles because of its universal assistance from well off countries to any in need, its focus on poverty, and of its empowerment of the weakest groups and states in the international system (1993:29).

Furthermore, whereas McKinlay (1979) had submitted that foreign aid provided the utilities of commitment and dependence, which a donor country employed to promote its political and economic interests, Lumsdaine asserted that:

> Foreign aid can not be accounted for on the basis of the economic and political interest of the donor countries alone; the essential causes lay in the humanitarian and egalitarian principles of the donor countries and in their implicit belief that only on the basis of a just international order in which all states have a chance to do well, was peace and prosperity possible (1993:30).

In essence, just as it was beginning to appear that all the pieces of the foreign aid puzzle had finally fallen into place, Lumsdaine's polemic on the humanitarian interests for aid rattled the puzzle board, knocked a few pieces out of place and repositioned some others. Yet, even with such laudable accomplishment, because Lumsdaine's study spanned only the period of the Cold War, some important slots in the foreign aid puzzle have neither been filled, nor has the relationship of each piece to the others been sufficiently explicated.

In a 1998 article, Schraeder, Hook and Taylor set out to clarify the foreign aid puzzle. Their study examined the foreign aid policies of the U.S., Japan, Sweden, and France toward Africa from 1980-1989. Using six independent variables - humanitarian need, strategic importance, economic potential, cultural similarity, ideological stance, and region - they examined the major determinants of the foreign aid practices of these four countries. They observed that although their cross-national analysis revealed a varied and complex pattern, there were, nonetheless, empirical similarities. Some of their findings were:

1. Contrary to the rhetorical claims made by the policy makers of the advanced democracies, altruism was not a determinant of their aid policies.
2. There was a clear linkage between the ideological posture of African states and the amount of aid they received from the donors.
3. Trade was an important determinant of foreign aid. (They found this to be particularly surprising in the case of Sweden, which is traditionally considered the darling of the Third World.) They concluded their study with a suggestion for further studies on the motivations for aid allocation, especially in the post-Cold War period.

Notably, this study, whose declared goal was to "clarify the foreign aid puzzle", supplied many useful insights into the nature of the foreign aid puzzle. It also identified some of the uses, limitations and problems with previous efforts. Equally noteworthy is the sophisticated time series method that Schraeder, Hook and Taylor (1998) adopted for their study. This present effort derived its methodological insights from their study. These observations notwithstanding, the explanatory value of their findings, particularly in relation to the extent to which their findings are generalizable across time is, undoubtedly, marginalized by the fact that their study only spanned the period of the Cold War. This is one crucial difference between their study and this present effort. Another difference relates to the issue of a recipient state's utility to a donor. Schraeder, Hook, and Taylor accurately surmised that donors would tend to provide more aid to recipient states that they consider to be of strategic importance to such donors. Their measurement of such strategic value is, however, restricted to conventional variables that tend to highlight military assets. In contrast, this present study expands the measurement of a recipient state's value to a donor to include the availability of strategic minerals in the recipient state.

With the theme pursued thus far, I should like to underscore the point that despite the density and impressiveness of the literature on foreign aid in general, it is indeed remarkable that in the post-Cold War period, few studies have attempted to examine the motivation question, especially in relation to Africa. Moreover, the few available studies that have sought to probe the subject in the post-Cold War era, for example, Hook (1995), Olsen (1996) and Schraeder, Hook and Taylor (1998) are impressive, but problematic in one respect or the other. Hook (1995), broached the motivation question in a thematic fashion but only discussed the subject in vague and broad terms. As Raymond Mikesell accurately noted in his review of Hook's book:

> Little attention is paid to the role of national economic interests in motivating foreign aid and to the way in which a particular form of aid was expected to achieve economic benefits for either the donor or the recipient country (Mikesell, 1996:100).

Olsen (1996), which set out to measure the relevance of ethics in the allocation of aid to Sub-Saharan Africa in the post-Cold War era is even more problematic. By his own admission, confronted with a choice of whether to test his hypothesis by empirical method, or by scrutinizing "the existing literature on the topic to find out if there exists a possibility that morality may play a role like the one described in the hypothesis" (Olsen, 1996:234), he opted for the latter method. Nonetheless, his work is flawed not so much because he chose the latter method, but rather that the works upon which his thesis rests focused on a different period. In essence, his thesis commits an ecological fallacy of a more disturbing variety – the tendency to extend the applicability of data from the Cold War period to the post-Cold War era simply because the works which cited such data were published in the latter era. The work of Schraeder, Hook and Taylor (1998), though more recent, is problematic for the reasons discussed earlier.

Another interesting point is that Lumsdaine's spirited argument of the liberal case about the relevance of morality in international politics has reopened the realist - liberal debate on the motivations for the allocation of aid to developing countries. By examining this subject with an exclusive focus on aid allocation to sub-Saharan African states in the post-Cold War era, this study hopes to rekindle interest in the factors which influence international cooperation between DAC member-states and sub-Saharan Africa. In summary, while drawing inspiration from the efforts of scholars who have labored in the foreign aid vineyard, this study differs from previous studies in the following ways:

1. A Focus on the post-Cold War period.

   The end of the Cold War presents ample opportunities to reexamine the motivations for the allocation of aid to sub-Saharan African states. By focusing on the post-Cold War period, this study controls for the effect of the probable 'abnormalities' in state behavior occasioned by the ideological competition between the Western alliance and the former communist bloc.

2. An exclusive focus on sub-Saharan Africa.

   Although a great deal of attention has been devoted to developing countries in the foreign aid literature, few post-Cold War studies have focused on sub-Saharan Africa. The argument here is not that sub-Saharan Africa is such a unique region, although much could be said for the marginal attention it receives in mainstream writings about the study of international relations. The point rather is that, in the examination of a subject like the motivations for the allocation of foreign aid to developing countries in the current phase of the evolution of the international system, a focus on sub-Saharan Africa merits attention for several reasons: First, the region is humankind's original home and a significant number of the world's current population of about six billion people live there. Second, while other parts of the world continue to experience impressive rates of development, the myriad issues of economic, political and social problems which foreign aid was originally conceived to address have attained acute dimensions in this region. Third, the dichotomy between the propositions of realism and liberalism are sharpest with respect to foreign aid to sub-Saharan Africa. Given these observations, a focus on sub-Saharan Africa enables one to observe the data on foreign aid allocation from a closer range and reveal important findings missed by aggregate data that only discuss aid to this region within the broader framework of aid to developing countries in general. By the same token, by focusing on a sub-continent notorious for harboring a significant number of the least developing countries (LLDCs)[11] in the world and yet coveted by some donors, in part because of the presence of strategic minerals in some of its constituent states, one can better test the theoretical assumptions of the realist and liberal paradigms.

3. The inclusion of crucial variables.

As comprehensive as the variables adopted in some previous studies were, with the possible exception of the collaborative efforts by McKinlay and Little (1979), and Meernik, Krueger and Poe (1998), they are remarkable for leaving out important variables like democracy and human rights. The inclusion of these variables can help shed additional light on the liberal position on the motivation for foreign aid. This study is therefore novel for the comprehensive character of its adopted variables.

4. The expansion of the universe of donors.

While many of the previous studies on the motivations for foreign aid allocations only test their models with a limited universe of donors, this present study has expanded this universe to include the ten key members of the DAC. Such expansion of the universe of donors enables me to use the motivation question as a panoptic lens that captures a panoramic view of the aid allocation landscape where many previous studies have sketched isolated and blurred images.

---

[11] Curiously, 68% of the 42 countries identified by the CIA World Fact Book as LLDCs in 1995 were in sub-Saharan Africa.

Why Realism and Liberalism?

Privileging liberal and realist theories over other available theories of international relations is warranted by (1) their durability, and (2) inherent in their durability, their utility as guide. It is curious that in the field of political science, especially in the sub-field of international relations, theoretical notions appear to be eternally in contention as evinced by the number of major textbooks with titles suggestive of the rivalry between theories.[12] In this process of theoretical competition, somewhat akin to the Darwinian process of natural selection, less fitting species either atrophy, fall into desuetude, or become embarrassingly disreputable as the fates of Dependency, World Systems, and Marxist theories of international political economy amply demonstrate. This is, perhaps, as it should be, for as Waltz (1979:6) reminds us, theories are speculative processes introduced to explain facts of observation. No matter how well supported they might be by prevailing facts, unlike the laws derived from experimental results (like those found in physics and chemistry), theories are impermanent – they come and go.

In the case of dependency theory, its principal argument that the global capitalist economy operates systematically to thwart the development aspirations of Third World countries could neither withstand overwhelming evidence that contradicted such position, nor could the import-substitution industrialization (ISI) policies that it prescribed serve as a catalyst for development in the Third World countries that adopted them. The rapid economic growth recorded by the newly industrializing economies (NICs) of South Korea, Taiwan, Singapore, Hong Kong, Brazil and others, at a time when other economies in Africa and Latin America were stagnating, suggests that active incorporation into the global capitalist system is an engine of development rather than the cause of underdevelopment. It is the benign neglect of regions such as Sahelian Africa, rather than their "dependent exploitation" by expansionary capitalism that better accounts for their lack of development (Gilpin, 1987:289). Furthermore, in the post-Cold War era, the normative argument by dependency theory that the development of the NICs is not "true development", an argument hitherto plausible among intellectuals in the Third World no longer holds water. Most Third World nations would gladly trade places with the NICs today.

More pertinent to my goal of theoretical evaluation are the methodological deficiencies of dependency theory. As Packenham (1976) points out, the fact that dependency theorists often conceptualize dependency

---

[12] Examples of such major international relations text books include: Dougherty & Pfaltzgraff, Jr. (1990); Kegley Jr. (1995); and Doyle (1997).

in dichotomous terms makes the measurement of its explanatory utility problematic. In addition, there is the consideration that many dependency arguments are non-falsifiable. As Biersteker (1993) observes, this makes it difficult to specify the types of data that would confirm or deny the central hypotheses of dependency theory. Equally problematic is the fact that the proponents of the theory are unable to account for pre-capitalist forms of dependence as well as dependency relations under socialism. Given these empirical and theoretical inadequacies, dependency theory falls short of the criteria for consideration in this study, hence its omission. In fact, given what we now know of development, what one finds surprising is not that dependency theory has atrophied, but that it survived for as long as it did. Despite occasional temptations to resurrect the theory to explain the North-South international relations every time the international capitalist system undergoes a crisis, dependency theory has lost the luster it once had.

Like dependency theory, Modern World Systems (MWS) theory, as popularized by Immanuel Wallerstein, does not meet the criteria for consideration in this study, because it is equally flawed in several respects. Essentially, its primary contention that the world economy has been static is erroneous because, it fails to take into account the dramatic changes in the structure of the system over the past several centuries. As Gilpin (1987:85) notes, while it is appropriate to view the world economy as a hierarchical structure composed of a core and periphery, it is also true that the geographic locus of the core and the global distribution of economic activities are not immutable. Historically, such geographical locus has shifted from the Mediterranean to the North Atlantic. And in contemporary times, with increasing globalization, we have been witnessing a shift in the locus of economic activity from the Atlantic region to the Pacific region (Gilpin, 2000). Moreover, contrary to the proposition of MWS theory, the example of the US is persuasive testament to the point that it is possible for a state that was once in the rearguard to move to the vanguard of the global capitalist system. A state's position within the world capitalist system is neither foreordained nor everlasting. The refusal of MWS theory to appreciate the simple fact that the nexus among states is primarily political and strategic rather than purely economic, renders its theoretical sketches of the international political economy patently out of sync with praxis. That it too - like its cousin, dependency theory - has not survived the Darwinian process of theoretical competition in international relations studies provides ample demonstration of its weakness, and the justification for its exclusion from consideration in this study.

As for Marxist theory, the primary source from which dependency and MWS theories derived many of their propositions, though it too is flawed in significant particulars, it has been more resilient. Shorn of its strident overtone about the inevitable doom of the global capitalist system, Marxism has much to recommend it. Karl Marx and Friedrich Engels, the originators of the theory accurately made the connection between politics and economics in their analysis of capitalism. The emphasis they placed on the role of economic and technological development in their explanation of the dynamics of the international capitalist system provided us with a theory of social change (Heilbroner, 1989). The law of uneven development, which Lenin derived from Marx's work constitutes an underlying cause of international political change.

Furthermore, Marx's description of the logic of capitalism – the drive towards accumulation and expansion via trade, the export of capital, and a cyclical tendency for the rates of profits to fall – remains the most persuasive analysis of the workings of the capitalist system. Yet, despite his impressive description of the capitalist system, Marx's inexorable political-economic theory was flawed in several ways. For scholars like Gilpin, its principal weakness as a theory of international political economy inheres in its failure to appreciate the role of political and strategic factors in international relations. The propensity to war which latter day Marxists ascribe to the uneven growth of national economies is more accurately explained by national rivalries that can occur regardless of the nature of domestic economies (Gilpin, 1987:53). For other scholars like Robert Heilbroner, an essential flaw in Marx's theory is its failure to perceive capitalism as an economic structure capable of considerable adaptation. The success of countries such as Norway, Denmark, Austria and even Japan in marrying private ownership of the means of production and egalitarian income redistribution has rendered the Marxist prophesy of an inevitable class struggle that would culminate in the triumph of socialism problematic (Heilbroner, 1989:169). An even more poignant point is that the collapse of socialism in the former Soviet bloc appears to have rendered the *Nunc Dimittis* to the prospects of a world of socialist states.

The above points being well taken, it bears emphasizing that the problems that Marx diagnosed with capitalism, especially, its tendency towards economic crisis and the concentration of wealth and power in the hands of a small elite in a few states are still very much with us. The disreputable status of Marxist theory, the reason why many of its propositions have become embarrassingly dated, stems not so much from the inaccuracy of Marx's observations about the world around him. Rather, Marxism has lost his persuasive edge and attraction because the capitalist system, which Marx railed so passionately against reformed itself and granted to labor concessions that Marx believed to be impossible in his time. Theorization about social phenomena must contend with temporal depreciation as the object of study undergoes both quantitative and qualitative changes. That Marx's intellectual heirs, blinded by the ideological competition between the US and the former Soviet Union, stubbornly refused to come to grips with this development, accounts in large part for the longevity of Marxism. With the benefit of hindsight, it is now easy to see how difficult it would have been for Marxism to survive.

In the light of the above observations, and the afterglow of the Cold War, when one surveys the theoretical battlefield of IR, two theories – realism/neorealism and liberalism – emerge as the last troops standing. While there are other notable contenders, and pretenders to explanatory prominence, for examples, feminist theory and the "constructivist approach", they have neither been sufficiently battle tested, nor do they yet command adequate followership in the discipline, hence their exclusion from consideration in this study. By contrast, it is safe to say that only liberalism and realism have so far survived the Darwinian process in the competition between theories of international relations, hence they merit privileged attention.

The second reason for selecting realist and liberal theories as the comparative theoretical framework for exploring the motivation question, owes much to their utility as reliable guides in the study of international relations. Because knowledge, as Imre Lakatos (1970) reasoned, is infinite in extent, to be able to gather information and order it so as to make it comprehensible, one needs some guide to help one separate the wheat from the chaff – the "relevant and necessary" data from the pool of "available and accessible" information. A part of the durability of realist and liberal theories is inherent in their utility, the other part is evident in the persuasive weight of their assumptions.

An assessment of the adequacy of realist and liberal theories on the motivation behind the allocation of aid by developed countries to sub-Saharan Africa will provide additional insights into their explanatory power and allow one to preserve their essential and meaningful elements while revising, reconstructing or rejecting their flawed particulars. Theories of international relations such as feminist theory, merely allow for normative descriptions of international relations. For the student interested in the ebb and flow tides of world affairs, especially the official transfer of resources from state to state, mere descriptions of such processes, even if done with unsurpassed accuracy, could at best provide highly reliable knowledge of the increases and decreases in such transfers, but would not, in the absence of coherent theory, enable one to probe the underlying motivations so as to better explain them. In essence, a full description of the history and process of foreign aid allocation by rich countries to poor ones, as many previous works have done,[13] and as the lesser

---

[13] Notably, there are at least four categories of works on the allocation of aid to Africa in the post-Cold War era. None of these, however, satisfactorily answers the research question raised in this study. First, there are works which examine the motivations for the allocation

theories of international relations would lead one to produce, is useful but of least explanatory power. A creative assessment of the theoretical elegance of realist and liberal theories as puzzle solving guides and explanatory tools of foreign aid is of most import.

By the same token, for a research study that primarily adopts a quantitative method of investigation, the choice of realist and liberal theories is defensible on the grounds that they are more susceptible to measurement. And because theory enables one to know what kind of data and connections to look for, knowledge of the motivation behind foreign aid allocation must proceed from knowledge of theory.

The Theories

Realism/Neorealism[14]

What is commonly referred to as the realist school of thought is home to two groups of scholars –realists and neorealists. Although these two groups of scholars "have different approaches and concerns, they adopt certain key assumptions that drive their work, and hence they can be thought of as a school" (Zakaria, 1992:191). I begin this section by discussing their shared beliefs and then proceed to underscore their differences.

The Realist/Neorealist Consensus

Realists and neorealists share the following assumptions about the nature of the international system and the behavior of its constituent actors.

---

of aid to developing countries in general with the use of independent variables inherent in the donor countries (public opinion, governmental orientation, and party composition of government) but discuss aid to Africa within this broad framework thereby missing the nuances in the aid policies of the different donors to various African states. Examples of such works are Noel and Therien (1995), and Opeskin (1996). Second, there are those with specific focus on Africa, which adopt a multi-donor comparison of aid allocations and yet utilize only data from the Cold War era. Examples of these are Schraeder (1995), Hook (1995), and Schraeder, Hook and Taylor (1998). Third, there are works that claim to offer post-Cold War explanations for the allocation of aid, but upon scrutiny are dubious rationalizations due to suspect methodology. Representative of this genre is Olsen (1996). Finally, there are works, which primarily focus on Africa, yet do so by examining the aid allocation practices of single donors. Cumming (1995), is representative of this sort of work.

[14] The origins of the term "realism" is traceable to the German word realpolitik *coined in the* Grundsatz der Realpolitik, *a famous treatise published by Von Rochau in 1853 which was largely inspired by the lessons of Frankfort (Carr, 1946:97 fn#2).*

1. States are the Primary Actors in the International System.
   The state is the centerpiece of realist and neorealist work because of their belief that states are the primary actors in international relations. They justify this belief on the grounds that the most important issues of war and peace revolve around the behavior of states. But although the term "international relations" itself lends credibility to this claim, some neorealists have argued: "that the state is ...the principal actor in international relations does not deny the existence of other individual and collective actors" (Gilpin, 1984:300).
2. The State is a Unitary Actor.
   Proceeding from their assumption that international relations are state centered, realists and neorealists assert that the fundamental unit of all social and political affairs is the group. The German sociologist, Ralf Dahrendrof (1959) referred to this as the conflict group. Realists and neorealists believe that while the precise nature of these conflict groups might change over the years, the primary definition of conflict remains group based. Whatever differences might exist among a state's policy makers, in the event of an external threat they often come together as a group to address such threats – hence the assumption of the state as a unitary actor.[15]
3. The International System is an Anarchic Realm.
   Realists and neorealists believe that international politics occur in an anarchic realm. By this they do not mean a Hobbesian state of perpetual war of all against all. Rather, they mean that the system is a self-help one that lacks a Leviathan: an "entity that holds a monopoly of the legitimate use of violence" (Aron, 1967:192) and can therefore impose its will on the competing state-actors in the system. States as self-interested units must therefore fend for themselves or risk inducing their own demise.
4. The Utility of Power in International Politics.
   Realists and neorealists underscore the primacy of power in the promotion and defense of a state's national interest. Because the international system lacks a super-ordinate power which can impose its will on the competing actors in the system thereby leaving states to fend for themselves as best as they can, the pursuit of power becomes an essential purpose for all states. Variation in the distribution of capabilities

---

[15] The 1990 example of the behavior of American policy makers prior to the commencement of "Operation Desert Storm" appears to lend credibility to this assumption. In that instance, despite the bitter division among members of Congress on the appropriateness and timeliness of going to War with Iraq, once President George Bush had committed US troops to battle, Congress and the American public rallied behind his policy.

among states requires that each state be concerned not with the intentions of other states, but with their capabilities. This assumption yields a realist/neorealist focus on the concept of "balance of power" as an underlying element in international relations.

The Realist – Neorealist Divide: Birds of a Feather Flying Separately[16]

Despite sharing the above beliefs, realists and neorealists have important differences. The first difference has to do with their conception of the meaning of anarchy. For realists, anarchy is a general condition. For neorealists it is an organizing principle. This difference is subtle, but important. The realist conception of anarchy as a general condition fixates international politics in Aron's (1967) sociological realm and renders, in Waltz's (1979) estimation, a theory of international politics impossible, if not unnecessary. This is because it imbues the actions of the constituent units in the system with the ability to impact the system – a one way causal arrow – but does not account for the effect of the structure of the system (as evident in the number of great powers and the distribution of capabilities between them) on the behavior of the constituent units. Since the international structure varies with the number of great powers, "when the number changes, consequently, the calculations and behavior of the states and the outcomes their interaction produce, vary" (Waltz: 1995:74). It is the injection of the structural element into the concept of anarchy, Waltz alleges, that made it possible for neorealists to devise a theory of international politics. Moreover, an accounting of the impact of structure on the system's constituent units enables neorealism to see that states are made functionally similar by the pressures of competitive interaction, despite the principal differences in their capabilities. While realism understood the concern for survival that anarchy imposes on the behavior of differently constituted units, it did not see how anarchy induces similarity among states. For neorealism, the process of competitive interaction, which the concern for survival renders necessary, brings about imitative socialization whereby the units in the system come to look or behave alike (Sterling-Folker, 1997:5). Hence, Waltz submits that the "idea that international politics can be thought of as a system with precisely defined structure is neorealism's fundamental departure from traditional realism" (Waltz:1995:74).

The other significant difference between realists and neorealists relates

---

[16] For a discussion of the realist position, see Thucydides (1954), Machiavelli (1950), Carr (1946) and Morgenthau (1973). For an enunciation of the neo-realist position, see Waltz (1979), (1995), Gilpin (1987), (1996) and Grieco (1995). For critiques of realism/neo-realism, see Ashley (1984), Buzan, Jones, and Little (1993), Griffiths (1992) and Lumsdaine (1993).

to their views on power. For realists like Hans Morgenthau, and before him, Thucydides and Niccolo Machiavelli, human beings are driven by the lust for power. Morgenthau (1946:192) labels this the *animus dominandi*. This lust for power is exacerbated by the competition for scarce resources. For neorealists such as Waltz and Gilpin, on the other hand, power is not an end in itself. It is "essentially instrumental to and necessary for the achievement of other goals like security and even liberal ideas" Gilpin (1996:6). Furthermore, while Morgenthau assumed the existence of an objective national interest defined in terms of power, neorealists admit the existence of a large subjective component to the definition of the national interest. Thus, whereas Morgenthau's conception of the national interest is resistant to changes in its definition that would reflect changes in the composition of the national elite in a given state, the receptivity of neorealists to the subjectivity of the national interest accommodates shifts in its definition. Finally, while the pursuit of absolute gain is a leitmotif in realists thought, neorealists draw attention to a state's concern for relative gain in its interactions with other states in the system.

Liberal Theory

Unlike realist theory which can be identified with a coherent set of assumptions, liberal theory, as Athur Stein (1990:7) correctly observes, is "multifaceted, and what is, or not at its core can be disputed". In part, this condition of liberal theory is attributable to the little time and effort that liberals spend on clarifying their assumptions.[17] Another reason for the poor state of liberal theory stems from the fact that until the mid-twentieth century, the major contributors to the formulation of the theory's essential elements were not international relations scholars, but people generally interested in international affairs (Zacher and Matthew, 1995:108). The core assumptions of liberal theory as synthesized by Zacher and Matthew (1995) are as follows:
1. Individual human beings are the primary international actors. On the surface, this appears to conflict with the realist assumption that states are the primary actors in world politics; but liberals, modifying their position, acknowledge that states are the most important collective actors in our present era. They are quick to add, however, that the present dominance of international relations by state-actors is not immutable.

---

[17] Mark W. Zacher and Richard A. Matthew, for instance, claim that until the publication of their article synthesized the common threads and divergent strands in liberal theory, no article or book described liberal international theory in a systematic way, provided an overview of its evolution, and linked current scholarship with the theoretical core of the older literature (Zacher & Matthew:1995:137).

Processes that tend to defy the logic of anarchy, such as globalization, liberals contend are rapidly changing the structure of the international system (Cerne, 1995). And, while realists perceive states as unitary actors, liberals contend that they are pluralistic actors whose interests and policies are determined by elections and bargaining among groups.
2. Contrary to the realist position that the primary goal of states is the selfish pursuit of power to defend their national interests, liberals contend that the interests of states are multiple, subject to change and both self interested and other-regarding.
3. Liberals believe that human and state interests are shaped by a wide variety of domestic and international conditions. Even though in the final analysis power plays a dominant role in how this state interest is conceived, defined and pursued among interest groups at the domestic level, modernization processes in the international arena – technological capabilities, patterns of interaction and interdependencies, transnational sociological patterns, knowledge and international institutions – all combine to constrain autonomous state action.
4. Whereas realists, arguing the case for the primacy of power in international relations claim that, "the network of international relations has not changed fundamentally over the millennia" (Gilpin, 1981:211), liberals contend that the relative influence of patterns of interests and coercion on international outcomes evolves over time, and that the impact of patterns of interests are growing. While some liberals agree with realists about the utility of coercion in a world once marked by colliding billiard balls, other liberals nonetheless submit that the processes of modernization, and a "quiet cataclysm" have mitigated the relevance and necessity of the use of force (Mueller, 1995). Such modernization process continues to engender the growth of cooperation and the reliance on non-coercive bargaining for the resolution of interstate conflicts (Keohane and Nye, 2001).

Table 2.1
Parallel Theoretical Perspectives on Aid to Sub-Saharan Africa

Theoretical Perspective	Evaluation about the Relevance of Africa to the Interest of the West by Prominent Authors	Prescriptions for the Uses and Future of Foreign Aid
Realism/Neorealism	By and large Africa is irrelevant to the interest of the US (Van Evera, 1990). African countries that are endowed with strategic minerals, or are located along major sea-lanes are of some relevance to the West (Desch, 1989).	Aid should be used as bribe to advance the interest of donors, or restricted to major humanitarian disasters that cannot be safely ignored (Morgenthau, 1962). Development aid should be drastically cut and linked to the efficiency of recipient states and "return on investment" (Bauer, 1972 & 1984); (Wolfson, 1979); (Eberstadt, 1988).
Liberalism/Neoliberalism	All regions of the world are important to humanity: "who can now ask where his country will be in a few decades without asking where the world will be? If we wish that the world be secure and prosperous, we must show a common concern for the common problems of all peoples" (Pearson, 1970:9). Morality matters in international politics (Lumsdaine, 1993).	Aid should be revamped to render it more effective (Lancaster, 1999). Recipient states should be rendered accountable for aid (Van de Walle, 1996). Aid should be tied to good governance and the commitment of the recipient states to democratization (Stokkes, 1996).

The above assumptions are the core beliefs of liberal theory. Undergirding these assumptions is a faith in the power of human reason and human action to change the world and make it possible for the most important actors in international relations (individual human beings) to more fully realize their potentials (Howard, 1978:11). The derivation of testable hypothesis from these propositions is, however, problematic. Of the seven strands of liberal theory that Zacher and Matthew (1995) identify in their study, only two differ sharply from realist theory to make testing worthwhile. These are republican liberalism and institutional liberalism.[18] It is from these two strands, therefore, that I have derived hypotheses to use in evaluating the assumptions of liberal theory on the motivations for the allocation of aid to sub-Saharan African states in the post-Cold War period.

Comparing the Explanatory Power of Rival Theories of International Relations: Notes and Observations

Appraising the adequacy of the propositions of rival theories of international relations with respect to the motivations behind foreign aid is an inherently problematic undertaking for several reasons. For one, the consideration that theory testing entails philosophical questions, which are primarily based on value judgment raises the key issue of what the acceptable criteria ought to be for such evaluations. An examination of one contemporary attempt to evaluate the propositions of realism on the balance of power propositions illuminates this point.

Troubled by the claim by some analysts that the dominance of the realist paradigm in the study of international relations is attributable to its fertility, compared to its rivals (for example, Elman & Elman, 1995), John Vasquez, in a 1997 article set out to evaluate the realist approach by the criteria speci-

---

[18] The other five strands of liberal theory identified by Zacher and Matthew (1995) are: interdependence liberalism, which they further divided into commercial and military liberalism, cognitive liberalism, sociological liberalism, and ecological liberalism. For the purposes of this study, the assumptions of commercial and military liberalism are not sharp enough in how they differ from the assumptions of realism to allow for a meaningful comparison. With respect to commercial liberalism, realists do not dispute its presuppositions about the growth of interdependence; they only disagree with the extent to which interdependence affects the relevance of power in both the resolution of conflict and the promotion of cooperation. Concerning military liberalism the views of liberals that technological advancements in the weapons of warfare have rendered a general war unthinkable overlap with those of realists. How the other question begging epithets – cognitive liberalism, sociological liberalism, and ecological liberalism – which are intuitively persuasive, might be developed into testable propositions is, by Zacher and Matthew's own admission, elusive.

fied by Lakatos (1970) for judging "progressive" or "degenerating" tendencies in research programs which he (Lakatos) preferred to call problem shifts.[19] In carrying out his evaluation of the realist program, Vasquez selected for review two notable books by two realists (Waltz 1979, and Walt 1987), two articles (Schweller 1994, Christensen and Snyder 1990), and an eleven-page letter to the editor of *International Security* (Elman and Elman 1995). He also made brief references to two historical case studies (Rosecrance and Stein 1993, and Schroeder 1994).

With respect to Waltz (1979) and Walt (1987), Vasquez claims that the latter's finding of a tendency by states to balance against a major power such states consider to be more threatening, contradicts the former's proposition that the anarchical nature of the international system "stimulates states to behave in ways which tend towards the creation of balances of power" (Waltz,1979:18). The thrust of Vasquez's argument, however, is that rather than admit this anomalous evidence as a falsification of the balance of power theory, realists summon semantic refinements to attempt to rescue the theory from falsification. Thus, rather than concede that his finding falsifies realist theory itself and not just Waltz's proposition, Walt introduces into the realist lexicon, the notion of balance of threat in an attempt to plug obvious errors in the theory. This, according to Vasquez, qualifies as an instance of a Lakatosian "theory shift" - a mere felicitous refinement intended to capture "all the connotations and emotive force of the balance of power [theory] while changing it only incrementally" (p.904).

Equally troubling for Vasquez is Randall Schweller's interpretation of his 1994 study which found that, contrary to Walt's suggestion that states tended to balance against threat, his review of European history revealed that bandwagoning was more common that balancing. But according to Vasquez, again, rather than concede that this finding provides contradictory evidence against realist theory, Schweller simply introduced the notion of balance of interest – the idea that states jump on the bandwagon of the most powerful state to gain rewards – to save neorealism from failure:

---

[19] According to Lakatos, a problem shift could be considered degenerative first, if in accommodating anomaly the movement from T to T^1 primarily involves the addition of auxiliary clauses to, or from semantic reinterpretation of the previous theory. Second, a series of theories constitutes a progressive problem shift if each new theory has some excess empirical content over its predecessor, meaning that it predicts some novel, hitherto unexplained fact by the previous theory. Third, and in tandem with the second point, a theory could be considered progressive if some of this excess empirical content is also corroborated such that each new theory leads one to actual discovery of some new fact. And fourth, a problem shift is progressive if it is both theoretically and empirically progressive, and degenerative if it is not (Lakatos, 1970:116-122).

Thus, Waltz moves from the idea of a balance of power to simply balancing power, even if it does not prevent war. Walt finds that states do not balance power but oppose threats to them selves. Schweller argues that states do not balance against the stronger but more frequently bandwagon with it to take advantage of opportunities to gain rewards (pp.905-6).

For Vasquez, the above points indicate the protean character of the evolution of the balance of power theory. But more than that, the way Christensen and Snyder (1990) have sought to fill the gap created by Waltz's failure to discuss the nature of his proposition under multipolarity, illustrates the degenerating nature of the realist paradigm. Critical of Waltz's theory on the grounds that it is too parsimonious and indeterminate, Christensen and Snyder (1990), specified that states will engage in buck passing (the reliance on third parties to bear the cost of stopping a rising hegemon) or chain-ganging (the unconditional commitment to reckless allies whose survival is deemed indispensable to the maintenance of the balance) depending on their perceived balance between offense and defense. They cited the European pattern of alliance formation, which led to WWI as an example of chain ganging and the pattern that occurred in Europe in the 1930s as an example of buck-passing. Vasquez, however, finds many problems with Christensen and Snyder's (1990) interpretation of their finding. The first problem he finds with them is that they assumed that Waltz's balance of power proposition is unproblematic for understanding alliance formation under bipolarity and therefore focused their attention on the explanation of balance of power under multipolarity. Second, and more problematic for Vasquez, was the way Christensen and Snyder went about filling the gap in Waltz's propositions. According to him, they try to cement the gap in Waltz's theory by importing a variable (the balance between offense and defense) from Van Evera (1984) who in turn got it from Jervis (1978), adorned it with fanciful labels (chain ganging and buck-passing) to give the false impression that neorealist theory is a cumulative and progressive enterprise. Upon close inspection, however, Vasquez contends, their finding reveals the degenerative tendency of the paradigm because:

> ...the argument that states will engage in buck passing or chain-ganging is an admission that in an important instance, such as the 1930s, states failed to balance the way Waltz (1979) says they must because of the system's structure (p.906).

Vasquez then submits that the emendation by Walt, Schweller, and Christensen and Snyder tries to salvage something of the balance of power theory, but does so only by moving farther and farther away from its original concept. For him, this observation, together with the lack of willingness on the part of realists/neorealists to specify what constitutes the true theory, which if falsified would lead to a rejection of the paradigm, provide ample evidence about the degenerating tendencies of the realist/neorealist research program.

Vasquez's effort in this article is quite bold and commendable. The primary problem with it, a difficulty that illuminates the problematics of comparing theories of international relations relates to his adoption of the Lakatosian criteria. Walt criticized him on this ground and asserted that Vasquez's "reliance on Lakatos's model of scientific progress is problematic, because the Lakatosian model has been largely rejected by contemporary historians and philosophers of science" (Walt 1997:931). The issue of how to operate Lakatos' criteria is rendered doubly difficult because Lakatos himself did not specify precisely what the operational criteria are, or should be. Scholars like Elman and Elman (1997:923), assert that although Lakatos himself did not specify the operational criteria for appraising research programs, there is a voluminous literature on his methodology, "including extended discussion of the operational criteria for appraising scientific research programs". They add that, the operational criteria which Lakotosians have specified address two sorts of problem shifts – "intra-or within program problem shifts which consists of modifications to the protective belt of auxiliary hypotheses, and inter-or between program problem shifts, which occur when, despite the prohibition against modification, elements of the hard core of the program are rewritten." They then argue that problem shifts are degenerative to the extent that they are ad hoc, and that Lakatosians distinguish among three notions of ad hocness: ad hoc_1, the theory predicts no novel consequences; ad hoc_2 the theory's novel predictions have not been corroborated; and ad hoc_3, the theory is obtained from its predecessor through a modification of the auxiliary hypotheses that does not accord with the positive heuristic of the program.Although Elman and Elman are right on this point, one should bear in mind that, it is the absence of consensus among Lakotosians on important elements, which constitute the operation of Lakatos's criteria that renders the operation of the criteria problematic. For example, as the Elmans themselves note, there are at least seven definitions of what constitutes novel facts among Lakatosians. And one might add that these do not all complement one another. Thus, a scholar's adoption of any one of these operational definitions of what constitutes novel facts would still render him/her vulnerable to criticism even from those who sympathize with Lakatos's criteria.

Another reason why the evaluations of theories of international relations is a problematic venture relates to the proliferation of different strands even within each rival school of thought such that it is difficult, if not impossible to nail down their propositions on the subject of inquiry without losing something of worth to the theories. Moreover, with respect to a subject like foreign aid, the rival theories hold similar perspectives on some issues, albeit for different reasons. For example, on a variable like imports, economic liberalism with its aversion to closed markets and protectionism would not frown at the finding of a positive correlation between the value of goods imported by an aid recipient country from a donor and the amount of ODA it receives from such donor. Similarly, realism because of its favorite disposition to protecting the national interest of donor countries would find such positive correlation appropriate. In assessing the motivations for foreign aid therefore, the issue about what variants of each theory merits consideration become subjective decisions. These are important issues to bear in mind.

Still, an evaluation of the propositions of realism and liberalism with respect to the motivations for aid allocation to sub-Saharan Africa in the post-Cold War era has at least two merits. First, given the opposing perspectives of the primary variants of each theory on whether aid should be given at all, and if so how much, it is of heuristic import to evaluate whether on balance the allocation of aid to one of the poorest regions on earth accords with the parochial motivations suggested by realism, or the universalistic ideals proposed by liberalism. A second consideration which is closely related to the first point is that, because the motivations for aid have strong bearings on the effectiveness of aid in promoting economic development in aid recipient states, it is proper to examine the positions of rival theories of international relations on the motivation question. Doing so promises to supply valuable insights that would allow one to proffer suggestions for either eliminating aid, or modifying it to rendering it more effective.

3 Variables, Hypotheses and Methodology

The Dependent Variable

The dependent variable in this study is bilateral official development assistance (ODA).[20] For the purposes of this research and because bilateral aid still represents the single largest source of foreign aid allocations from advanced industrial countries (AICs) to developing countries (LDCs), multilateral aid and aid from Non-Governmental Organizations (NGOs) are excluded from consideration.[21] The donor countries whose aid policies have been selected for comparative examination are the G7 countries (Canada, France, Germany, Italy, Japan, UK and the US), and the three Scandinavian countries of Denmark,

---

[20] The Development Assistance Committee (DAC) defines this as: "Those flows to developing countries and multilateral institutions provided by official agencies, including states and local governments, or by their executive agencies, each transaction of which meets the following tests a) it is administered with the promotion of the economic development and welfare of developing countries as its main objective; and b) it is concessional in character and conveys a grant element of at least 25 percent" *(Geographic Distribution of Financial Flows to Aid Recipients. DAC, 1997:249).*

In calculating the value of the dependent variable (ODA), I have departed from the example of previous studies such as, Schraeder, Hook and Taylor (1998), which used per capita ODA. Instead, I have emulated Poe (1991 and 1992) and Poe & Meernik (1995:409) by adopting net ODA as my dependent variable. In defending this method, Poe & Meernik argued that because decision makers in donor countries must concern themselves with budgetary constraints inherent to the aid allocation process, it seems that these decision makers would be more likely to think of foreign aid output in terms of their actual size. I agree.

[21] I shall, nonetheless, make comparative references to trends in the allocation of multilateral aid by the donors in the study. Although multilateral aid is widely regarded as having a larger public goods component than bilateral aid (Bobrow and Boyer, 1996), in some cases, multilateral aid serves the national interest of the donor as effectively as bilateral aid. Such "benefits include the enhanced credibility donors achieve by such collaborations. In other cases, particularly those involving environmental policy, multilateral agencies address regional or global problems of consequence to the donor states that cannot be resolved through bilateral channels" Hook (1995:29). It is also note worthy that in recent years, there have been significant increases in the volume of aid to NGOs. This volume, however, is still comparatively less than the flow of bilateral aid.

Norway and Sweden.[22] There are thirty-six sub-Saharan African states in the study.[23]

The Independent Variables

Ten independent variables are included in the study. These ten variables are organized into five clusters: (1) The strategic importance of recipient to donor, (2) Economic variables, (3) The Humanitarian needs of recipient States, (4) Ex-colonial ties between donor and recipient, and (5) Democracy.

(1) Strategic Importance

The notion of strategic importance resides at the core of realist assumptions about the motivations for foreign aid.[24] Three variables are used to test the correlation between aid allocations and recipients' strategic importance to donors. These are:

Foreign Military Presence. The decision by a donor to station a significant number of its troops in an aid recipient country, and conversely, the willingness of such recipient state to host foreign troops from a particular donor state is herein referred to as foreign military presence (FMP).[25] FMP indicates the existence of important ties between such donors and recipients. Aid by a donor

---

[22] My original goal was to include all the DAC members in the study. Doing so, however, raises problematic issues of validity and reliability. For example, although countries like Ireland, New Zealand and Austria have impressive foreign aid programs, they do not allocate aid to many of the countries in this study. Their inclusion would yield missing data for too many cases that it could the statistical results derived from the multiple regression analysis suspect.

[23] As Przerworski and Tenune (1989) reminds us, the critical problem in cross national research is that of identifying "equivalent phenomena and analyzing the relationship between them in an equivalent fashion". Therefore, I have used two criteria in determining whether to include an aid recipient, sub-Saharan African state in the study: First, that such a state was an internationally recognized sovereign state by 1989 in other to accommodate the one year lag time built into the regression analysis. Second, that it had a population of at least one million people as at 1989. The countries which met these criteria are: Angola, Benin, Botswana, Burkina Faso, Burundi, Cameroon, Central African Republic, Chad, Congo, Cote d' Ivoire, Ethiopia, Gabon, Ghana, Guinea, Kenya, Lesotho, Liberia, Madagascar, Malawi, Mali, Mauritania, Mauritius, Mozambique, Niger, Nigeria, Rwanda, Senegal, Sierra Leone, Somalia, Sudan, Tanzania, Togo, Uganda, former Zaire, Zambia, and Zimbabwe.

[24] For examples of works discussing this point, see Wittkopf (1972), Organski (1990), Van-Evera (1990), Mansour (1994) and Poe & Meernik (1995).

[25] In this study Foreign Military Presence is considered significant if it involves the stationing of at least five hundred troops from a donor's country. Troops stationed as part of a multinational effort, such as UN peacekeeping missions, are not considered as FMP, because

to states where it has a military presence could help sustain a regime friendly to such donor, or it could be used as reward to the recipient state for hosting the donor's troops for the furtherance of the donor's interests in that particular region. The hypothesis derived from realist theory therefore is that the pattern of aid allocation by a given donor should reflect a preference for countries hosting its troops. For liberal theory, which serves as the null hypothesis, FMP should not influence aid allocation. This variable is operationalized as a dummy variable.

Recipient States' Defense Expenditures. The rationale for using this variable to measure a recipient state's strategic importance to a donor is premised on the assumption that because security issues are central to realist theory, donors interested in promoting their security would seek out states which have the military capability to assume the role of surrogates for the pursuit of the donor's political interests. Liberal theory again serves as the null hypothesis.

In the post-Cold War era, such donor-interest runs the gamut from anti-terrorism, through nuclear non-proliferation, to the containment of the growth of religious fundamentalism (Huntington, 1996). With respect to some sub-Saharan African states, especially those in the Horn of Africa, US foreign policy during the Cold War, although primarily motivated by its ideological competition with the former Soviet Union, reflected some of the concerns mentioned above.[26] It is equally note worthy that, as much as a recipient state's defense expenditure is revealing of its strategic value to a donor, it could also be an indication of the levels of repression, or of internal conflict, or of civil war in such aid recipient state. Given the peculiarities of authoritarian regimes in sub-Saharan Africa, this is particularly worrisome. Bearing this in mind necessitates a cautious interpretation of the multiple regression coefficients for this variable.

Presence of Strategic Minerals in Recipient State. Minerals such as uranium, manganese, platinum, bauxite, and chromium, are considered vital to the national security of advanced industrial states. It is equally true that many AICs manifest acute dependence on these minerals, some of which are abundant in some African states. The United Kingdom, for instance, is 100 percent dependent on imported chromium, cobalt and iron ore; 74 percent dependent on aluminum; and 67 percent dependent on copper (Crowson,

---

an aid donor's decision to participate in such multilateral operation could be more of a reflection of its support for the efforts of such international organization than its interest in the host state.

[26] For examples of works which discuss this point, see Lefevbre (1991), and Mansour (1994).

1997).[27] I have constructed a strategic mineral index (SMI) to measure this variable. (See the mathematical computation of this index in Appendix I.)

If the proposition of realist theory about the influence that parochial interest exert on foreign aid allocation is correct, the aid allocation policies of donor states should evince a pattern whereby, recipient states with higher scores on the strategic mineral index receive more aid than others who are not similarly endowed. On the other hand, the hypothesis derived from liberal theory is that scores on the SMI would make no difference in the amount of aid states received.

(II) Humanitarian Need

Population. The size of a state's population is commonly believed to be representative of its actual power capabilities (for industrialized countries) or potential power capabilities (for developing countries). Realists and liberal theorists agree about the relevance of population in the determination of foreign aid allocation. Realists, however, perceive population as a measure of a state's potential political and economic capabilities, while some liberal scholars view population only as indicative of an aid recipient-state's relative need for such aid, (Lumsdaine, 1993). Because the allocation of foreign aid promotes cordial relations between aid donors and recipients, a hypothesis derived from realist theory is that donors would tend to preferentially allocate aid to large, relatively wealthier states that have the potential for becoming regional powers. Liberal scholars, on the other hand, emphasizing the humanitarian motivation behind aid allocation, hypothesize that larger poor states should attract more aid to meet their relative need for such assistance. In interpreting the regression results as to whether realist or liberal propositions are at work with respect to the population variable, I examine how the coefficient sign for this variable combines with the coefficient signs for other variables that are less ambiguous with respect to the predictions of the two theories.

Recipient States' Per Capita Gross Domestic Product (GDP). For some liberal scholars, for example Lumsdaine (1993), the humanitarian needs of recipient states provide stronger insights into the motivations for aid allocation than the real-politik propositions by realists. Other liberal scholars such as Noel and Theiren submit that the results of their study show that states with strong domestic welfare programs tend to have strong foreign aid programs. They

---

[27] See Appendix I: Table I for the dependency ratios of countries in the European Union, the US and Japan. Also, Tsousoplides (1991), and Paone (1992), shed some additional light on this point.

further suggest that such findings vindicate the position espoused by scholars like Friedrich Kratochwil about the impact of domestic transformations on international interactions (Noel and Theiren, 1995:552). Still, other scholars like Bobrow and Boyer suggest that the humanitarian imperative behind the allocation of aid is a:

> ...far better explanation (albeit, an incomplete one) of the foreign aid behavior by the members of the OECD than narrow economic motives of trade and investment, competition with the Soviet Union, donor pursuit of prestige, or hegemonic American leadership (Bobrow and Boyer, 1997:86).

From the above propositions, I derived the liberal hypothesis, which specifies that poorer states would receive more aid from donors than relatively richer ones.

Whereas the humanitarian need thesis of foreign aid motivation argues that aid allocation correlates with short falls in the domestic resources of the recipient state and therefore uses Per-Capita GDP as an indicator of the relative need of such states, realist theory suggests an opposite correlation between GDP and aid allocation. It hypothesizes that donors concerned with protecting their profitable economic interests would tend to preferentially allocate aid to wealthier states, as aid would help to promote the profitability of such donors' export trade and alleviate the economic difficulties of its major trading partners.

(III) Economic Variables

Donor's Trading Interest. One of the strongest criticisms of foreign aid has been the tendency of some donors to tie their aid allocation to recipients' procurement of goods from such donor states, thereby promoting the profitability of the donors' export trade. This observation provides some justification for the realist position about the national interest motivation behind foreign aid allocation. The hypothesis derived from realist theory therefore is that, one should find the pattern of such donors' aid allocation favoring states importing relatively higher values of goods from such donors. Alternatively, aid could be used by donors to gain access to hitherto closed markets, as Vengroff (1982) observed in his study of the US food aid to sub-Saharan Africa.

On the other hand, although many liberals argue against the practice of tied aid on the grounds that it promotes inefficiency and distorts the market for such goods, liberal theory as a whole does not frown at the prospect of a positive correlation between aid and trade. The humanitarian variant of liberal theory, however, leads one to expect that the finding of a strong positive correlation between aid and the value of recipient states' import of goods from such donors would be problematic if it takes away from the poverty-reduction focus of aid. Data for this variable were obtained from the *Direction of Trade Statistics* published by the International Monetary Fund (IMF).

Donor's Investment Interest This variable assumes that a self-interested donor would allocate more aid to countries where its national firms either have, relatively substantial investments, or to countries where they seek such investments. Aid to such countries would, therefore represent an external subsidy to ensure the profitability of the foreign investment of such donor country's multi-national corporations (See Maizels and Nissanke, 1984:884). Essentially, there are two principal methods of measuring FDI. The first method, which yields a more accurate result, uses the stock of the FDI of a donor's national firms in an aid-recipient state. The second method takes note of the number of affiliations and subsidiaries of multi-national corporations (MNCs) originating from the donor's country and located in the recipient-state. This latter measure is less accurate because it does not take into consideration differences in the size of the MNC affiliates involved (Tsoutsoplides, 1991). The first and more accurate method was adopted for this study. Because of the peculiar problems of data gathering in sub-Saharan Africa, however, accurate information about the annual changes in the stock of donors' FDI in recipient states are not available. I have therefore utilized the reported FDI for 1993 and 1994 for most donors. Such data were obtained from the *World Directory of Foreign Investment* published by the United Nations.

(VI) Colonial Ties

Donor's Ex-Colony. Schraeder, Hook and Taylor (1998) accurately observed that, because the heritage of colonialism exerts significant influence on the culture of African states, especially as it affects their international relations, it is imperative to measure the effects of culture on the aid policies of donor countries. While their observation is correct, for the purposes of this study, how one should classify this variable becomes problematic. Realists, with their emphasis on the national interest motivation behind aid allocation, could accurately claim that the allocation of aid to a donor's former colony furthers such donor's national interest to the extent that it allows her to exert control over the former colony's economy, enhances its international stature, increases its stock of goodwill and generally provides it with significant leverage over the international relations of the former colony. Liberals, on the other hand could equally argue that the interpretation of cultural similarity as a national interest variable constitutes an overly expansive definition of national interest. Logically speaking, almost everything under the sun could be given a national interest interpretation. But doing so would render the term analytically useless. Moreover, a donor's demonstration of preference for its ex-colonies in its aid allocation could be a mere case of "charity beginning at home", rather than summoning aid to serve any specific national interest. These objections are well taken. Still, in measuring variables in order to properly test hypotheses, it is imperative to eliminate as much as possible definitions that are vague, fluctuating, and confusing.

Furthermore, a strong argument could be made for the realist position that whatever a state's immediate aim, if the ultimate goal of its policy is the enhancement of its power with its scarce resources, to the extent that its disbursement of aid to other countries increases its prestige, such expenditure of its resources augments the intangible components of its national power. Here it is particularly to heed *Occam's razor*.[28] Thus, I consider it more analytically useful to classify ex-colony as a realist rather than a liberal variable. In this study, I treated this variable as a binary one, where 0=No and 1=Yes.

(V) Democracy

Levels of Democracy. The end of the cold war has witnessed the emergence of democracy as a crucial variable in the study of international relations. So pervasive, and some would say persuasive, is the liberal thesis on the importance of this variable that the propositions of democratic peace theorists have emerged as the new orthodoxy in the study of international relations. Many liberals hail democracy as a powerful predictor of a state's behavior. With particular reference to foreign aid, a 1989 published statement by the Development Assistance Committee (DAC) of the OECD directly linked development with democracy:

> There is a vital connection, now more widely appreciated, between open, democratic and accountable political systems, and individual rights. And the effective and equitable operations of economic development implies more democracy, a greater role for local organizations and self-government, respect for human rights, including accessible legal systems, competitive markets and dynamic private enterprise (Quoted in Stokkes, 1996:75).

In light of the above points, the hypothesis I derived from liberal theory

---

[28] Occam's razor (named after William of Occam, an English scholar and philosopher who died about 1349) is the maxim that assumptions introduced to explain a thing must not be multiplied beyond necessity.

is that in the post-Cold war period the level of a country's democracy would be an important determinant of the amount of aid it receives from donor countries.

Realists, on the other hand, dismiss the connection between democracy and peace on several grounds. First, they note the paucity of cases substantiating the democratic peace propositions. Second, they argue that contrary to the assertion of the proponents of the theory, democracies have indeed sometimes fought other democracies. The American-British war of 1812, for instance, they argue, "was fought by the only two democratic states that existed, and conflict and bitterness between them persisted through the century and beyond" (Waltz, 1993:78). Third, realists recall that a Germany with a pluralistic democracy fought two major wars with other democracies.[29]

There are additional arguments for using levels of democracy as an independent variable to tap into the motivation question. In recent years, the strong links between democracy, accountability, rule of law, open markets, and an aid recipient state's ability to use aid effectively have received renewed attention. Equally important is that most aid donors have signified their intention to use democratization as a condition for disbursing their aid funds. In his State of the Union address in 1994, US President Bill Clinton referred to the promotion of democracy and human rights as the corner stone of his administration. Moreover, recent trade legislation such as the African Trade and Opportunity Act passed by the US Congress in 2000 make a vital link between American aid and the institution of democracy in recipient states.

In this study, I operationalized this variable by using the seven-point scale of political rights developed by Freedom House. For notes on how this scale is defined and measured, see *Freedom in the World*, 1994-1995: (672-677).[30]

---

[29] There is a burgeoning literature on the relevance of democracy in the explanation of foreign policy behavior. For a general enunciation of the impact of democracy on foreign policy behavior, see Doyle (1996). For works arguing the specific case for the "democratic peace", see Babst (1964), Chan (1984), Dixon (1994), Gleditch (1992), Levy (1989), Maoz and Russett (1993), Owen (1996), Rummel (1983), Russet (1996), Weede (1983), (1984), (1989), (1992). For challenges to the "democratic peace" prepositions, see Layne (1996), Meashaimer (1990), and Spiro (1996). For works discussing democracy as a conditionality for foreign aid, see Meenik, Kreuger and Poe (1998), Riddell (1993), Sorensen (1995), and Stokke (1995).

[30] In the Freedom House scale, which runs from one through seven, a score of 1 represents most democratic and 7 least democratic. To facilitate statistical measurement, in my regression analysis, I have revised the order of this scale in the opposite direction.

Methodology

This study adopts a statistical method of inquiry to evaluate the explanatory power of realism and liberalism on the aid motivation question. The choice of this methodology stems from its utility in probing the relationships between variables for a universe through the manipulation of samples drawn from it. Statistical methods also allow one to perform a variety of operations, some of which can be used to check the significance of others. There is a variety of statistical approaches, which one could use to investigate a given question, but the one most appropriate for this study is the pooled time series, multiple regression method. Charles Ostrom, Jr. (1978:9) defines time series as a collection of data X_t (t=1,2,...,T) where the interval between observations X_t and $X_t + 1$ is fixed and constant. The use of this method requires that the data be ordered into cross sections – a unit of analysis at a single point in time for which there are observations on a set of variables ($X_1...X_n$). When the variables for a number of different cross sections are observed over time, the resulting data matrix is known as pooled time series (Sayrs, 1989:7). Multiple-regression helps in the isolation of relationships between variables so that one could "tell whether or not they (relationships) exist, and their strength even after one controls for other variables" (Handwerker & Bogatti, 1998:576).

The pooled time series multiple regression approach is preferable to the old, "separate regression-multiple years" method used by scholars such as Maizels and Nissanke (1984), Tsousoplides (1991), and Lumsdaine (1993) for at least two important reasons: First, there is the consideration that running separate regressions is like doing separate zero-order correlation coefficients. This is problematic because, other than the fact that one capitalizes on chance to find low probabilities, one is unable to control for other potential influences.

The second reason is that, the chronologically ordered format of time series data comes closest to familiar notions of history. For inquiries such as the motivations behind foreign aid, such proximity to history is invaluable. In this regard, the advantage of time series, as Janoski and Isaac (1994:31) point out, is that, rather than simply describing "one damn year after another", time series allows one to test for the strength of relationships over a period of time while controlling for the influence of other variables.

The combination of pooled time series with multiple-regression, however, gives rise to important methodological problems. For one, in the pooled time series structure, data for one year's value is often closely related to the previous year's value, thereby violating the basic assumption of ordinary least square (OLS) which states that the error terms corresponding to different points in time are not correlated. The existence of such serial correlation causes the coefficients to be inefficient, the estimated standard errors to contract, and the significant errors to inflate. Thus, the results of an insignificant equation may appear to be significant. This study dealt with these problems by utilizing the modified OLS procedure that lagged the endogenous variable. I then performed tests for autocorrelation/serial correlation by using the time series analytical tools in SYSTAT. Where there was significant autocorrelation, differencing the series produced more efficient estimates. In addition to this procedure, I performed the generalized least square error component (GLSE) procedure with the aid of the SAS program and then compared the results to the ones from SYSTAT. As expected, there was no significant difference in the two results.

In the pooled time series for this study, there are eight observational years spanning 1990-1997. The combination of the 10 donor states, the 36 recipient states and the 8 series years yields a total of 2880 observational points. In measuring the effect of the independent variables on changes in the values of the dependent variable, I built in a one-year lag time to account for the lag between the availability of information on the hypothesized causal variables in the recipient state and the reflection of that information in the formulation of the donors' aid policies.

In calculating the multiple regression coefficients, I employed the natural log transformations[31] for the dependent variable (ODA) and those for the independent variables to enhance my observation of a linear relationship between the variables. The exceptions to this procedure were those for the variables strategic mineral index (SMI), and foreign military presence (FMP) and Ex-Coly which are binary variables. For the treatment of the missing data for the values of recipient states' defense expenditure, I used the linear interpolation method in SPSS and then imported the results into SYSTAT. In this procedure, "the last valid value before the missing value, and the first valid value after the missing value are used for the interpolation" (SPSS: 1996:79). I also used SYSTAT for the production of the scattergrams included in the case studies.

---

[31] The advantage of using the natural log transformation is that it reduces vast disparities in the data values without destroying the relative order of the observation vis-à-vis one another. The use of the natural log transformation also means, however, that the relationship between the dependent and independent variables is curvilinear rather than linear (i.e., curvilinear in the raw data, but the relationship is still linear in the parameters of the regression model). Because of this the regression coefficients can no longer be interpreted as the slope of a line fitted through data points, where a one unit increase in the independent variable produces a change in the dependent variable equal to the regression coefficient. Nonetheless, the regression coefficients are still directly interpretable, this time as elasticity coefficients (Wittkopf, 1972:34).

4 The Findings: Realist Lore and Liberal Principles: Another Case for Muted Optimism

The transfer of financial resources in the form of foreign aid by advanced-industrial countries (AICs) to less developed countries (LDCs) represents a rational decision on the part of the former to incur the opportunity costs that prevent such resources from being allocated to alternative uses. A scrutiny of such spending behavior provides valuable insights into the motivation for different donors, and it allows one to evaluate the positions of rival theories of international relations on these motivations. True, the foreign aid policies of the developed countries do not fall neatly into the dichotomous categories suggested by rival theories of international relations. This observation is even more pertinent given that the proposition of the rival theories considered in this study come with caveats which while being somewhat question begging, nonetheless represent important admission of the diversity of interests which push and tug foreign aid policies in particular directions.[32]

The task of this chapter is to sort out the degree of influence, which humanitarian, other-regarding principles, or/and narrow self-interest exert on the foreign policies of the different donors. Here I present the findings of the study, followed by a general discussion of what these findings imply for the propositions of realism and liberalism. In addition to my presentation of these findings, I briefly discuss the post-Cold War patterns of aid allocation for six important donors – Canada, Denmark, Germany, Italy, Sweden, and

---

[32] Thus, arguing the case for the liberal position on the motivations for foreign aid Lumsdaine reiterated his assertion several times that "foreign aid cannot be accounted for on the basis of the economic and political interests of the donor countries *alone* (emphasis added), the essential causes lay in the humanitarian and egalitarian principles of the donor countries, and in their implicit belief that only on the basis of a just and international order in which all states had a chance to do well was peace and prosperity possible" (1993:30). In a similar vain, while articulating a neo-realist position of foreign aid Gilpin maintained that: "Although humanitarian and developmental concerns do play an important role, the primary motives for aid by individual governments have been political, military and commercial" (1987:311-12).

the United Kingdom – to sub-Saharan Africa. I defer the discussion of the aid policies of the other four donors – France, Japan, Norway, and the United States to the four subsequent chapters in part two where more detailed study of the cases for these donors are presented and discussed. Before turning to the regression results it is useful to underscore some basic facts about foreign aid in general.

First, as Lumsdaine (1993), correctly points out, the idea of strong states providing financial assistance to weak states is a relatively new phenomenon in interstate relations. Historically, rather than promote the outward flows of financial and technological resources to weak states, strong states often sought protection money from weak states (Lumsdaine, 1993:33).[33] The origins of the contemporary foreign aid regime[34] are traceable to the European Economic Recovery Plan, otherwise known as the Marshall Plan, named after then US Secretary of State, George C. Marshall whose address at Harvard University in June 1947 contained the original idea. Marshall proposed the establishment of a program of economic assistance by the United States to help European governments and their people rebuild their World War II ravaged economies. By the end of the summer of 1947, however, it became apparent that the prospects of a quick European Economic Recovery were bleak. United States bilateral aid to states, such as the United Kingdom and France, were quickly depleted and existing international institutions, such as the International Bank for Reconstruction and Development (IBRD), were inadequate for the task. The establishment of a multilateral regional institution was proposed by Marshall to replace the previous US bilateral programs. The United States then requested European states to consult together, coordinate their efforts, and provide the US with specific, statistically based information about their needs. The subsequent coordination between European states gave birth to the Organization for European Economic Recovery (OEEC). In due course the OEEC evolved into the Organization for Economic Cooperation and Development (OECD) at a convention signed by twenty states in Paris on December 14, 1960. The current OECD includes three major countries that were not members of the OEEC: the United States, Japan, and Canada. From

---

[33] It should be noted, however, that there were significant exceptions to the historical pattern of strong state-weak state relations observed by Lumsdaine. A striking example relates to French aid to American founding fathers during the American revolutionary war against Great Britain. French aid, which was not tied to exploitative conditionality was critical to American victory.

[34] A regime refers to the "set of implicit or explicit principles, norms, rules, and decision making processes, around which actor's expectations converge in a given area of international relations", Krasner (1982:186). A more state-centric perspective defines regimes as "governing arrangements constructed by states to coordinate their expectations and organize aspects of their behavior in various issue arrears", Kratochwil and Ruggie (1986:759).

the outset, development was stipulated as a central concern of the OECD (Evans and Newnhan, 1997). In 1963, members of the OECD formed the Development Assistance Committee (DAC) to coordinate the transfer of bilateral and multilateral resources to developing countries to assist them in their development efforts. Since its inception, the DAC has been the leading forum for rich nations to discuss their mutual interests in aid administration.

From its Marshall plan beginnings, foreign aid has grown in quantity and quality such that by the end of the twentieth century, virtually all developing countries and the former Soviet republics received one form of aid or the other from developed countries. Scholars now talk about the existence of a foreign aid regime. Increasingly too, the provision of foreign aid by the developed democracies has come to be viewed as one of the services which they render to developing countries - a public good contribution - to the maintenance of the stability of the international system (Bobrow and Boyer, 1997).

It is equally worth noting that the provision of aid by the members of the Development Assistance Committee (DAC) of the OECD, unlike the practice of other international institutions like the International Monetary Fund (IMF), has been a public and open process in terms of the public accessibility of their reports.[35] In addition, the foreign aid in question here has been offered on two important concessional terms – as outright grants, or as loans bearing such low interest as to have a very high grant element.

On the surface, these observations about some of the basic characteristics of foreign aid provide strong justification for the position of liberal scholars on the humanitarian motivation behind aid allocation. True, there is a persuasive ring to such position. On the other hand, such claim provides strong reasons to gauge how well the pattern of aid allocation to sub-Saharan Africa, one of the poorest regions on earth, correlates with the liberal position in the post-Cold War era. Moreover, as Baldwin (1966:5) observes, foreign aid is first and foremost a technique of statecraft, a means by which some nations attempt to influence other nations to act in desired ways. One should also bear in mind that the ten donors whose aid policies are examined in this study have incorporated their aid programs into their broader economic, political, and security relations with sub-Saharan African states.

---

[35] The DAC publishes periodic reports on the volume, terms and allocation of aid by its members to recipient states and international institutions. Although a few of these reports contain inconsistent figures, perhaps, attributable to the problems inherent in the gathering of such comprehensive data, they are impressive and thorough.

Table 4.1
Results of Pooled Time-Series Regression for Bilateral ODA and Independent Variables (1990-1997)

VARIABLES	CANADA Beta	t Scores	DENMARK Beta	t Scores	FRANCE Beta	t Scores
Constant	2.403	.699	13.002	1.369	9.979	3.741
FMP	-.029	-.430	-.109	-1.935	.088	1.676
FR-EXCOLY	.207	2.306*			.444	5.938*
DEFEXP	.021	.312	-.088	-1.492	-.004	-.081
FDI	.083	1.309	.218	3.979**	-.046	-.862
GDP	-.071	-1.001	-.283	-4.328**	-.103	-1.605
IMPORTS	.150	2.264*	.070	1.223	.142	2.159*
POP	.211	2.644*	.149	2.189*	.120	2.022*
PR	.070	1.041	.157	2.549*	.041	.760
SMI	.020	.314	.036	.592	-.017	-.328
UK-EXCOLY	.142	1.666			-.164	-2.529*
R^2	.123		.225		.443	
Adjusted R^2	.092		.202		.422	
F	3.896		10.100		21.986	
F Significance	.000		.000		.000	

* = p < .005
** = p < .001

Table 4.1
Results of Pooled Time-Series Regression for Bilateral ODA and Independent Variables (1990-1997)

VARIABLES	GERMANY Beta	t Scores	ITALY Beta	t Scores	JAPAN Beta	t Scores
Constant	11.448	3.191**	-10.753	-1.666	13.944	1.910
FMP	.108	1.930	.050	1.011	.027	.454
DEFEXP	.049	.842	.087	1.544	-.190	-2.967**
FDI	-.054	-1.021	.040	.785	.150	1.973*
GDP	-.285	-4.385**	-.185	-3.008**	-.070	-.966
IMPORTS	-.115	-1.972*	-.090	-1.557	-.009	-.137
POP	.299	4.334**	.388	5.906**	.260	3.200**
PR	-.038	-.648	-.161	-2.877**	.265	4.122**
SMI	.163	2.849**	.070	1.294	.072	1.152
R^2	.315		.390		.158	
Adjusted R^2	.295		.373		.133	
F	16.023		22.316		6.524	
F Significance	.000		.000		.000	

Table 4.1
Results of Pooled Time-Series Regression for Bilateral ODA and Independent Variables (1990-1997)

VARIABLES	NORWAY Beta	t Scores	SWEDEN Beta	t Scores	UK Beta	t Scores
Constant	-16.659	-2.179*	-10.341	-1.231	1.402	.303
FMP	-.150	-2.935**	-.215	-3.796**	-.180	-3.536
FR-EXCOLY					-.304	-4.091*
DEFEXP	.058	1.022	.060	.928	.067	1.318
FDI	-.200	-3.708**	.134	2.298*	-.075	-1.289
GDP	-.154	-2.487**	-.104	-1.535	-.135	-2.217*
IMPORTS	.125	2.439**	.156	2.428*	.004	.063
POP	.242	3.798**	.077	1.056.222	3.345	*
PR	.075	1.306	.063	.990	-.068	-1.310
SMI	.200	3.612**	.074	1.180	-.064	-1.212
UK-EXCOLY					.207	2.952*
R^2	.342		.191		.484	
Adjusted R^2	.323		.168		.465	
F	18.098		8.208		25.967	
F Significance	.000		.000		.000	

Table 4.1
Results of Pooled Time-Series Regression for Bilateral ODA and Independent Variables (1990-1997)

VARIABLES	UNITED STATES Beta	t Scores
Constant	7.517	1.665
FMP	.072	1.300
DEFEXP	.109	1.744
FDI	.000	.002
GDP	-.316	-4.445**
IMPORTS	.017	.250
POP	.163	2.160*
PR	-.027	-.447
SMI	.083	1.394
R^2	.231	
Adjusted R^2	.209	
F	10.480	
F Significance	.000	

Canada

As evident from Table 4.1, the independent variables in this study account for only about 12 percent in the variance of Canada's aid to sub-Saharan Africa in the post-Cold War era. Notwithstanding this low proportion of explained variation, it is possible to make important observations about the nature of Canadian aid to the sub continent. The first observation is the finding of a statistically significant positive correlation between Canadian ODA and former French colonies (t=2.306).[36] Given Canada's bicultural heritage, this finding is not surprising. What is interesting, however, is what appears to be a shift from the preference for former British colonies to former French colonies.[37] While the correlation between Canadian ODA and former British colonies is also positive, it is only significant at the 90 percent p value. A plausible explanation for this finding is the fact that Canada is the only DAC donor, which belongs to both the Commonwealth and *La Francophonie*. This has therefore brought a unique dimension to its worldwide development assistance program. Given that it shares this trait with the sub-Saharan African region where the majority of states are either former British or French colonies, for many years Canada sought to provide nearly two thirds of its bilateral assistance to countries in those two groups.

Equally notable are the positive correlation between Canadian aid and the population of recipient states (t=2.644), coupled with the value of their imports from Canada (t=2.264). These findings point to the mixed motives behind Canadian aid. On the one hand, while the disbursement of aid to more populous countries suggests a policy of allocating aid according to need, the positive correlation between Canadian ODA and the value of recipient states imports from Canada suggests a tendency on the part of the Canadian government to employ aid in the service of its economic interest. This finding also indicates that, of the humanitarian, political, and economic dimensions

---

[36] Some studies, for example, Vengroff and Tsai (1982) chose to report the beta coefficients in the presentation of their results. I elect to report the t statistic for the multiple regression equation in this study.

This does not present any problems because, in multiple linear regression, there are many statistics that are equivalent. Choosing to report the variable that results in the largest increase in R^2, for example, is the same as choosing the variable that has the smallest observed significance level for the test of its partial regression coefficient. This is also the same as choosing the variable with the largest absolute value for the t statistic, the variable with the largest absolute value for its partial correlation coefficient, and the variable which results in the smallest residual sum of squares (Norusis, 1997:461).

[37] See DAC Report for the years 1980-89.

which have represented the trinity of motivations behind Canadian aid policies toward sub-Saharan Africa in the past, the post-Cold War period is witnessing a shift towards economic interests.

Another notable finding by this study is the absence of a statistically significant correlation between the record of recipient states on democratization and the allocation of Canadian aid. This finding is at odds with Bencivengal (1984) that found a correlation between Canadian aid flows and the political legitimacy of the government in the recipient states.[38]

The degree of its dispersion among the thirty-six states in this study is another notable feature of Canadian aid. With an average concentration level of forty percent, Canadian aid evinces one of the most dispersed patterns of aid giving among the ten donors whose policies are considered in this study. Even the DAC has raised concerns about the high levels of the dispersion of Canada's aid efforts because of the negative impact that such dispersion tend to exert on aid effectiveness.[39]

There are three primary reasons for the high levels of the dispersion of Canadian aid in sub-Saharan Africa. First, there is the peculiar nature of the origins of Canadian aid. Canadian aid began in the early 1960s under the liberal government of Prime Minister Lester Pearson with the intention of projecting the liberal government's values of humane internationalism abroad.[40] This policy goal necessitated that Canada exclude very few countries (in most cases, only the steadfast Soviet bloc countries) from its aid programs in order for it to maintain an aid presence in every country.

The second reason relates to the nature of Canada's domestic society mentioned earlier. Canada's bilingual heritage (British and French) mirrors the case of sub-Saharan Africa, where most countries are either former British, or French colonies.[41] Thus, the desire to project abroad Canada's image as a

---

[38] Bencivengal's study assessed political legitimacy in recipient states by using political party variables, which measured the non-exclusion of opposition parties from domestic politics. In contrast, I adopt the political rights scale developed by Freedom House. This is a more comprehensive measurement of levels of democratization than the one used by Bencivengal.

[39] See Development Cooperation: Efforts and Policies of the Members of the Development Assistance Committee, 1998.

[40] Humane internationalism is frequently used to refer to that component of the political cultures of industrialized countries which accepts that these countries have an obligation to act to alleviate global poverty and to promote the development of Third World countries. This is usually linked to the conviction that effective action to meet these obligations is also in the long-term interest of the industrialized countries (Pratt, 1989:3-23).

[41] Some sub-Saharan African countries are former Belgian colonies. French is, however, their official language. These former Belgian colonies are Burundi, Rwanda and the former Zaire, now the Democratic Republic of the Congo. And although Portuguese is the official language of the former Portuguese colonies of Angola and Mozambique, French is also widely spoken.

bilingual and bicultural country necessitates fostering links between Anglophone and Francophone Africa.[42] This trend, which now appears to be favoring former French colonies, was clearly evident in the pattern of Canadian aid during the Cold War. A 1978 study by Dudley and Monmarquette, for example, found that a significant predictor of who received Canadian aid was membership in either the Commonwealth or the Francophone communities. The nature of Canadian society, therefore, tends to impel the country's aid allocation towards relatively high levels of dispersion. Perhaps too, as Lavergne (1989:58) observes, spreading aid thinly over a large number of countries "allows the government to satisfy as large a constituency (of advocacy groups) as possible without unduly antagonizing any group".

Denmark

An examination of Danish aid to sub-Saharan Africa reveals important differences between Denmark's approach to development assistance and many of the other donors in this study. One of these differences is that, unlike donors such as France, Japan, and Germany, Danish aid concentrates on countries in southern and eastern Africa. Together, the independent variables in this study account for about 23 percent of the variance of Denmark's bilateral aid to sub-Saharan Africa in the post-Cold War era. The value of the gross domestic product (GDP) of the recipient states accounts for a larger share of this explained variance than any other variable, and the inverse correlation between GDP and ODA ($t = -4.328$) indicates the poverty amelioration focus of Danish aid.

The regression result also shows a positive correlation between the population of recipient states and the allocation of Danish aid ($t = 2.189$), revealing that Denmark preferentially allocates aid to more populous countries. This observation is in line with what liberal theory would lead one to expect. Although realist theory similarly predicts that aid would be allocated to more populous countries, the absence of a statistical significance in the correlation between ODA and defense expenditure - a corollary to realist proposition about the significance of large population - indicates that the principles of liberal humanitarianism, rather than realist calculations provide a far better explanation of Danish aid to sub-Saharan Africa. In fact, for Denmark, the correlation between ODA and the defense expenditure of recipient states is negative.

---

[42] J. Stephen Hoadley observes that although Canada has never acquired colonies, or extensive overseas territorial commitments, it is "obliged by its particular ethnic composition and delicately balanced federal politics to give token aid to both Commonwealth and Francophone recipients with which it would otherwise have little contact" (1980:126).

The regression result further reveals a positive correlation between the levels of democratization in recipient states and their receipt of aid from Denmark (t =2.549). This finding provides support for pronouncements by the Danish Government that its aid would be preferentially allocated to states taking more meaningful strides toward democratization (Development Cooperation, 1996).

Equally notable is the finding of a statistically significant positive correlation between the allocation of Danish aid and the stock of the foreign direct investment by Danish firms in aid its recipient countries (t =3.979). This finding could be interpreted as supportive evidence for the proposition of realist theory about the national interest motivation behind foreign aid. Danish authorities, however, claim that investment in its aid recipient states is in line with the country's comprehensive approach to development assistance, and that Denmark is one of the few countries that encourages its national firms to invest in its aid-partner countries (Svedson, 1989).

The outstanding Danish ODA performance has been facilitated through the existence of a revolving five-year planning procedure with expenditure frames submitted once a year to the Parliament by the government. Denmark is also one of the few donors whose aid program is governed by a special law. This law, the Danish Law on international development cooperation of 1971, articulates the broad objectives of Danish aid and obliges the Minister for Development Cooperation to submit to Parliament annually, five year expenditure plans for cooperation programs. The law specifies the objective of Danish aid to be: "to assist developing countries to achieve sustainable and balanced economic and social development based on improved living conditions, and to promote equal and free opportunities for the individual in accordance with the aims and principles of the United Nations Charter" (Development Cooperation, 1996:133).

Historically, Denmark has provided ample support for multilateral institutions. Its contributions to international institutions in 1995 amounted to 45 percent of its ODA disbursements. Beginning in that same year, it announced a policy of "active multilateralism", whereby its contributions to international organizations would be concentrated on activities having higher priority for Denmark. In this regard, the United Nations Development Program (UNDP) remains the largest single recipient of Danish multilateral ODA (18 percent in 1996), followed by the International Development Agency (IDA), which received 16 percent of Denmark's total ODA contribution for that year.

With respect to aid concentration, Danish aid manifests a duality of concentration: globally, it is concentrated on a limited number of sectors in twenty program countries - thirteen in Africa, five in Asia and two in Latin America. Then within Africa, it is concentrated on a few countries in Southern and Eastern Africa. Development experts argue in favor of aid concentration on the ground that it makes for more effective management and actualization of the declared objectives of such aid.[43] While the majority of the recipients of Danish aid have historically been in Eastern and Southern Africa, in the post-Cold War period, the West African states of Niger, Ghana and Burkina Faso have been among states favored to receive Danish aid.

According to Danish authorities, the important criteria for selecting program countries are the prospects for attaining sustainable development, and efforts made to promote the respect for human rights and democratic values. Denmark's relation with Kenya illustrates this point. At a 1996 meeting on development cooperation between the Danish and Kenyan Governments, Denmark was openly critical of Kenya's breaches of the human rights of its citizens, its negligence, or refusal to take action against the frequent complaints by Kenyans about police brutality, continued corruption within the Kenyan government, and its failure to live up to democratic standards.

Among DAC members, Denmark has built up a very good reputation in both the volume and quality of its aid efforts. The principle of recipient ownership, i.e., the primacy of recipient's own development efforts and direction, are considered central to all Danish aid programs. This partially explains the preference for Tanzania over many other countries as a recipient of Danish aid. Under the leadership of late President Julius Nyerere, the proclamation of the Arusha Declaration resonated positively with the Danish authorities who identified strongly with its paradigm of a people centered development. Ironically, however, the principles of self reliance encapsulated in the Arusha Declaration which rendered Tanzania an attractive aid recipient to many donors have been eroded by Tanzania's high dependency on foreign aid such that, its receipt of ODA as a percentage of its gross national product (GNP) rose steadily from 5 percent in the 1970s, to over 57 percent by 1992 (Bagachwa, 1997).

---

[43] See Lancaster (1999:70-3) for a discussion of this subject. Bagachwa et al. (1997:181-82), evaluation of the performance of Danish aid in Tanzania calls into question Denmark's alleged commitment to aid effectiveness. While praising Denmark for its concerted attention to issues of development, they criticized her for procurement practices that tended to tie aid to Tanzania to purchases of goods in Denmark, thereby undermining the effectiveness of such aid.

Germany

In the post-Cold War period, when measured by volume, Germany has been the second largest aid donor to the sub-Saharan African states in this study. The independent variables in this study accounts for about 32 percent of the variance in German aid. The direction of the statistically significant regression coefficients suggests that a mixture of humanitarian and parochial goals are the motives behind Germany's aid.

The most important variable in the explanation of Germany's aid to sub-Saharan Africa is the GDP of the recipient states. The inverse relationship that GDP has with ODA (t = -4.385) indicates the poverty reduction focus of Germany's aid. Pertinently too, the more populous states tended to receive relatively higher volumes of German aid (t =4.334). Together, these two variables - GDP and population - underscore the tendency on the part of Germany to direct aid to countries like Ethiopia, Mozambique, Tanzania and Rwanda where aid is most needed.

Another interesting finding of this study is the positive correlation between the scores of recipient states on the strategic mineral index (SMI) and their receipt of Germany's aid (t =2.849). This finding suggests that Germany also employs ODA in the service of its economic and security interests, and it explains the relatively high volumes of aid allocated to countries, such as Zaire and Zimbabwe, states abundantly blessed with strategic minerals.

The three basic objectives of Germany's aid are poverty reduction, protection of the environment and natural resources, and education and training. Poverty reduction, and the protection of the environment are raised as crosscutting tasks to permeate all Germany's aid activities. The German concept of poverty reduction focuses on structural reform, self-help and economic efficiency. It also emphasizes the importance of the participation of the citizens in government. The German administration considers private development as a key to poverty reduction, and it also initiates aid program intended to help needy countries, while at the same time providing jobs for Germans.

Proceeding with its emphasis on poverty reduction, in 1993, Germany began to increase the flexibility and cost effectiveness of its technical cooperation for developing countries and the main implementing agency of its ODA, the GTZ, started to decentralize its activities and to call upon local expertise and personnel. It strengthened the mainstreaming of poverty and gender issues through the creation of a cross-departmental advisory team on poverty alleviation, gender and process management. New ministerial guidelines for poverty alleviation specified in 1998 that thenceforth, every one of Germany's aid projects would be examined and classified with respect to its expected direct impact on poverty (Development Cooperation, 1998).

With respect to the levels of concentration, just as Germany's global ODA is characterized by a wide dispersion, its aid to sub-Saharan Africa is also widely spread among all states, giving her one of the most dispersed aid allocation patterns of all DAC members. Globally, Germany's aid covers over 130 countries, with some 20 recipients accounting for about half of its allocable bilateral ODA. In the 1980s, the major recipients of Germany's aid included Egypt, Turkey, India, China, Brazil, Indonesia, Pakistan, and Bangladesh. In the post-Cold War era, there has been no significant deviation from this global pattern except that now, countries of Central and Eastern Europe (CEECs), and the newly independent states (NIS) of the Caucasian and Central Asian Republics have become major recipients of Germany's aid. In 1993, the German government created two new divisions within the Ministry for Economic Cooperation and Development (BMZ), to handle development assistance relations with these countries, and Germany remained by far the largest donor among DAC members to these countries (Part II CEECs/NIS). Total German aid disbursement to this group was $3.3 billion and $2.4 billion in 1992 and 1993 respectively, and this figure represented 35 percent of aid from all DAC members to this group.

Within sub-Saharan Africa, however, there were slight changes in the countries receiving up to 2 percent of Germany's global bilateral aid. In 1980-81, only Sudan and Tanzania received that much aid from Germany, 3.3 and 3.1 percent respectively. In the early years of the post-Cold War period (1991-1994), Zaire, Ghana, Zambia, Mozambique and Ethiopia sometimes received between 2.1 and 4.0 percent of Germany's total bilateral aid to all countries.

In 1991, the German government established policy conditions for its aid allocation to developing countries. The conditions stipulated that the volume and structure of its bilateral assistance would depend on:

1. The respect for human and legal rights in the recipient country.
2. Participation of the recipient country's population in political and development process.
3. Respect for the rule of law by the recipient states.
4. Liberalization of economic policy and promotion of private enterprises by the government of the recipient states.
5. The broad commitment of the recipient states to development oriented actions.

With respect to the extension of these guidelines to sub-Saharan Africa, it is remarkable that they did not register in the findings of this research. This is probably due to the fact that Germany applies these conditions with some degree of flexibility. As the DAC observed in its 1994 issue of Development Cooperation Report, the five conditions are seen as a whole, and a country's serious efforts to meet them tend to justify continued or increased cooperation with Germany. Some countries that are in the process of democratization and economic reforms, but do not meet all five criteria, such as many states in sub-Saharan Africa, still receive assistance to encourage their commitment to the reform process. Expenditures for military purposes by aid recipient states have been a recurring issue in Germany's consultation with developing countries in general. Excessive spending for this purpose is viewed as an indication of a lack of development commitment that could lead to reduction of Germany's assistance. On the other hand, developing countries making efforts to reduce their military sector could still receive German support for purposes such as the training of their demobilized forces. In essence, with respect to poor regions like sub-Saharan Africa, Germany emphasizes and rewards the efforts of its aid recipient states in meeting its aid conditions. This practice contrasts sharply with the pattern for donors, such as Japan, which tend to penalize states failing to meet its aid conditions by either reducing the aid allocated to them, or canceling their aid programs outright.

With respect to other trends in the allocation of Germany's aid, although Germany remains one of the largest sources of aid to sub-Saharan Africa, and indeed to all developing countries, the volume of its aid has been falling significantly in recent years. As a share of GNP, its global ODA net disbursements fell from 0.42 percent in 1990 to 0.28 percent in 1997. Similarly, its aid to sub-Saharan Africa declined from about $1.3 billion in 1990 to about $826 million in 1997. Although this decline was related to general budget cuts associated with the Maastricht criteria, to the extent that they indicate future trends, they do not augur well for many sub-Saharan African countries looking forward to external support for their liberalization and democratization efforts.

Italy

In the post-Cold War period, measured by volume, Italy has been the sixth largest aid donor to sub-Saharan Africa. The variables in this study accounts for about 39 percent of the variance in Italian aid to the region. The regression result suggests that the chief motivations behind Italian aid are humanitarian concerns. One of the primary determinants of Italian aid to sub-Saharan Africa has been the size of the population of the recipient states. The positive correlation between this variable and ODA ($t = 5.906$) indicates that Italy tends to allocate aid to the more populous countries in the region.

The regression result also showed a statistically significant inverse correlation between the GDP of recipient states and the allocation of Italian aid (t = -3.008) suggesting a humanitarian concern to utilize aid to alleviate the poverty of recipient states. Given the history and objectives of Italian aid to the region, this finding is not surprising. For example, Ethiopia, which has been a traditional favorite recipient of Italian aid is at once one of the poorest and most populous states in sub-Saharan Africa. The idea of directing Italian aid to address basic needs in sub-Saharan Africa was concretized in a 1987 Italian comprehensive legislation - Public Law 99 (Bollini and Reich, 1994). PL 99 was itself the culmination of several preceding efforts championed by a coalition of concerned Italian groups and citizens - the Radical Party, the Christian Democrats and college students. Outraged by images of starving children in Ethiopia and other Sahelian countries due to the drought and famine which ravaged that part of Africa in the early 1980s, this group soon formed a powerful coalition of aid advocates, and they began to exert pressure on the Italian government to come up with an effective response to the food crises in Africa.

The levels of democratization by recipient states also registered as a significant determinant of what countries received Italian aid. Contrary to what liberal theory leads one to expect, however, this variable had an inverse correlation with ODA, suggesting that less democratic states in sub-Saharan Africa tend to receive more aid from Italy (t = -2.693). At first cut this finding is puzzling. But when one considers the fact that Italian aid is highly concentrated on Ethiopia, Zaire, Mozambique, Somali, Congo, and Sierra Leone - all states with dismal records of democratization in the period covered by this study, the finding becomes less puzzling.

An equally notable finding by this study is the positive correlation between Italian aid and the amount allocated by recipient states to defense expenditures. While this finding is in sharp contrast to the practice of other members of the DAC, it is consistent with the finding of an inverse correlation between the levels of democratization in recipient states and their receipt of Italian aid noted above. For much the same reasons as suggested above, Italian aid tend to go to countries with high defense expenditures and poor record on democratization. The persistence of civil strife and ethnic conflict in some sub-Saharan African countries tend to compel governments in those countries to allocate significant portions of their countries' meager resources to the defense sector. Coincidentally, these countries for reasons associated with either historical ties (Ethiopia and Somalia), or poverty (Mozambique, Angola, and Sierra Leone) tend to command relatively substantial aid from Italy. Thus, while these findings might suggest that Italy undermines development in sub-Saharan Africa by providing aid to authoritarian states, the opposite is most probably the case. Perhaps, the Italian government tends to support these states not because they are non-democratic, but in spite of the fact that they are non-democratic, for primarily humanitarian reasons.

During the decade of the 1980s, Italy's bilateral aid focused on eastern sub-Saharan Africa, with Ethiopia and Somalia perennially receiving 15-20 percent of its bilateral aid disbursements. Italian aid to sub-Saharan Africa during this period was twice the DAC average. Even though its aid to the region has declined somewhat in favor of Latin America, in 1990, its disbursements to its favorite states in sub-Saharan Africa amounted to about $1.03 billion. Its favorite five countries - Ethiopia, Zaire, Somalia, Mozambique and Tanzania - received over 60 percent of this amount.

After soaring in the 1980s, however, Italian aid budget suffered a broad collapse in the mid-1990s. For example, its global net ODA disbursements fell dramatically from $2.7 billion in 1994 to $1.6 billion in 1995, representing a mere 0.15 of its GNP, compared to the 0.27 percent of GNP the previous year. This was the second lowest ratio in the DAC for that year, next to the United States. Similarly, in that year, its aid to sub-Saharan Africa was about a third of its 1990 volume. This steep decline was attributable to a combination of factors, including the erosion of the Italian public's confidence in aid, and the government's introduction of new and strict expenditure controls in the wake of corruption investigations into widespread abuses of the Italian fund for development.[44] Italian global bilateral aid declined from $665 million in 1994 to $608 million in 1995, with most of this amount going to emergency assistance, food aid, and a few scholarships.

In 1996, Italy's global aid effort recovered considerably as its aid volume performance increased by 35 percent in real terms to reach $2.4 billion. This amount corresponded to 0.20 percent of its GNP (after 0.15 percent in 1995). Its aid to sub-Saharan Africa that year, however, fell further to about $240 million. Although this rose slightly to about $260 million in 1997, it is doubtful that its aid to the region would again approximate its late 1980s- 1990 levels.

With respect to the future trends of Italian aid in general, major reforms continue to reorient its efforts. In Africa, this has meant a concentration on actions aimed at reducing poverty and boosting sustainable development. In Southern Europe and the Middle East, the aim has been to rebuild institutional capacities and develop the private sector. More than half of Italy's ODA now funds programs and projects devoted to improving the living conditions of the poor as it seeks to capitalize on its experience and expertise in primary health care and social sector activities. A major Reform Bill was approved by

---

[44] See Norland, R., "Cleaning House", Newsweek 8 March (1993:6-12). For a more scholarly discussion of the government response to the scandal, see Bollini and Reich (1994).

the government in 1997 and tabled before Parliament in 1998. The centerpiece of the reform is the establishment of a new public agency to take responsibility for implementing programs planned and negotiated by the Ministry of Foreign Affairs. Poverty reduction has also been a central concern in the allocation of voluntary contributions to multilateral organizations. These are all welcome changes, but volume wise, the retrenchment in Italy's aid efforts, especially in sub-Saharan Africa continues to raise concerns about its future commitment to development cooperation.

Sweden

Even though only about 19 percent of the variance in Swedish aid is explained by all the variables in this study, the signs of the statistically significant coefficients tell an interesting story about the nature of Swedish aid to sub-Saharan Africa in the post-Cold War era. Curiously, the variable FMP (foreign military presence) accounts for a larger portion of the variance in Swedish aid. This variable has an inverse relationship with Swedish ODA ($t=-3.796$), indicating that Sweden tends to direct its aid away from the sub-Saharan African states hosting foreign troops. On the surface, this finding appears odd. When one recalls, however, that the countries in sub-Saharan Africa that hosted foreign troops in the period covered by this study are all former French colonies, this finding is not surprising. This is because Sweden tends to direct its aid away from former French colonies; like other Nordic countries, it concentrates its aid efforts in southern and eastern Africa. This behavior is in consonance with Sweden's expressed belief in a division of labor, or equitable burden sharing of the development assistance effort by members of the DAC. This concern was a primary motivation behind its recent project - *Development Finance 2000*. In this document, Sweden spelt out and analyzed the actions needed to achieve a strong and effective multilateral system on the basis of equitable burden sharing among DAC members.

Other significant revelations made by this study relate to the finding of statistically significant positive correlations between Swedish aid and foreign direct investment (FDI) ($t =2.298$), coupled with the value of goods imported by its aid recipient states from Sweden ($t =2.428$). Given Sweden's popular reputation as "the darling of the Third World" (Schraeder, Hook and Taylor, 1998), this finding is quite surprising. There is the consideration that Sweden, together with other Scandinavian countries seek to maintain a uniform approach to aid giving, and therefore tend to adopt a comprehensive approach to development assistance by encouraging trade and investment with their partner countries. This point is, however, not persuasive. This is because in as much as this study found a statistically significant inverse correlation between the GDP of the recipient states and Danish and Norwegian aid, the same is not true for Sweden. The correlation between Swedish aid and the GDP of its aid recipients in sub-Saharan Africa is negative though not statistically significant (t = -1.535). The assertion that Swedish aid has traditionally expressed its welfare, poverty reduction values, and the country's desire to be the conscience of the world,[45] while being persuasive for the behavior of its foreign aid during the Cold War era, must now be taken with a pinch of salt.

Equally curious is that the regression result of this study did not reveal a statistically significant positive correlation between the record of recipient states on democratization and the allocation of Swedish ODA. Again a plausible explanation for this finding is the observation that Sweden directs its aid away from former French colonies, which tend to have relatively more impressive records on democratization than countries in eastern and southern Africa, Sweden's favorite regions. Nonetheless, in its global ODA program, Sweden tends to accord high priority to democracy and human rights. A specific budget line for such activities in 1994/95 amounted to $70 million. Sweden makes wide use of NGOs and multilateral organizations as intermediaries for aid delivery in this area. In 1995, it began an innovative program of providing support for political parties in developing countries and the CEECs/NIS through bodies associated with political parties represented in the Swedish Parliament. Moreover, Sweden is the host country for the International Institute for Democracy and Electoral Assistance (International IDEA), founded by 14 countries in February 1995, with the objective of promoting sustainable democracy worldwide.

Comparing the Swedish aid efforts in sub-Saharan Africa with the global thrust of its aid program yields additional insights into the nature of its ODA. Among other crosscutting objectives of Swedish aid worldwide, particular emphasis has been placed on the promotion of women in development. In 1985, the government adopted a plan of action for Women in Development (WID) assistance, aimed at ensuring a fuller integration of WID concerns into all Swedish bilateral aid projects and programs.

Furthermore, in response to the recommendations of the International Conference on Population and Development held in Cairo in 1992, Sweden began to adopt policies, which address issues concerning population from a broad perspective, including activities to promote the empowerment of women, sexual and reproductive health, and the sustainable use of natural resources.

During the Cold War era, Sweden maintained an aid policy that had a

---

[45] See the discussion of this point by the Swedish people themselves in "Nordic Voices", Daedalus 113, No.2 (Spring, 1984).

geographic concentration on 17 major recipient countries. It developed a country programming procedure to implement this policy, and the total number of its aid recipient countries worldwide remained around 70. During the decade of the 1980s, Swedish bilateral aid to sub-Saharan Africa declined from 40 percent of its net bilateral disbursements in 1980 to 36 percent in 1989. During the same period, the share of its bilateral assistance to Latin America, geared towards the promotion of democratization and peace in that region, increased from 3 to 10 percent. The favorite destinations of its aid to sub-Saharan Africa remained fairly consistent.

Since 1994, the volume of Swedish aid to sub-Saharan Africa, and indeed its aid to all developing countries has been declining. In 1994 for examples, its global net ODA disbursements amounted to $1.82 billion. As was the case in 1993, 75 percent of this figure was provided under its bilateral aid program. In comparison with 1993, however, this was a decline of about 1 percent in real terms, and its ODA/GNP ratio also fell to 0.96 percent from 0.98 percent in 1993. That same year, its aid to sub-Saharan Africa fell from about $412 million the previous year to $345 million, and represented about 25 percent of its aid to all LDCs. Then in 1995, its global net ODA disbursement fell to about $1.7 billion. Its aid to sub-Saharan Africa also declined to $328 million. And although it remained the fourth ranking DAC donor, its ODA/GNP ratio slipped to 0.77 percent. Also in 1995, the Swedish Parliament, citing tight budgetary constraints decided to suspend efforts to maintain the domestic 1 percent ODA/GNP target.

In response to criticisms about the declining trend in its development assistance efforts, in the mid 1990s, Sweden began to introduce far-reaching reforms in its aid management. In 1995, its five separate aid agencies – the Swedish International Development Authority (SIDA), the Swedish Agency for International Technical and Economic Cooperation (BITS), the Swedish Agency for Research Cooperation in Developing Countries (SAREC), Swedcorp and Swedish Center for Education in International Development (Sando U-centrum), which hitherto carried out the development program with relative autonomy were merged into one organization, the Swedish International Development Agency (SIDA). The merger of the agencies was expected to refocus its aid on poverty amelioration, and the promotion of gender equality in developing countries.

There is another interesting dimension of Swedish aid to sub-Saharan Africa. Although the Cold War did not exert any major influence on its aid to this region, the end of the Cold War has given rise to new concerns which now compels Sweden to direct significant parts of its aid efforts away from the alleviation of poverty in the sub-continent into the service of new objectives in Central and Eastern Europe. Whereas during the Cold War period, a primary motivation behind Swedish aid was its desire to foster a "feeling of solidarity with the poor peoples of low income countries [in order to] counterbalance the capitalist and neo-capitalist forces that threatened equitable development in poor countries" (Redetzki, 1991: 242), in the post-Cold War period Central and Eastern European countries have become the primary recipients of its aid. Swedish aid to these countries that the DAC refers to as Part II CEECs/ NIS, is concentrated on the closest neighboring countries and region with whom Sweden has long established historical and cultural ties and with whom it shares common environmental and security problems. Thus a major share of Swedish aid to the CEECs/NIS support has been channeled to Poland, northwest Russia, Estonia, Latvia and Lithuania. A Swedish government bill in 1995 specified four objectives for this component of Swedish aid program: to promote a democratic culture, to promote common security, to support a socially sustainable economic transition, and to support environmentally sustainable development. In 1994, its aid to these countries totaled $91 million, a doubling of the 1993 amount. And in 1995, this amount rose to $105 million.

In comparison to other DAC members, Sweden has a liberal aid-tying performance. In the most recent ten-year period, its tied aid has equaled approximately 20 percent of its bilateral commitments, compared to total DAC average in 1992/93 of 38 percent. The Swedish International Development Agency (SIDA) has reiterated its goal of increasing the procurement ratio in its bilateral program without modifying its traditional untying policy by encouraging the involvement of Swedish industry in exporting goods and services to developing countries.

In addition to its programs in developing countries, SIDA has also worked on ways of cooperating with more advanced economies. This was the subject of a report to the Government in 1996. Another report suggested ways to promote the development of the capital markets and financial institutions. This work builds on SIDA's strength in developing trade and industry directed towards small and medium size companies in the private and public sectors. One of its declared objectives is to create strong alliances between companies in developing countries with Swedish firms using a small-scale approach which promotes cost sharing and the provision of technical assistance to developing countries. Given the paucity of direct investment by the advanced industrial countries (AICs) in sub-Saharan Africa, this is a promising development.

United Kingdom

The variables in this study accounts for about 48 percent of the variance in British aid to sub-Saharan Africa in the post-Cold War period. The most important variable for the prediction of British aid in the study was FR-

EXCOLY (former French colonies). As expected this variable had an inverse correlation with British aid (t = -4.091). This finding, apart from confirming widely held beliefs about the influence of colonial ties on the allocation of British aid suggests that the United Kingdom is more concerned with allocating less aid to former French colonies than it is with allocating more aid to its own former colonies. This practice is the direct contrast to the pattern of French aid allocation to the region. Britain discriminates against former French colonies more than France discriminates against former British colonies in its foreign aid policy.

The regression result further reveals a significant positive correlation between the size of the aid recipients' population and the allocation of British aid (t =3.345). Furthermore, while there was no significant correlation between British aid and the defense expenditure of recipient states, there was a significant, inverse correlation between British ODA and the GDP of aid recipients (t = -2.217), indicating that larger, poorer states tend to receive more aid from the United Kingdom. In this respect, the objectives of British aid evince remarkable continuity. Since 1975, when a British white paper, *More Help for the Poorest*, specified that British aid would be targeted toward helping poorer states around the world, Britain has consistently oriented its aid toward poorer countries, especially its former colonies.[46]

An equally notable feature about the pattern of British post-Cold war aid allocation to sub-Saharan Africa is that states hosting foreign military troops (FMP) tend to receive less aid from the United Kingdom (t = -3.536). Given that the sub-Saharan African states with FMP are overwhelmingly former French colonies such as Cote d'Ivoire, Senegal and Gabon - states where France has relatively large investments - this finding is not surprising.

A curious revelation by the regression result is the absence of a statistically significant positive correlation between the performance of recipient states on democratization and their receipt of British aid. Given that the United Kingdom proclaims this as one of the determinants of its aid policies, this finding is notable.[47] A possible explanation for this anomalous finding is that the influence of colonial ties prevails over other considerations in the motivations for British aid. Were levels of democratization the dominant metric for determining its aid recipients in the region as a whole, Britain would find more of its aid going to former French colonies, which tend to have relatively more impressive records on democratization. Moreover, when one restricts the analysis to former British colonies alone, the variable, Political

---

[46] The observation made by Lancaster (1999) provides additional support for this finding.
[47] See Bose and Burnell (1991), and Healey (1996) for more detailed discussions of the determinants of British aid.

Rights (PR) becomes significant and one observes Britain employing the denial, or reduction in aid levels to punish states like Nigeria and Sierra Leone who had appalling records on democracy during the period covered by this study.

In terms of the global thrust of its aid efforts, the United Kingdom has a highly concessional, bilateral aid program largely oriented towards the poorest countries of the world. It is also a major contributor to multilateral institutions and the European Community. It has many prominent institutions in the development field and an enormous amount of expertise, building on its long experience in developing countries. During the Cold War years, British aid was largely tied to procurement in the United Kingdom and its bilateral aid program had one of the highest proportions of tied aid among DAC members. By the middle of the 1990s, however, it had taken steps to liberalize procurement for the poorest countries and untied a significant portion of its program aid.

Essentially, compared to what obtained during the Cold War era, the fastest growing instrument of British development cooperation in recent years has been the Joint Funding Scheme (IFS) through which the United Kingdom supports about 116 British NGOs in about 1800 projects in developing countries by providing co-financing for them. In 1994/95, for instance, it disbursed over $55 million under the IFS through British NGOs alone. Its total disbursements through world wide NGOs amounted to almost $300 million in that year and these were mostly for emergency aid and personnel cost for aid volunteers.

Between 1990 and 1992, sub-Saharan African states received about 38 percent of British total aid to LDCs, which amounted to $1.8 billion and $1.7 billion in 1991 and 1992 respectively. In 1993, global British net bilateral ODA increased by 1 percent in real terms to $2.9 billion ($3.3 billion in 1992 prices and exchange rates) while its multilateral ODA rose by 2 percent, largely due to contributions to regional development banks and the European Community programs. At 0.31 percent its ODA/GNP ratio remained unchanged from the previous year. Its aid to sub-Saharan Africa dropped from about $642 million in 1992 to about $418 million in 1993, representing about 28 percent of its $1.5 billion aid to all LDCs. Britain's official aid to Part II CEECs/NIS for that year was $285 million, and this represented 0.03 percent of its GNP.

Britain's net global ODA disbursements increased in real terms by 5 percent to $3.2 billion in 1994. Its bilateral disbursements rose by 11 percent to $1.76 billion while its multilateral disbursements decreased by 1.3 percent to $1.44 billion. Its aid to sub-Saharan Africa also increased to about $566 million, and the ODA/GNP ratio for its global aid effort remained at 0.31

percent. Also in 1994, it provided $293 million in official aid to countries on Part II of the DAC list. During the mid 1990s, British emergency aid continued to rise.

Pertinently, since the end of the Cold War, British aid has increasingly gone to Part II CEECs/NIS. Its aid appropriations for assistance to this group are included in the budget of the Overseas Development Administration. It provided about $1.52 billion in official net aid disbursements to CEECs/NIS between 1990- 1994, and an additional $406 million in 1995. Comparatively, its aid to sub-Saharan Africa declined from $566 million in 1994 to $541 million in 1995. It rose slightly in 1996 to $568 million, but fell again to $558 million, or 28 percent of its total aid to LDCs in 1997.

With respect to the future trend of British aid to sub-Saharan Africa, although it appears that the Part II (CEECs/NIS) will continue to defeat the region in the competition for British aid, the election of a Labor government in May 1997 showed some signs of renewed attention to the goal of poverty reduction in the region. The government of Prime Minister Tony Blair immediately created the Department for International Development (DFID) upon assuming power in 1997. The Department is headed by a Secretary of State within the Cabinet and also has a Parliamentary Under-Secretary of State. In November 1997, the DFID published the first British White Paper on international development in twenty years. Entitled *Eliminating World Poverty*, the White Paper made clear the government's commitment to the DAC's international development strategy and targets, especially the goal of halving the proportion of people living in extreme poverty by 2015. The concept of partnership was stated as central to this goal and the role of DFID within the government was redefined to emphasize working for coherence on all policies affecting developing countries, instead of the sole administration of a development program. The Blair government has sent promising to signals to the development community that it intends to keep its election pledge of reorienting the direction of British aid to help the poorest countries. The government has provided an additional $2.7 billion of its global aid expenditure over the three financial years 1999/2000 to 2001/2002 (Development Cooperation, 1999 Report).

With respect to sub-Saharan Africa, five of the top ten recipients of British aid in 1999 were from the region. These countries were Tanzania ($113 million), Zambia ($93 million), Uganda ($92 million), Mozambique ($67 million), and Ghana ($62 million).[48] These are welcome and promising signs. In particular, the Blair administration's emphasis on a coherent approach to development cooperation could not have come at a more opportune time.

---

[48] See Development Cooperation Report (1999: 102).

Sub-Saharan African states have begun to open up their economies by encouraging foreign investors to participate in the development of productive sectors of their economies. The establishment of a coherent approach to development promised by the British Labor Government could indeed mark the beginning of a new partnership between the United Kingdom and the region.

Discussion

Realist Lore and Liberal Principles: Another Case for Muted Optimism[49]

This section addresses two sets of analytical questions on what the above findings mean for the propositions of realist and liberal theories. With respect to realism, three questions come to the fore: First, what do the above findings tell us about the parochial national interest motivations behind foreign aid (the classical realist explanation)? Second, what do they tell us about the structural arguments tendered by neorealists? Or phrased differently, has the transformation of the international system produced changes in the pattern of aid allocation to sub-Saharan Africa in the direction that the neorealists' ideas about the relative gains problematic would lead one to expect? Furthermore, has the logic of anarchy produced "sameness" in the behavior of donor states with respect to their allocation of aid?

As for liberal theory, the following questions merit attention: First, to what extent have moral principles informed the allocation of aid by DAC donors? Or alternatively, has the humanitarian goal of poverty reduction been a pervasive one among donors? Second, with respect to the democracy-development cooperation link, how has the shift toward democratization by recipient states, or lack thereof, informed the donors' patterns of aid giving? And finally, on balance, does the post-Cold War trend in the allocation of aid to sub-Saharan Africa rekindle optimism in liberal principles, call for a circumscription of its claims, or reinforce the trained skepticism of the realist/neorealist? Before turning to the discussion of these issues, it is imperative to underscore what, perhaps, is the most important observation by this study - the increasing marginalization of sub-Saharan Africa in the international system.

---

[49] The phrase - muted optimism - is borrowed from Bobrow and Boyer's (1998) study of contemporary developments in the foreign aid regime. In that piece, they concluded that contrary to the propositions of hegemonic stability theory, American decline, with respect to the production of foreign aid public goods, has not resulted in the broad collapse of the foreign aid regime because of the increased contributions by other states.

Despite the diversity of motivations behind the foreign aid policies of the ten donors in this study, my findings speak with a single voice about the increasing marginalization of sub-Saharan Africa in the international system. This marginalization is evident at two levels: First, there is the post-Cold War trend whereby donors are diverting their aid resources away from the region, even though many states in the region have embraced the liberal values of free market economy and democratization. Given the paucity of other sources of development finance available to the states in sub-Saharan Africa, this trend is quite unsettling. In 1992, for example, for the first time in the contemporary history of international financial flows, private financial flows, which amounted to $90.5 billion, exceeded global foreign aid transfers by more than $20 billion. Also, International Bank lending to state entities more than tripled between 1991 and 1992 from $11 billion to $37 billion (OECD, 1994:65). Meanwhile, sub-Saharan Africa, a region that has never been able to attract significant private capital (because such capital tends to shy away from development projects whose profitability are not readily measured in short term profits) must now contend with the diversion of aid to other regions.

Second, there is the consideration that the variables conventionally used in the study of international relations appear to register poorly on the African radar screen, hence the low proportion of the variance explained by the exogenous variables in this study. On the one hand, this observation suggests that the concentration on an African sample is a poor test of the dominant and rival theories of international relations. Ironically, however, for cogent reasons a concentration on an African sample represents as potent a test as any other sample. Not only are the differences between the propositions of the rival theories examined in this study - realism/neorealism and liberalism - sharpest in relation to sub-Saharan Africa, but also, foreign aid, the subject of investigation here was officially intended to promote development and address the issues that engender marginalization – authoritarian governments, poverty, and benign neglect by rich countries. A focus on sub-Saharan Africa, therefore, allows one to observe the temperament of these theories with respect to an important subject like foreign aid from a close range, while at the same time gauging how well the objectives of development assistance are being met. That the variables in this study, especially those generated from realist theory are poor predictors of foreign aid recipients speaks as much to the marginalization of sub-Saharan Africa as it does about the poverty of realism as a comprehensive paradigm for understanding international relations.

Moreover, the rival theories spotlighted here share a common ground on the need for AICs to maintain foreign aid programs in developing countries. What they do not agree on, however, are the purposes that such aid ought to serve. In one of the few articles written by a prominent realist to primarily focus on the subject of foreign aid, Hans Morgenthau, "the *paterfamilias* of American postwar academic realists" (Ruggie, 1995:64), presented a strong case for why an advanced industrial country like the United States should maintain a foreign aid program:

> It is in fact pointless even to raise the question whether the United States ought to have a policy of foreign aid as much as to ask whether the United States should have a foreign political or military policy. For the United States has interest abroad, which cannot be secured by military means and for the support of which the traditional methods of diplomacy are only in part appropriate. If foreign aid is not available, they will not be supported at all[50] (Morgenthau, 1962:301).

Morgenthau then identified six types of foreign aid: humanitarian foreign aid, subsistence foreign aid, military foreign aid, bribery, prestige foreign aid, and foreign aid for economic development. Although he conceded that even humanitarian foreign aid could serve political objectives, his discussion of economic foreign aid muddied the water on the motivation question when he veered from a discussion of the motivations behind such aid to an incoherent analysis of why such aid would not produce development in the underdeveloped regions of the world.

With respect to the national interest consideration tendered by realists as the motivation behind aid allocation, of the six donors discussed above only the pattern of Denmark's aid allocation had a positive correlation with foreign direct investment (FDI). The nature and history of Danish aid in sub-Saharan Africa, however, cautions against attributing this to the prediction of realist theory. A more persuasive explanation of this finding is that because Denmark adopts a comprehensive approach to development assistance, it not only concentrates on a few countries, but also encourages its national firms to invest in such countries in order to stimulate their economic growth. That Denmark tends to gain from such investment is salutary to the positive-sum benefits for donors and recipients that aid is supposed to promote. Moreover, there was no significant correlation between the value of goods imported by recipient states from Denmark and the amount of aid they received. Given the past instances where Danish authorities pressured aid recipients to procure goods from Denmark (Bagachwa, 1997:182) such finding is encouraging news.

---

[50] While neorealists like Waltz (1993) and Gilpin (1987) tend to see foreign aid as a foreign policy instrument designed to satisfy donors' parochial national interests, it is remarkable that a classical realist like Carr (1946:239) argued the case for using foreign aid to satisfy social ends beyond the donors' national frontiers.

With respect to other donors, however, the aid allocation patterns for Canada, France, Germany, Norway and Sweden had, as predicted by realist theory, positive correlation with the value of goods imported by aid recipients from these countries. This finding provides some support for realist theory.

In addition to the above points, there was a surprising positive correlation between Italian ODA and the defense expenditure of its aid recipient states. This is, perhaps, readily explained by the historical tendency of Italy to concentrate its aid on Somalia, Ethiopia, Rwanda and other states in eastern Africa whose governments, for reasons related to the persistence of ethnic conflict in those countries tend to allocate significant portions of their meager resources to the defense sectors. When one excludes these cases from the regression calculation for Italy, the positive association between ODA and defense expenditures disappears. And in any case, the notion that donor states, (with the exception of France), have strategic interests in sub-Saharan Africa, the defense of which warrants either the establishment of military bases, or the propping of authoritarian leaders in the post-Cold War period is not tenable. The end of the Cold War has severely discounted, if not eliminated the need for the establishment of military bases in sub-Saharan Africa. During the Cold War, the need for military bases was, for donors like the United States, strongly linked to an exaggerated communist threat, the desire to secure strategic shipping lanes, and the imperative of maintaining access to oil (Desch, 1993). With the end of the Cold War, sub-Saharan African states have become less important because, unlike the Middle East, they do not have large oil reserves. Nigeria and Gabon who boast significant oil reserves are much too weak and dependent on the West for the sale of their oil to pose a major threat to western interests.

Strategic (non-oil) minerals is a different matter altogether. Strategic minerals was another realist variable that registered on the motivations radar for Germany and Italy. Historically, the quest for access to strategic minerals was a raison d'être for the competition by developed nations for direct investment in Africa. This was "exemplified by Germany's tenacious efforts to secure high grade ore in Algeria" (Polanyi, 1957:12). It was also one of the reasons why the US supported the late President Mobutu of Zaire despite his repressive regime. True to the expectation of realists, this study found a positive correlation between the scores of aid recipients on the strategic mineral index (SMI) and the amount of aid they received from Germany and Norway. While this finding provides some support for the national interest rationalization submitted by realists, the finding of an inverse correlation between these donors' ODA and the GDP of recipient states indicates that at least mixed motives, rather than purely parochial interests are the motivations for their aid giving.

What about the neorealists position on the motivation question? There are three dimensions to the neorealists argument. The first dimension relates to the powerful influence that international anarchy exerts on the interaction between the units populating the system. Neorealists assert that through the process of imitative socialization and competitive interaction, actors in the anarchic international system come to discover what behaviors are more, or less supportive of their survival. Thus, by emulating the behavior of the successful actors, the states populating the international system come to look and behave alike (Sterling-Folker, 1997:5). The extension of this logic to the foreign aid arena yields a legitimate question: If anarchy exerts such a powerful influence on the behavior of the states in the system, why is there such a divergence in the foreign aid behavior of the above donors? Why, for example, do Danish and Swedish aid cut a different trajectory than German aid? The retort that Germany and Sweden have dissimilar aspirations because of their size and power credentials is unpersuasive because even the United Kingdom which ought to be as concerned as Germany and Italy are about securing access to strategic minerals strikes a different foreign aid posture from these countries in this regard.[51] The proposition of neorealism is therefore problematic on this count.

Ironically too, and more damaging to the neorealists position is the finding of inverse correlation between the ODA from almost all donors and the GDP of recipient states. Poverty amelioration has been an important feature of the foreign aid programs of almost all donors. What this finding suggests is that the "sameness" effect tendered by neorealists is at work here, but not for the selfish, and competitive reasons they claim. Rather, it illustrates the emergence of a foreign aid regime that has influenced the behavior of even the large and dominant states in the international system in ways neorealists like Mearsheimer (1995) allege to be improbable. While it is true that some donors have steadfastly resisted incursions against their sovereign authority to dispense their aid funds as they see fit, by and large they have adhered to the rules of the foreign aid regime, and they have expected fair play on the part of others (Hook, 1995). This observation lends credence to the contention that the concepts, which according to neorealists flow from anarchy - self

---

[51] In one study that supplies valuable insights into the behavior of small states in the foreign aid arena, J. Stephen Hoadley contends that the differential in power capabilities between large and small states constrains the latter group such that their foreign aid policies, especially with respect to generosity of terms and concentration, tend to exhibit peculiar patterns (Hoadley, 1980). Even if this claim is plausible, it neither accounts for the significant differences one observes in the foreign aid pattern of similarly constrained small states, nor does it explain why some large states behave like small states on such measures like aid concentration, percentage of tied-aid, and ODA/GNP ratio.

help, power politics, and competitive security - are socially constructed concepts rather than essential features of anarchy (Keohane, 1990). True, the absence of a leviathan that can impose its will on actors in the international system leaves states to fend for themselves as best as they can. Contrary to the claims by neorealists, however, this fact neither eliminates the proclivity of differently constituted states to engage in other-regarding behavior, nor does it dictate that among the varied actions a state engages in, only those actions calculated to reap parochial benefits are the ones deserving of attention in the study of international relations.

The tendency to perceive anarchy as the organizing principle of international relations (Waltz, 1979) is not problematic in itself. There is a substantial difference, however, between the conception of anarchy as the organizing principle of international relations, and the tendency to imbue such reality with the expectation of only, or primarily selfish behavior on the part of state actor. To do so understates the inherent ambiguity of anarchy, and overestimates its explanatory power, for as Wendt (1992) accurately observes, anarchy is what states make of it.

The contention by neorealists that the transformation of the international system from bipolarity to an increasingly multipolar structure would produce such "consequential shift"[52] as to alter the behavior and preferences of the actors in the system fares a little better; but it only scorches the liberal thesis on foreign aid without demolishing it. Neorealists argue that the constraints of anarchy lead states to worry not simply about how well they fare from cooperative arrangements themselves (absolute gains) but about how well they fare compared to other states (relative gains). Because states are ever so conscious of the distribution of gains from cooperative arrangements, they tend to orient their foreign policies to the maximization of their relative gains. Waltz, (1979:105) articulates this perspective tersely:

> When faced with the possibility of cooperating for mutual gain, states that feel insecure must ask how the gain will be divided. They are compelled to ask not "will both of us gain?" but "who will gain more?" If an expected gain is to be divided, say in the ratio of two to one, one state may use its disproportionate gain to implement a policy intended to damage or destroy the other. Even the prospect of large absolute gains for both parties does not elicit their cooperation so long as each fears how the other will use its increased capabilities.

Neorealists equally assert that bipolarity was the decisive variable in the long peace experienced by the West because it removed the security

---

[52] Waltz (1979:162) defines a consequential shift as "variation in number (of principal actors) that leads to different expectations about the effects of the structure on the units".

dilemma and the relative gains problem from the agenda of relations among western powers[53] (Layne 1990:41). Other (non-realist scholars) have asserted that within the Western alliance the Cold War also made possible, a division of labor in international cooperation whereby the United States, because of its political comparative advantage specialized in the production of security goods, while other alliance members specialized in the supply of other public goods such as foreign aid (Boyer, 1993). With the end of the Cold War the problems of relative gains are expected to severely constraint relations among AICs. Extending the neorealist reasoning on the relative gains problematic to the foreign aid arena leads one to expect that: (1) there will be significant reductions in the volume of aid to sub-Saharan Africa as new and more attractive potential recipients emerge from other regions, (2) there will be systematic increases in the aid allocation to these newly emerged, more attractive aid destinations where aid allocations are expected to yield future higher returns, and (3) The logic of relative gains will impel all donors to engage in behaviors I and 2 above, because a state that fails to redirect its ODA in such manner risks losing out in future gains from cordial ties with these new aid destinations that ODA helps to cement.

Remarkably, there is strong evidence of the above behavior on the part of some donors. Canada, Italy, Germany, and Sweden have all cut back their aid allocations to sub-Saharan Africa at the same time that they have systematically increased their aid allocation to the DAC's Part II countries. Of the ten donors in this study, France and Norway are the only donors who have so far failed to redirect their ODA away from sub-Saharan Africa to the Part II countries in ways which compromise their efforts in the sub continent.

The reasons for this behavior on the part of Germany and Sweden are, however, more nuanced than the naked pursuit of relative gains. Both countries have extensive geographical, cultural and psychosocial ties to many countries of the former Soviet bloc. The reorientation of their foreign aid programs toward these countries is, therefore, less surprising. The Italian case is also understandable in the propinquity context, at least with respect to its aid to Romania, Hungary, and Poland.

The Canadian case, on the other hand, is a much different story. It is difficult to rationalize the decline in Canadian aid to sub-Saharan Africa and the corresponding rise in its aid disbursements to countries like Poland and the Ukraine outside the light of its relative gains concerns. The consideration appears to be that if Canada maintains its humane internationalist posture and continues its hitherto significant aid presence in sub-Saharan Africa, while

---

[53] For a neorealist discussion on how anarchy limits international cooperation, see Grieco (1995).

other donors reorient their aid to the Part II countries (CEES/NIS), it risks weakening its future competitive abilities with other donors on gaining access to the emerging markets of these new aid destinations. Given these points, the finding of significant shifts in the aid allocation pattern of some donors provide some support for the neorealist position on the effect of relative gains concerns on development cooperation.

Turning to the liberal record, three points merit consideration. The first point is the remarkable inverse correlation between ODA and the GDP of recipient states for almost all the donors in this study, suggesting that poverty amelioration has been a primary concern for them.[54] This finding provides strong support for the liberal thesis on the humanitarian motivation behind foreign aid. In addition to the positive correlation between ODA and the population of recipient states, this finding confirms Lumsdaine's observations about the flow of aid to all developing countries for the Cold War period: "Aid went preponderantly and increasingly to those countries where the poorest people lived, and where a lot of them lived" (1993:94).

The second point about the liberal thesis on the motivations behind aid is that this study did not find a strong democracy-aid link. This makes it tenuous to substantiate the republican strain of liberal theory that predicts a greater degree of cooperation between donors and relatively more democratic states. Denmark and Japan were the only donors whose patterns of aid allocation had statistically significant positive correlation with the recipients' level of democratization. While this finding increases skepticism about the democratic peace theory, it will be interesting to revisit the subject in a few years when the seeds of democracy would have taken firmer roots in the recipient countries and see what changes emerge in one's observations.

A third way of accessing the propositions of liberal theory on the motivations behind foreign aid is to look at which countries were strong aid donors, that is, the donors who bore relatively higher aid burden measured by the ODA/GNP ratio in the period covered by this study. Measured by this criterion, Denmark, Norway and Sweden again come to the fore as the strongest aid donors. For the eight year period covered by this study (1990-1997), with an ODA/GNP average of 0.32, 0.29, and 0.29 Denmark, Norway and Sweden respectively, were all donors whose ratios exceeded the United Nations recommendation specifying that developed countries should earmark 0.15 percent of their GNP as aid to the least developed countries (LLDCs). With an average ODA/GNP ratio of about 0.20, France was the only G7 country to

---

[54] The inverse correlation between ODA and GDP is statistically significant for all donors save Canada and Sweden in the multiple regression model. The bivariate correlation between ODA and GDP is, however, significant for Sweden.

exceed the UN recommendation. By contrast, the average ODA/GNP ratios for the other donors were: Canada 0.05 percent; Germany 0.07 percent; Italy 0.05, Japan 0.04; UK 0.06; and the US who came last at about 0.02 percent. Canada's low ODA/GNP ratio is surprising given its claims to the principles of humane internationalism. It is also notable that Denmark, Norway and Sweden - three states with strong aid programs - also have strong domestic welfare programs to aid poor people in their countries. By comparison, Canada, an otherwise democratic-welfare state also appears to be retrenching its hitherto impressive welfare programs at home.[55] It is possible that the domestic policy orientation of donor countries is a primary determinant of their allocation of foreign aid. This dimension of the aid motivation question was not, however, explored by the variables in this study.

Conclusion

In the post-Cold War era, a strong case could be made for the liberal position that the practices of international politics, with respect to the allocation of foreign aid by advance industrial countries to sub-Saharan Africa, are not simply devices to be taken up and abandoned as technical instruments to national ends. The findings of this study show that the realist position about the parochial national interest motivation behind foreign aid is at best only weakly supported. Morality, it appears, does count in international relations at least with respect to answering the question of why rich countries extend economic assistance to poor countries.

Moreover, a persuasive case could be made for the liberal position that once a few donors adopted the goal of poverty reduction in sub-Saharan Africa, its compelling moral logic began to influence and modify the actions of other donors. This is the production of the "sameness" effect not brought on by competitive interaction, but rather by the contagion of moral concerns. True, other donors might have jumped on the development assistance moral bandwagon just to look good. But even if that were the case, that would still be an argument for the power of moral principles, for as La Rochefoucauld states, and Lumsdaine (1993:67) reminds us, "hypocrisy is the tribute that vice pays to virtue".

This record of how humanitarian concerns for poverty alleviation have so far influenced the allocation of aid to sub-Saharan Africa is encouraging, and in a sense it refurbishes recent statements by many donors about their commitments to the broad objectives championed by liberal theory - good

---

[55] See Pratt (1994) and Therien and Noel (1995) for additional discussions of this point.

governance, elimination of illiteracy, democratization, and the deperipheralization of the sub continent.[56] This encouraging finding is, however, muted by evidence of a redirection of aid resources away from the region to other areas, perhaps for reasons that are not together unrelated to the neorealist notion of relative gains. This trend threatens to further marginalize sub-Saharan Africa in spite of the apparent humanitarian patterns one observes in the foreign aid kaleidoscope. Among the different donors, there are strong similarities and significant differences in the patterns of their aid allocation to the region that nourish hope, and yet simultaneously fan the embers of skepticism about the prospects of mitigating the marginalization of the sub-continent. The study of the four cases - France, Japan, Norway, and the United States - in the next four chapters illuminates these points.

---

[56] See Development Cooperation Report, 1998 for the consensus of opinion among DAC members on the need to intensify their efforts in regions like sub-Saharan Africa.

Part Two

Part Two

Introduction to Part Two

The Study of Four Cases

The behavior of nation-states, which remain the most consequential actions in the international system, despite the increasing influence of non-state actors, can be compared on many counts. Scholars of the neorealist persuasion contend that states "armament policies and their interventions abroad are two of the most revealing" (Waltz, 1993:46). Even if this assertion held true for most of the Cold War period, "[T]he post-Cold War world no longer has ideological fissures and an unrestrained arms race to preoccupy its attention and encourage a fixation on power politics" (Kegley, 1993:134). Current realities in the international system appear to have diminished the adequacy of privileging bombs and wars issues, (the so called high politics)[57] over issues of the international political economy. This section examines the behavior of four prominent members of the DAC - France, Japan, Norway, and the United States - in the foreign aid arena.

My approach to comparing the foreign aid policies of these donors focuses on three essential features of foreign aid – volume, degree of concentration or dispersion, and the relative share of the aid burden borne by each of the four donors. These three aspects of foreign aid are considered essential because they shed important light on the priorities that influence the foreign aid policies of various donors. Apart from deciding on the amount of its national resources to allocate as foreign aid to specific regions of the world, each donor must make the important determination about the particular states on which to concentrate relatively greater shares of its aid money. Probing the degree of such concentration and the types of recipient-states such donor privileges offer valuable insights into the motivations behind the donor's foreign aid policy.

Another reason for choosing to highlight these three aspects of foreign aid stems from the relative ease by which they can be measured. While many

---

[57] It should be noted that Waltz breaks ranks with many realists when he urges that "the distinction between high and low politics, once popular among international political economists, is misplaced. In self help systems, how one has to help oneself varies as circumstances change" Waltz (1993:63).

concepts in international relations – for example the issue of relative gains, the degree of a system's polarity, and the degree of autonomy allowed foreign aid agencies in donor states – are easier to describe than measure, the three features of foreign aid selected here are more amenable to systematic and comparative measurement. I begin by examining the foreign aid relations of each donor to sub-Saharan Africa against the backdrop of these three dimensions of foreign aid. In doing so, I locate the international relations of each donor with the region within the historical context of their evolution, and link the finding of this study with previous efforts. A more proximate examination of the aid policies of France, Japan, Norway, and the United States raises important questions. If, for instance, "the imagery of gift giving embedded in most discussions of foreign aid becomes questionable when other benefits to the donor are taken into account" (Wood, 1986:14), what are such benefits to a donor like France? What impact does the national role conception of a donor such as Norway have on the pattern of its aid giving? And how does one reconcile the simultaneous retrenchment in American aid with its assumption of the hegemonic responsibilities of maintaining the stability of the international system in the event of episodic crises in sub-Saharan Africa? What role does aspiration to the ranks of the great powers have on Japan's foreign aid policies? These are some of the interesting questions tackled in the following four chapters.

5 France: The Enduring Salience of *Besoin de Rayonnement*

Colonialism gave impetus to the pattern of France's global aid allocation as the French government sought to finance large portions of the capital formation, and in some cases, the current budgets of the states in its colonial empire. With respect to sub-Saharan Africa, a mixture of humanitarian and parochial concerns has exerted contradictory pressure on French aid to the region. In 1964, for instance, the Jeanneney Report commissioned by the government of President Charles de Gaulle advocated for France's benevolent approach to foreign aid:

> Even if France thought the poverty of others threatened neither her own development, nor her security, she would have to assist them simply because it would be intolerable for her to ignore their fate (Quoted in Hook, 1995:54).

One decade later, the Abelin Report rationalized a mixture of parochial and humanitarian motives for French aid:

> Our aim is one of mutual benefits and we must affirm in frankness and without any sense of guilt that France intends to develop its commercial and cultural relations with those regions of the world whose human development it wishes to foster, not only for the reasons of their raw materials but also for their human resources, their geographic importance and their historic echoes (Quoted in Evans, 1989:136).

The finding of this study reveals a continuation of the twin pressures that concerns for humanitarian and parochial interests exert on French aid. In the post-Cold War period, France has been the largest single source of foreign aid to sub-Saharan Africa, although its aid is concentrated on its former colonies.[58] Together, the variables in this study account for about 44 percent

---

[58] The former French colonies in Africa include Benin, Burkina Faso, Cameroon, Central African Republic, Chad, Comoros, Congo [Brazzaville], Cote d'Ivoire, Djibouti, Gabon, Guinea, Mali, Madagascar, Mauritania, Senegal, Seychelles, and Togo.

of the variation in French aid to the region. As expected, the variable FREXCOLY(former French colonies) accounts for a significant portion of this explained variance (t =5.930). This finding confirms widely held beliefs about the influence that former colonial ties exert on the allocation of French aid. Furthermore, the inverse correlation between UK-EXCOLY (former British colonies) and French ODA (t = -2.529) provides additional support for the above assertion.

Another significant finding by this study is the positive correlation between French ODA and the value of its aid recipients' imports from France (t =2.159). Again, this finding is not surprising given the economic and commercial objectives, which studies such as the Abelin report have proposed for French aid. Globally, about half of French aid is tied to the procurement of French goods and services, including experts and consultants by its aid recipients. Notably, compared to its interests in Europe and other prosperous regions of the world, France's commercial interests in sub-Saharan Africa are quite small. They include, however, some powerful firms that are quite strident in promoting their interests with the French government. Such firms include Elf Aquitane (the highly influential French oil monopoly formerly owned by the French government), Alcatel, Dassault, Thompson, and other numerous small firms whose activities are primarily aimed at the African market. It is widely believed that many French firms, protected from competition by trade restrictions and other commercial concessions afforded them by African governments would be uncompetitive if their monopolies were lost (Lancaster, 1999).

The regression result of this study also reveals that French aid favors the more populous states in sub-Saharan Africa (t =2.022). This finding, when corroborated with the finding of an inverse correlation in the coefficients between French ODA and the GDP of the recipient states (t = -1.605), (though not statistically significant), suggests that blatantly parochial interests were insufficient in themselves in sustaining French aid.

The absence of a statistically significant correlation between French ODA and the democratic record of the recipient states is another curious finding by this study. This finding is curious because, at the sixteenth Franco-African summit held in La Baule, France in June 1990, then President Francois Mitterrand announced that thenceforth, French aid would favor those countries that were either democratic, or seriously pursuing democratic change (Schraeder, 1995:551). At the time, this statement was widely hailed in the development community as the harbinger of a new paradigm in France's foreign aid policy towards Africa. Subsequent events, however, revealed otherwise. For example, in the wake of a military coup in Niger in 1996, France initially stopped the provision of aid to that country. But within a very short time, it resumed its aid, even though Niger's military regime was notorious for its political repression. It is believed that France's desire to maintain access to the significant uranium deposits in Niger colors its policy towards that country.[59]

Furthermore, Schraeder (1995) observed that apart from failing to offer incentives to democratic reformers at the expense of recalcitrant leaders, France's aid to some states have sometimes been inversely proportional to their democratic efforts. Benin, for instance, received $580 million in French aid in 1989, but only $300 million in 1990, after taking steps toward democratization. On the other hand, Togo, the Democratic Republic of Congo (former Zaire), and Cameroon that remained authoritarian regimes saw their aid receipts from France increased from $628 to $925 million; $305 million to $519 million; and $659 million to $1002 million respectively.

In order to understand the nature and motivations behind French aid, it is necessary to underscore how the possession of colonies in Africa enhanced France's word wide grandeur, especially the promotion of French civilization and culture. During the colonial period, unlike the British policy of association that emphasized the adaptation of British rule to the cultural peculiarities of its colonies, France pursued the policy of *assimilation*, which stressed the permanence of political ties between the mother country and the colonies, and sought to assimilate the African elite into French society (Ake, 1996). Despite this difference in policy, British and French rule in Africa were similar in their rhetoric. The British policy of association, despite its claims to tailoring British rule to the cultural peculiarities of the colonies, (for example, its simultaneous pursuit of direct and indirect rule in southern and northern Nigeria respectively), sought to assimilate a small class of pliant natives into British society by investing them with royal titles and perquisites. On the other hand, in contradiction of its general policy of uniform assimilation, France sought to tailor key features of its colonial policies, especially with respect to economic and military affairs, to the peculiar nature of its colonies. Moreover, the broad claims by the French government that the inhabitants of Francophone Africa were black French men and women were neither taken seriously by the majority of Africans who bore the brunt of French rule, nor did French citizens in the home country look favorably on the few Africans who sought to cash in on such claims.

Perhaps, more than any singular event, the end of the Second World War produced significant changes in the way the French government related to its colonies. Participation in the war had exposed Africans who fought on

---

[59] About 2 percent of the world's known deposits of uranium are located in Niger (Crowson, 1998).

the side of the Allies to social, economic and political conditions in Europe. The sharp contrast of European conditions with what obtained back home imbued Africans with the courage to begin to agitate for better conditions from the colonial governments, and eventually independence (Coleman and Rosberg, 1970). To dampen the drive of the nationalists for independence, France responded by providing subsidies for the development of infrastructure and education in its colonies. But in the 1950s, the agitation for decolonization intensified. To further dissuade Africans from seeking independence, the French government warned African nationalists to consider the penalty for independence as "one can not conceive of an independent territory and a France continuing to help it" (Hayter, 1966:29). While this threat weighed heavily on the minds of African nationalists, it could not halt the momentum of the independence movement.

Outside Africa, French rule also had to contend with challenges to its quest for the actualization of *La Francophonie*.[60] After a 56 day siege, the French army was defeated by Vietminh troops in the battle of *Dien Bien Phu* on May 7, 1954, and France was compelled to begin its withdrawal from Indochina. Soon, in North Africa, France was also forced to relinquish its hold on Morocco on March 2, 1956, and Tunisia eighteen days later. The French law (*Loi Cadre*) passed by the French National Assembly that year, which invested the president with the power to grant colonial independence by executive order facilitated these events.[61]

In a 1958 referendum, a majority of the people of Guinea rejected membership in a French community and opted for independence. The French government granted Guinea its independence, but it angrily terminated its aid and withdrew its officials from the territory (Lancaster, 1999). Other French colonies, however, voted for association but, later opted for independence. Initially, France also terminated aid to many of these states. But by the mid 1960s, with its remaining colonies in west and central Africa having gained independence, and the Cuban missile crisis having intensified the Cold War, France decided to continue aid to countries like Guinea to which it had cut

---

[60] *La Francophonie* – the cultivation of a large French speaking community – was once so potent that one scholar dubbed it " a language based movement in world politics" (Weinstein, 1976).

[61] Algeria, however, proved to be the exception to this process of rapid decolonization. The huge number of French citizens who had permanently established their homes in Algeria, and who, aided by the French government had secured more abundant lives for themselves than they had in France were not eager to surrender their new found prosperity. This set the stage for their bitter confrontation with Algerian freedom fighters, a confrontation that soon escalated into a bitter war and occasioned a constitutional crisis in France. In the end Algerian nationalists prevailed, and France acceded to Algerian independence on July 5, 1962.

aid, and initiate foreign aid programs to its other former colonies. Although the independence of these states transformed their political relations with France, their economic relationships remained functionally intact.

With respect to the global thrust of its foreign aid programs, since the end of the Second World War, French aid has manifested a dual emphasis - the promotion of French language and culture; and the legitimization of its claims to great power status. France has consistently used foreign aid to support the promotion of the French language and culture. In the mid 1960s, when it reinstated aid to many of its former colonies, large shares of its aid went to the education and technical assistance sectors, which primarily entailed the supply of French literature teachers and textbooks to these former colonies. Furthermore, the French, with a strong sense of nostalgia and a healthy dose of atavism, frequently express a *besoin de rayonnement* - the need to shine - which they measure by how widespread the French language is spoken, and how well the glories of French culture are recognized throughout the world (Kolodziej, 1974). Former French President Georges Pompidou summarized the psycho-social rationale for *besoin de rayonnement* in the following passage cited in Lancaster (1999:116):

> Of all countries, France has held most profoundly to the export of its language and culture. That trait is truly unique to us. When a French man in a foreign country meets someone else who speaks French, who has read French literature, he has the impression of finding a brother. This is the ambition of our intellect, perhaps, our genius. Our cooperation is without doubt, oriented fundamentally towards expanding our language and culture.

The desire to expand *La Francophonie* also accounts for the high volume of French aid to the former Belgian colonies in central Africa where French is, at least, one of the official, or popular languages. During the decade of the 1980s, the Mitterrand government provided significant amounts of ODA to the Democratic Republic of the Congo (former Zaire) ($461 million), Burundi ($243 million), and Rwanda ($199 million). Then, in the early years of the post-Cold War period, the annual amount to Rwanda, which was approximately $20 million was doubled to $40 million (Schraeder, 1995:556).

Remarkably, apart from fostering the perception of Francophone Africa as falling within France's sphere of influence, if not a *chasse gardie* - an exclusive hunting ground - France's pursuit of *besoin de rayonnement* has sometimes soured its relations with other members of the DAC, especially the United States. Lancaster (1999) observes that the French became highly suspicious of US intentions in Africa when Congress and President Harry Truman began pressuring Europeans to grant independence to their colonies after the Second World War. The quickness with which the US moved in to establish embassies in many African states once France granted them independence confirmed the fears of the French government. In response, France sought to discourage what it perceived as US encroachment into its sphere of influence by supporting the efforts of African governments to limit the freedom of movement of American diplomats and aid officials. This behavior prompted observers of the African scene such as Kaye Whiteman to remark that the real Cold War in Africa was between the Americans and the French (Whiteman, 1982).

Since the end of the Cold War, an important feature of the management of French aid is the fact that recipients outside of DOM/TOM (its dependent territories) divide into two categories. In the first category are countries that fall within the ambit of the ministry of Cooperation and Development (MCD), and are provided with a wide range of funding schemes, investment projects, adjustment assistance, and technical cooperation implemented by the MCD and the Caisse Centrale de Cooperation Economique (CCCE). The second group of countries falls outside of the ambit. The non-ambit countries receive either project or balance of payments aid under treasury loan agreements (loans, or grants which may or may not be associated with private credits) or benefit from the technical cooperation schemes managed by the Ministry of Foreign Affairs. During the end of the 1980s, France was an important donor for certain non-ambit countries such as Indonesia, which received $109 million in 1989, and Egypt, which received $85 million in 1988. The ambit countries which include 30 in sub-Saharan Africa and 7 in the Caribbean region, receive about two thirds of France's bilateral aid, excluding aid to DOM/TOM.

France's aid to sub-Saharan Africa in the 1980s rose almost twice as fast as its over all ODA. Since the June 1990 France African summit in *La Baule*, the instruments used in favor of the ambit countries (covered by the Ministry of Cooperation) have been modified. Thenceforth, the poorest countries only receive grants managed in close coordination between the Ministry of Finance (the Treasury), the Ministry of Cooperation and the Caisse Centrale de Cooperation Economique (CCCE), joined together in a program orientation committee. Moreover, one third of France's total ODA net disbursements go to technical cooperation, including trainees and technical assistance. This is one of the highest percentages for any DAC member state.

As previously stated, measured in absolute dollar amount, France is unquestionably the most generous donor of aid to sub-Saharan Africa. Comparing its aid efforts in the region with its global aid program yields interesting findings. First, in France, the provision of development assistance is considered an essential element of French policy, in which several ministers, as well as the Prime Minister and the President of the Republic take an active interest. During the decade of the 1980s, France's net ODA disbursements increased annually by 4.9 percent, earning her the fourth most rapid growth rate among DAC members. The grant element in its total ODA commitments for this period exceeded the 86 percent norm stipulated in the DAC terms recommendations. The grant element of its aid to LLDCs at 89 percent was, however, slightly below the DAC's recommended term of 90 percent.

In 1990, France's ODA net disbursement to developing countries (again excluding flows to its overseas departments and territories – DOM/TOM) grew by 6 percent in real terms to $6.6 billion. This figure included its forgiveness of export credit claims to many of its aid recipients, which amounted to $166 million, and of structural adjustment lending classified as Other Official Flows (OOF) of $128 million. Its bilateral ODA increased by 8 percent, while its multilateral contributions decreased by 2.5 percent mainly because of its reduced contributions to the World Bank group and regional development banks. Its ODA/GNP ratio increased from 0.54 percent in 1989 to 0.55 percent in 1990, and its bilateral ODA to sub-Saharan Africa amounted to about $2.5 billion.

It is worth noting that in the 1990s, France progressively adapted its aid procedures and modalities to new directions. At the second UN Conference on the Least Developed Countries (LLDCs), held in Paris in September 1990, it announced the conversion of all its LLDC ODA loans into grants. It also expanded its cooperation in the fields of environment, humanitarian, and emergency aid. The Caisse francaise de development (CFD) – the former Casisse centrale de cooperation economique (CCCE) - broadened its operations to include more countries in North Africa and Indochina.

In 1992, France's global net ODA disbursements increased by 2.3 percent in real terms to $8.3 billion. As in 1991, virtually all the growth was accounted for by its increased contributions to multilateral organizations, which rose by 11 percent in real terms in 1992. While regional development banks received $225 million, compared with $36 million in 1991, France's contributions to the European Community fell by 8 percent in real terms.

France's ODA to GNP ratio rose by one point in 1992 to 0.63 percent. Its ODA to sub-Saharan Africa that year amounted to $2.57 billion. Aid to five of its former colonies – Cote d'Ivoire, Cameroon, Senegal, Guinea, and Madagascar, however, accounted for over fifty percent of this amount.

In 1993, France's net ODA disbursements amounted to $7.9 billion, the same amount in real terms as in 1992. While its contributions to multilateral organizations dropped by 7 percent, its bilateral assistance rose by 2 percent. Its ODA/GNP ratio was 0.63 percent, the same as in 1992. Also in that year, its official aid to Part II CEECs/NIS rose from $364 million the previous year to $605 million and attained 0.05 percent of its GNP. France's aid to sub-

Saharan Africa in that year declined slightly to $2.55 billion.

Globally, the distribution of French bilateral ODA among its aid recipients favors middle income countries (54 percent in 1993-94), while low-income countries (including LLDCs) received a smaller portion (40 percent). This distribution pattern, which is almost the inverse of the DAC average (low income: 58 percent; middle income: 38 percent), is influenced by the weight of African middle-income recipients in the distribution pattern of French ODA. The six top ranking recipient countries and territories of French bilateral ODA in 1993-94 were Cote d'Ivoire, Cameroon, New Caledonia, Egypt, French Polynesia, and Senegal. Together, these countries received 29 percent of total French ODA (gross). Traditionally also, a substantial portion of French aid has been provided in the form of loans, although this share has recently been decreased. In 1994, the overall grant element of French ODA, at 89 percent, was lower than the DAC average of 92 percent. France's aid to sub-Saharan Africa amounted to about $2.63 billion in 1994. And that same year, it provided $650 million in official aid to the DAC's Part II (CEECS/NIS) countries.

Pertinently, 1994 witnessed the devaluation of the franc - the official currency of France's 14 former colonies in sub-Saharan Africa that comprise the African Financial Community (CFA). The devaluation of the franc positioned these countries to continue their efforts towards structural adjustment, including the reform of the public sector, and resume development cooperation with other donors and international financial institutions. France supported the efforts of these countries by providing them with substantial ODA. In particular, it waived all the debt resulting from its ODA loans to low-income countries and half of the ODA debt of the middle-income countries in the franc area. While this French gesture is praise worthy, it ought to be properly understood, that the conditions which led to the over valuation of the CFA franc in the first place were partially the result of France's economic policies toward the region.

By the mid-1980s, it had become clear to most observers of Africa's political-economic relations that the CFA franc was seriously overvalued. The effect of the unrealistic value of the CFA franc was to inhibit the exports of the CFA countries, while at the same time encouraging the elite in these countries to increase their imports from France. The French government was not unaware of this fact, because it had intervened several times since the late 1980s to bail out many of its former colonies from foreign exchange crises and finance their balance of payments deficits. Sometimes, France even paid the salaries of its former colonies, which could not pay their external debts. In 1993, for instance, it transferred over $1 billion to support the CFA franc. The effect of such "assistance" was to encourage the leaders in the CFA countries to continue their flawed economic policies. So long as an overvalued franc allowed them to enjoy cheap imports of consumer goods, vacation abroad, and educate their children in France, Francophone Africa's political elite had no incentive to devalue the CFA franc. Four factors, however, combined to forge a new reality on the currency issue: First, in January 1994, the World Bank terminated most of its aid to the CFA countries. This decision stepped up the pressure on France, which was itself contending with budgetary difficulties, to shoulder the burden of subsidizing the financial problems of its former colonies. A second factor was the ascendance of a new personality to the French prime ministership. Prime Minister Balladur, in contrast to previous French leaders, had few ties to Francophone Africa, and so he wondered why France would persist in pursuing the patently failed policy of shoring up the CFA franc. Third, although France's substantial aid program dates back to decolonization, by the mid-1990s, these extensive activities were being subjected to more intense scrutiny and questioning by the French public because of the wide spread belief in many AICs that aid to developing countries, especially countries in Africa, has been grossly ineffective.[62] A final reason for the devaluation of the CFA has been attributed to the death of President Houphouet Boigny of Cote d'Ivoire, a long-term president who had strongly opposed devaluation (Lancaster, 1999). Given these points France's decision to support the devaluation of the CFA franc becomes perceivable in a new light.

In France, development cooperation is considered to be an essential element of foreign policy, in which several ministers, as well as the Prime Minister and the President of the Republic take an active interest. The aid program has had a high political profile in debates about France's international responsibilities and implications. France's aid is also linked to its economic and commercial objectives. Recall that this study found a statistically significant correlation between the value of goods imported from France by its sub-Saharan African states and the amount of aid they received from the French government. Just under half of French bilateral ODA is tied to the procurement of French goods and services (including experts and consultants). This percentage, however, does not tell the whole story about the benefits which France derives from its ODA. France's seemingly generous ODA efforts in sub-Saharan Africa contribute to forging stronger links between French elite and the ruling class in its former colonies. Via these relations, France is able to create a web of fiscal, monetary and commercial linkages with its former colonies, such that, even if France untied all of its aid to the region, the existence of this nexus of economic relations, practically guarantees that

---

[62] In comparison to other members of the DAC, however, public opinion in France has been supportive of foreign aid. See EUROSTEP, ICUA, and InterAction (1995).

these states would derive most of their imports from France.

In essence, the pattern of France's post-Cold War aid to sub-Saharan Africa reveals a striking continuity with what obtained during the Cold War period. And while France continues to concentrate its aid on its former colonies, it has broadened its aid presence in sub-Saharan Africa by extending significant amounts of aid to former British colonies. Furthermore, while France continues to make extensive use of bilateral aid, it also made notable contributions to multilateral institutions, especially the European union.

In 1995, French global net ODA amounted to $8.4 billion. In real terms, this was a decline of 12 percent from the 1994 figure. This decline was partly accounted for by the timing of its payments to multilateral agencies and reduced outflows following the devaluation of the CFA franc in January 1994. Its ODA/GNP ratio fell to 0.55 percent in 1995 after peaking at 0.64 percent in 1994, ranking her fifth place among DAC members, after Denmark, Norway, the Netherlands and Sweden on this measure of burden sharing. French aid to sub-Saharan Africa in 1995 amounted to about $2.22 billion, a slight decrease from the $2.63 billion figure for the previous year. A relatively small portion of French ODA – 24 percent in 1995 – was provided in the form of contributions to international institutions. Nearly half of this multilateral ODA consisted of the assessed French contributions to the European Union, that is, the Community's aid budget and the European development Fund. The World Bank group and regional development banks together received 8 percent and the UN just under 1 percent of French ODA in 1995.

Essentially, in contrast to other donors, such as Norway and Denmark, the French foreign aid program has never had a development doctrine to guide it. There is no general framework to provide a strategic focus for its aid efforts; no means of prioritizing the activities funded under the name of development, and no basis for holding aid agencies accountable for their activities (Lancaster, 1999). This fact accounts for the high politicization of French aid, and consequently the reasons for the sub-optimal performance of its aid programs despite involving an enormous amount of money.

In the past, the multiplicity of policy objectives in France's relationships with developing countries and the dispersion of ministerial responsibilities for different categories of aid recipients among various ministries and institutions have resulted in a highly complex management of the French aid program. Many observers (including the DAC), and increasingly, the French Government itself, have raised questions about whether this system has reduced the effectiveness of France's aid programs. Recognizing this flaw, the French Government decided in February 1996 to "improve the integration of development aid policy into France's foreign policy; to clarify the responsibilities of all those involved in development aid to enhance the efficiency of the organization and operation of official development assistance".[63]

In the later years covered by this study, French global aid effort began to decline significantly. Its global net ODA volume fell, in absolute terms, from $8.4 billion dollars in 1995 to $7.5 billion in 1996, a decrease of 11.8 percent in constant (1995) dollars, leaving France in the fourth place, after Japan, the United States and Germany. Its aid to sub-Saharan Africa that year also declined to $1.82 billion, and represented about 32 percent of its total aid to LDCs. Then, in 1997, this aid volume further fell to $7.1 billion in constant dollars (a 4.4 percent decrease). Also, in that year, its aid to sub-Saharan Africa at $1.70 billion, fell to its lowest levels since 1990. Despite this decline in the absolute volume of its net global ODA, France moved up from the fourth place in 1996 to third place among DAC members, ahead of Germany. In addition, although its ODA/GNP ratio slipped to 0.45 percent, it still ranked first place among the G7 countries in this respect.

In 1998, France's net ODA disbursement declined again to $5.7 billion, and was the third largest donor in the DAC. Expressed as a share of its GNP, France's ODA for that year was 0.40 percent – a steep fall from the 0.64 percent it posted in 1994, but nonetheless the highest ratio among G7 Countries. The list of its ten favorite recipients remains fairly consistent, except that Poland is now numbered among the lot.

Table 5.1 Top Ten Recipients of France's Global ODA in 1998

Rank	Country	(US$ m)
1	French Polynesia	392
2	New Caledonia	381
3	Egypt	302
4	Cote d'Ivoire	299
5	Cameroon	271
6	Morocco	235
7	Madagascar	225
8	Senegal	184
9	Poland	169
10	Congo, Republic	164

Source: *The DAC Journal. Development Cooperation, 1999 Report.* Vol.1. No.1 (2000): 84.

---

[63] See Press Communiqué issued by the French Prime Minister, February 7, 1996. Also quoted in Development Cooperation: Efforts and Policies of Members of the Development Assistance Committee (1996:141).

Figures 5.1 and 5.2 are pie charts showing the pattern of France's global gross ODA allocation in 1998 by income group and region. The least developed countries (LLDCs) and sub-Saharan Africa account for the largest shares of France's bilateral ODA by income group and region respectively.

Additional insights into the post-Cold War pattern of French aid to sub-Saharan Africa could be gained by comparing the number and type of countries that received at least 2 percent of its aid in the region, to what obtained during the Cold War era.

France 99

France's Gross Bilateral ODA Allocation (1998)

Figure 5.1 By Income Group (US$ m)

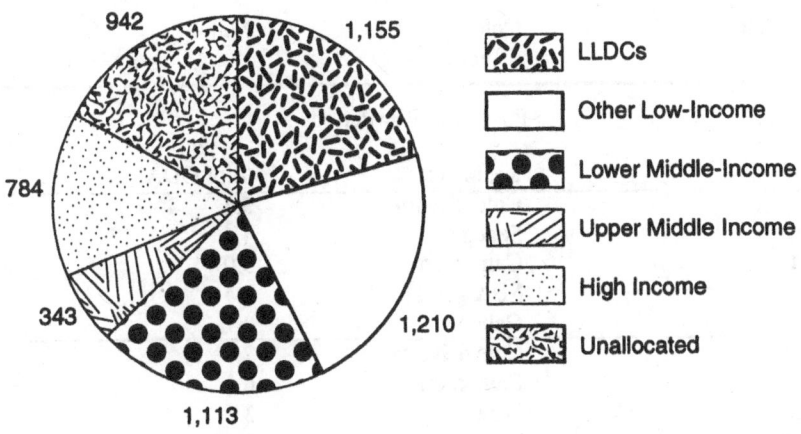

Figure 5.2 By Region (US$ m)

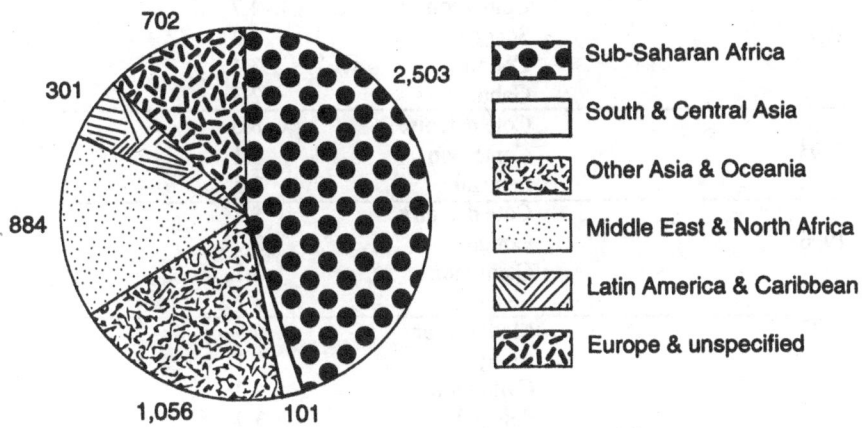

Source: The DAC Journal. Vol. 1, No. 1 (2000: 84)

Table 5.2 Comparison of Favorite Recipients of France's ODA to Sub-Saharan Africa (Cold War Years v Post-Cold War Period)

Cold War Years

1970-71	% of ODA[64]	1980-81	% of ODA	1985-86	% of ODA
Cote d'Ivoire	2.6	Senegal	2.7	Senegal	2.7
Madagascar	2.2	Cote d'Ivoire	2.3	Mali	2.0

Post-Cold War Period

Year	Recipients	% of ODA
1991	Cote d'Ivoire	5.4
	Senegal	4.4
	Cameroon	3.0
	Madagascar	2.4
	Gabon	2.1
1992	Cote d'Ivoire	7.0
	Cameroon	6.5
	Senegal	3.6
	Guinea	2.3
1993	Cote d'Ivoire	10.0
	Cameroon	6.9
	Senegal	3.1
1994	Cote d'Ivoire	10.0
	Cameroon	4.7
	Senegal	4.2
	Congo	3.4
	Gabon	2.3
1995	Cote d'Ivoire	8.0
	Cameroon	4.1
	Senegal	3.5
1996	Cote d'Ivoire	5.2
	Congo	3.7
	Cameroon	3.1
	Senegal	3.1
1997	Madagascar	6.5
	Congo	5.1
	Cameroon	4.2
	Senegal	3.0
	Cote d'Ivoire	2.8

Source: Development Cooperation Report. Paris, OECD (Various Years).

[64] This is calculated as the percentage of the donor's total ODA to all developing countries (LDCs).

As Table 5.2 amply demonstrates, in the post-Cold War period, there has been an increase in the number of sub-Saharan African states receiving at least 2 percent of the total French aid to developing countries. Equally worth noting is the fact that Cote d'Ivoire, Senegal, and Madagascar continue to be France's favorite aid recipient states in the post-Cold War era. In fact, France has increased the concentration of its aid on these countries, even as it has extended such favoritism to Cameroon and Gabon.

Another notable feature of French aid to sub-Saharan Africa revealed by Table 5.2 is the tendency by France to direct its aid to the relatively more prosperous states in the region. Compared to other states, Cote d'Ivoire, Cameroon and Gabon are all middle-income countries. This practice contrasts sharply with the foreign aid policy of the Nordic states, such as Denmark and Sweden who tend to target their aid to poorer countries.

With respect to burden sharing, France appears to contribute a significant proportion of its gross national product as aid to sub-Saharan Africa, although one should bear in mind that this is preferentially allocated to its former colonies. Table 5.3 illustrates this point.

Table 5.3 Dimensions of France's ODA (1991-1997)

Dimension	1991	1992	1993	1994	1995	1996	1997
Total ODA to All LDCs ($millions)	5772	6304	6154	6611	6429	5754	4775
ODA to SSA as % of ODA to All LDCs	41	41	42	40	35	32	36
ODA to SSA as % of GNP	0.23	0.26	0.24	0.24	0.16	0.15	0.14
% of Concentration on Top Five Recipients SSA	43	52	49	61	55	53	61

Source: Geographic Distribution of Financial Flows to Aid Recipients, 1960-1997. (CD-ROM). Paris, OECD (1998).

As Table 5.3 makes clear, between 1991 and 1994, about a quarter of 1 percent of France's GNP was allocated as aid to its former colonies in sub-Saharan Africa. But beginning in 1995, the percentage of French aid to the region dropped markedly such that by 1997, the final year covered by this study, its aid to the sub-continent was about 0.14 percent of its GNP. Moreover, this diminished proportion of its GNP became more concentrated on its former colonies. Figure 5.3 illustrates this point fuller.

Figure 5.3 Scattergram Showing the Favorite Recipients of France's Bilateral ODA (1990-1997)

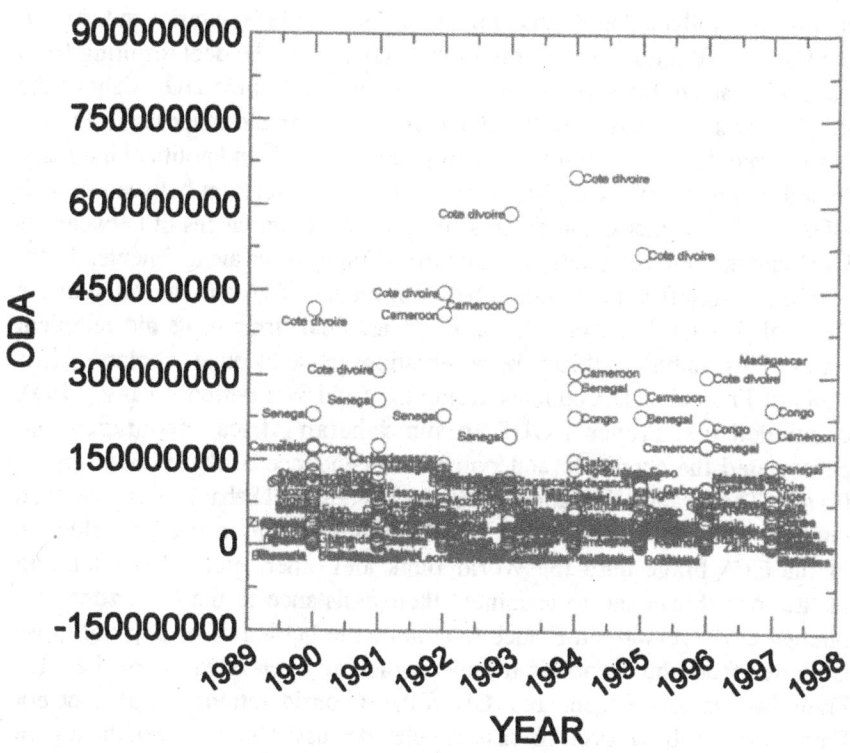

Source: Geographic Distribution of Financial Flows to Aid Recipients, 1960-1997. (CD-ROM). Paris, OECD (1998).

With respect to the question whether, on balance, French aid to sub-Saharan Africa in the post-Cold War era reflects humanitarian, or parochial motivations, the answer is mixed. On the one hand, France has played, and continues to play an important role in the development of the region, especially its former colonies. Among the members of the DAC, it is the highest aid donor to the region in terms of absolute dollar amount. And globally too, France's ODA volume has consistently ranked among the DAC's top donors in absolute dollars, and it ranks highest among the G7 countries in terms of the ODA/GNP ratio. In addition, France has waived the debt resulting from its ODA loans to the low-income countries and half of the ODA debt of the middle-income countries in the Franc area. Yet, on the other hand, France has utilized its ODA to further its parochial economic and political interests. In addition to a statistically significant, positive correlation between French ODA and its former colonies, this study found a similar result between its ODA and the value of goods imported from France by its aid recipients. There was also a significant correlation between French ODA and the value of the stock of foreign direct investment of its national firms in its aid recipient states. This finding confirms the observations made by other scholars. In his study of France's ODA policies during the Cold War period, Evans (1989), concluded that France's ODA to sub-Saharan Africa encouraged and perpetuated the economic and political dependence of these countries on France. This strain in the pattern of France's foreign aid behavior has continued into the post-Cold War era. Recall that France did not consent to the devaluation of the CFA Franc until the World Bank and other international lending institutions threatened to terminate their assistance to the CFA zone and intensify the pressure on France to assume the burden of bailing out those countries from the economic troubles which an over-valuation of the CFA Franc had, in part, engendered. Given these considerations, whether or not French aid to sub-Saharan Africa is calculated to assist the people of the region more than it promotes the parochial interest of French firms, and the sizable number of French nationals in francophone Africa, especially the middle-income countries, is a debatable point. What is not so disputable, however, is that France continues to utilize its aid and investment policies to preserve its political, and economic ties to its former colonies. At the same time, France is expanding its influence into former British colonies, thereby promoting the goal of *la francophonie*. If successful that could nurture, if not help actualize, France's enduring dream of *besoin de rayonnement*.

Conclusion

It is notable that this study found no statistically significant inverse correlation between French ODA and the GDP of its aid recipient states. This finding is, however, neither particularly surprising, nor does it demolish the liberal thesis on foreign aid. France has been traditionally known to target its aid to middle income countries, especially those in its former colonies. Moreover, the mere characterization of French aid as self-interested does injustice to another consideration: of the ten donors in this study, France allocated by far the most amount of aid to sub-Saharan African states. In addition, while the cultural and parochial benefits which France derives from its aid to sub-Saharan Africa are self evident, unlike donors such as Canada, Germany, the United States, and Sweden, who have significantly reduced their aid to the region, while at the same time increasing their allocation to other regions, France remains the most consistent source of aid to many states in sub-Saharan Africa. Indeed, it is doubtful whether countries such as Gabon, Cote d'Ivoire, and Cameroon, long ignored by other donors, but now considered to be middle income countries would have achieved this status in the absence of French assistance. This is not to deny, however, that the way the development cooperation between France and its partner countries currently operates could use some improvements. In particular, France's economic and fiscal policies with respect to the CFA zone which still discourages local production, despite the devaluation of the CFA in 1994, needs to be revamped to encourage trade with other developed countries. Currently, France's economic policy toward the zone invests her with a virtual monopoly over the markets of these countries. Such protectionist policies discourage competition and efficiency. They also foster government corruption.

6 Japan: A Rear Entry into Great Power Rank

The post-Cold War period has witnessed increased international activity on the part of Japan. In the realm of international development finance, Japan has emerged as the world's largest foreign aid donor (measured in absolute dollars). It surpassed the United States to attain this position for the first time in 1989. In 1996, Japan's share of the total official development assistance (ODA) disbursed by the OECD member states amounted to 17.1 percent, or $9.4 billion. More recently, in 1998, Japan disbursed $10.6 billion of net ODA, making it the largest donor (in absolute dollars) in the Development Assistance Committee (DAC) for the sixth consecutive year.[65] With respect to sub-Saharan Africa, although Japan has been only the fourth largest aid donor (behind France, Germany, and the United States) to the sub-continent in the 1990-1997 period, it has taken notable steps to engage the region in a new development partnership. Examples of Japan's effort in this area include its sponsorship of two international conferences – the Tokyo International Conference on African Development (TICAD I & II), and its enactment of a 1992 ODA Charter where it specified the support for democratization and reduction in military spending by developing countries as some of the criteria it would thenceforth consider in its allocation of aid. What accounts for these initiatives on the part of Japan? Given the hegemonic decline of the United States and the implication of this decline for the maintenance of international regimes, does Japan's increased international activities raise important matters about the resilience of regimes and the behavior of other states in the face of a hegemon's retrenchment of its support? Does Japan's behavior attest to the triumph of liberal principles, and by implication, the diminishing utility of the realist paradigm, as many liberal scholars contend?[66] Alternatively, does Japan's behavior in the foreign aid arena reflect its calculated pursuit of its parochial national interest, thereby vindicating the realist framework? And there is yet a larger and equally important question: What does Japan's foreign

---

[65] See The DAC Journal. Development Report, 1999. 2000, Vol. 1, No. 1. (p.90)

[66] Even during the era of the Cold War, scholars such as Krasner (1982) argued that the growth and influence of regimes circumscribes the utility of a purely realist framework in the

aid behavior in sub-Saharan Africa tell us about the character of the emerging structure of the international system? These are important questions to which an examination of the extension of the logic of the realist/neorealist and liberal propositions promises useful insights, and they represent my primary task in this chapter.

Japan's Aid to sub-Saharan Africa: An Historical Overview

The origins of Japanese global aid program are traceable to two post-World War II factors: first, following its surrender to the allied powers after the US detonated the atomic bomb on Hiroshima and Nagasaki in 1945, Japan became a major recipient of reconstruction aid from the United States and the newly formed International Bank for Reconstruction and Development (IBRD, or the World Bank).[67] By dint of determination, and external assistance, Japan's economy recovered so rapidly that, by 1955 it commenced the payment of reparations (*baisho*) to the countries it had occupied during the war, including Burma (1955), the Philippines (1956), and Indonesia (1958). Over the years, these payments metamorphosed into foreign aid.[68]

The second impetus for Japanese aid was a direct product of the Cold War competition between the then Soviet bloc and the Western alliance. In 1949, Chinese political leader Mao Zedong, who had founded the Chinese Communist Party in 1921, successfully proclaimed the People's Republic of China. This development was widely perceived in the West as supportive evidence for the Soviet Union's avowed goal of spreading the communist ideology to all corners of the globe. In 1951, in a bid to stem the growing tide of communism in Asia, the United States spearheaded the establishment of the Colombo Plan for Cooperative Economic Development in South and South East Asia. The Colombo Plan included sixteen Asian countries and six external governments including the United Kingdom and Japan. Its primary mission

---

comprehension of international relations. More recently, other scholars, such as, Bobrow and Boyer (1998) have contended that contrary to the assertions of hegemonic stability theorists, the decline of the United States has not occasioned a broad collapse of the international system with respect to the provision of public goods like foreign aid. Other liberal scholars such as Lebow (1994), Russett (1996), and Doyle (1996) contend that the long peace and the end of the Cold War attest to the failure of realism and the diminishing utility of that paradigm for understanding international relations.

[67] It is often forgotten that not too long ago, Japan was itself the second largest recipient of external assistance, right after India. It was only in 1990 that Japan finally paid back the last installment on its loans from the World Bank and was taken off the World Bank's borrowers list (Orr, 1990:476).

[68] Arase, 1995.

was to coordinate aid to Asian countries and thereby incorporate them into the global orbit of the capitalist ideology. One of the conditions for membership in the Plan was the provision of development assistance to poor Asian countries. Japan was encouraged to contribute assistance to India and other poor countries in South East Asia. This region was, and has remained the primary focus of Japanese aid. More than one decade would elapse before Japan's aid ventured into Africa.

Essentially, the extension of Japan's aid to Africa is attributable to the pursuit of economic nationalism by Nigerian statesmen in the 1960s. Upon independence in October 1960, Nigeria's trade with the United Kingdom, Japan and other European countries grew rapidly. The terms of this trading relations though more profitable to the Europeans were not unfavorable to Nigeria, since European countries were the favorite destinations of Nigeria's agricultural exports. Nigeria's trade with Japan, however, was more problematic. Japanese exports to Nigeria, which mainly involved textile products, increased rapidly while Japan's imports from Nigeria remained negligible. The Nigerian government made several attempts to persuade the Japanese government to correct the imbalance in its trade with the country. When these efforts failed to yield meaningful results, Nigerian statesmen resorted to coercive diplomacy and began to threaten the Japanese government with economic sanctions. In a 1963 statement bearing striking resemblance to contemporary pronouncements by some members of the US Congress, the Premier of the Western Region of Nigeria, Chief Obafemi Awolowo, summarized the urgency of Nigeria's concerns:

> Unless the Asiatic countries undertake right now to buy from us equivalent value of goods in return for what we buy from them, our national interest dictates that we should cease forthwith buying from them... Of all the Asiatic countries, Japan is the chief culprit in this matter. We cannot afford to go on year in year out to lose money to a very rich country – almost over rich country - like Japan. We must insist on equitable trade with our overseas customers.[69]

In 1963, the Nigerian government followed through with this threat and imposed limits on the import of certain goods from Japan. When this limited action failed to wrest concessions from Japan, in 1966 the Nigerian government imposed an embargo on all imports from Japan with the exception of some textile products. Japan then responded with an offer of a loan to the tune of ten million pounds to Nigeria to offset the trade deficits. Cognizant of how the Nigerian government had successfully used the threat of economic

---

[69] Awolowo, *Daily Sketch* (Lagos), December 16, 1963. Also cited in Lancaster, 1999: 167.

sanctions to wrest concessions from Japan, other African states – Kenya, Tanzania and Uganda – followed the Nigerian example, and they too received offers of assistance from Japan. Thus began Japanese foreign aid in Africa.

During the Cold War era, two states, Tanzania and Zambia, were Japan's favorite aid recipients in sub-Saharan Africa. The privileged status which these two countries enjoyed from Japan stemmed from the role they played in shielding Japan from criticisms by other developing countries – criticisms which resulted from Japan's lucrative commercial relations with South Africa during the anti-apartheid years when the international community imposed comprehensive sanctions against South Africa. As Kweku Ampiah accurately observed, because of the leadership position commanded by Tanzania and Zambia in the anti-apartheid movement, Japan's policy makers sought to cultivate good diplomatic relations with these "frontline states". The intention was "to use the bellwether of African public opinion and the moral voice in the region's politics to assuage African anxiety over Japan's expanding economic relations with South Africa".[70] Japan's continuation of aid to these countries in the post-Cold War period represents an acknowledgment of these efforts. Recent trends in Japan's aid to the region, however, signal a shift in its ODA focus from these countries to the relatively more economically progressive states like Ghana and Cote d'Ivoire. As Atsushi Kungano, head of an independent task force that contributed to a recent Japan's Ministry of Foreign Affairs evaluation of Japan's aid asserted, "Japan can no longer afford to spend ODA broadly. It needs to spend it more strategically, taking national interest into full account".[71]

Additional insights into the pattern of Japanese aid to sub-Saharan Africa could be gained by locating its aid to the region within a comparative framework of its global aid effort. During the 1980s, Japan's aid to sub-Saharan Africa doubled to reach 15 percent of its global aid allocation by the end of the decade, but this still constituted only about one half of the DAC average. Japan's global ODA net disbursements increased in 1990 by 4 percent in real terms to $9.1 billion with bilateral and multilateral disbursements increasing by 3 percent and 8 percent respectively. Loans, which made up more than 40 percent of its ODA increased by 4 percent while its bilateral grants increased by 3 percent. Its aid to sub-Saharan Africa was about $814 million for that year. The ODA/GNP ratio of Japan's global aid effort stood at 0.31 percent, the same as it was in 1989.

In the post-Cold War period, developing countries in Asia continue to

---

[70] Ampiah, 1995: 123.
[71] Quoted in Hook and Zhang (1998:1066). See also, "Japan's ODA at Historic Crossroads", Daily Yomiuri (March 14, 1998:11).

receive close to two-thirds of Japan's bilateral aid. Here, the operation of Japanese development assistance has been referred to as the "flying geese" pattern of development whereby Japanese aid dovetails its trading interests, and is aimed at strengthening its global economic position.[72] Pertinently too, just as it has traditionally done in Asia, in the post-Cold War period, Japan has also sought to use its ODA to open up new markets in sub-Saharan Africa.

In 1991, Japan's global ODA net disbursement increased by 10 percent in real terms to $11 billion. This increase was attributable to its bilateral disbursements, which rose by 19 percent in real terms. Its aid to sub-Saharan Africa also increased to $931 million, representing about 10 percent of its total aid to LDCs. Also, in 1991, while Japanese grants increased by 2 percent, its loans increased by 32 percent in real terms and its ODA/GNP ratio increased by one point to 0.32 percent. More than any other member of the DAC, Japan frequently disburses its ODA as loans. While it has been sharply criticized for this behavior by others in the aid community on the grounds that it diminishes the quality of such aid, Japan has defended its policy. As Kenko Sone, an economic official in the Japan government stated:

> We believe aid quality has more than one meaning. In our view, lending money enforces some discipline on the part of recipients and encourages them to use the resources more prudently than if we just gave them away. Countries sometimes get used to simply taking money. Receiving loans often makes them work harder and become more efficient. In this sense, we consider loans as of greater quality than grants, particularly since through emphasizing loans we can make more money available to developing countries (Hook, 1995:80).

That the Japanese authorities place high importance on the repayment obligations associated with its ODA loans explains, in part, its reluctance to render such assistance to many sub-Saharan African countries that are often unable to fulfill their loan obligations. Several factors account for the inability of African states to repay their loan obligations. These include the poor performance of their export products, which is itself partially attributable to the economic policies of AICs that tend to discriminate against the region's non-mineral exports. There is also the fact that the majority of Africans live in abject poverty. This fact compels African governments to allocate high proportions of their national budgets to address social service needs, such as education, health care and the provision of basic infrastructures. Massive corruption by government officials is another drain on the resources of African states, although with the new wave of democratization sweeping through the

---

[72] Arase, op. cit.

continent, some progress has been made in controlling this social malady.

Despite a decline of 6 percent from its 1991 aid volume, Japan, with net ODA disbursements of $11.2 billion in 1992 remained with the United States at the top of all foreign aid donors in the world. Its bilateral loans fell by 22 percent in real terms to $4.6 billion, following its high growth (nearly 20 percent) in the previous two years. Its grants rose by 3 percent in real terms to $3.76 billion and its contributions to multilateral agencies increased by 22 percent to $2.8 billion. Japan's ODA to GNP ratio slipped from 0.32 percent to 0.30 percent in 1992 and remained below the DAC average of about 0.42 percent. Its aid to sub-Saharan Africa declined in that year to about $844 million. Its Fourth Medium Term ODA Target of $50 billion was successfully met at the end of 1992. Notwithstanding major increases in its aid effort in 1992, Japan continued to lag in DAC financial terms.

Japan's net disbursements of ODA in current dollars increased from $11.2 billion in 1992 to $11.3 billion in 1993 despite a 12 percent decline in real terms, giving her the highest net disbursements of all DAC members. Its ODA/GNP ratio fell to 0.26 percent in 1993, and its bilateral ODA loans dropped sharply by 33 percent. The decline of its net disbursements of ODA loans was attributed to two main factors: the number of quick short term loans (mainly used for structural adjustment support) which dropped sharply; and its collection of repayment of previous ODA loans, which increased substantially (Development Cooperation, 1994). During this period, a large portion of Japan's ODA disbursements was in the form of untied loans to finance large infrastructural projects in Asia, such as the Port of Colombo in Sri Lanka.

As previously mentioned, Japanese assistance has long emphasized the centrality of self-help efforts on the part of developing countries, hence Yen loans have been an important instrument in its approach to development. Such practice, however, represents an inadequate response to the needs of least developed countries (LLDCs). Cognizant of this fact, in 1994, Japan began expanding its grant programs. The grant element of its ODA commitments rose from 79 percent in 1993 to 82.5 percent in 1994 although it was still below the DAC recommendation on Terms (Development Cooperation, 1995). Another notable aspect of Japan's relations with Africa is its encouragement of the idea of South–South cooperation, whereby developing countries are encouraged to cooperate with other developing countries in the exchange of knowledge and development experience through the establishment of training programs and exchange of experts coordinated from Tokyo.

Furthermore, in 1995, Japan's net loans decreased by 11.6 percent in real terms to $4.1 billion, while its grant allocations increased by 9.8 percent to $6.3 billion. Its aid to sub-Saharan Africa also increased to about $1.26

billion that year. This apparent effort to steer Japan's ODA policy toward less parochial goals was also evident in its multilateral contributions for that year. Japan's total multilateral ODA increased by 2.3 percent from its 1994 figure to $4 billion in 1995.

In 1996, however, Japan's global net ODA dropped sharply by 25 percent in real terms to $9.4 billion, with the ODA/GNP ratio declining from 0.28 per cent in 1995 to 0.20 percent that year. This drop reflected increases in Japan's budget stringency. Its aid to sub-Saharan Africa declined to about $1.02 billion. Then in 1997, this fell deeper to about $715 million, the lowest level since 1990. While the declining trend in Japan's aid allocation to sub-Saharan Africa raises concerns about the future of its aid to the region, it has, however, signaled its commitment to a new development cooperation partnership with the sub-continent by organizing the second Tokyo International Conference on African Development (TICAD II) in 1998 - a follow up to the first one it organized in 1993.

At the 1998 conference, which Japan jointly organized with the United Nations Organization and the Global Coalition for Africa, Japan articulated the Tokyo Agenda – a policy framework expressing a clear commitment by Africans and their partners to agreed goals and priority actions. The ten specific elements of the Tokyo agenda are:

- An overall goal of reducing poverty and integrating Africa with the global economy through accelerated economic growth and sustainable development.
- A reduction in the proportion of the region's population living in extreme poverty by at least half by 2015.
- Promotion of the concept of recipient ownership and global partnership as the principles underlying the Agenda for Action.
- The achievement of universal elementary school education by 2015.
- The reduction of adult literacy to half of the 1990 level by 2005.
- The elimination of gender disparity in elementary and secondary education by 2005.
- The provision of safe water for at least 80 percent of the population by 2005.
- The reduction of mortality rates for children under age 5 to one third of the 1990 levels by 2015.
- The improvement of the production and competitiveness in the agricultural and mining industries in light of their potential to create jobs and products for export.
- The promotion of confidence building measures to help in the prevention of regional conflicts (Development Cooperation, 1999).

As ways to achieve these common goals and objectives, the conference focused attention on strengthening coordination among all the actors in Africa's development, including an enhanced role for civil society, regional cooperation within Africa, and Asia-Africa cooperation. The participants at the Tokyo conference also promised to maintain the momentum generated by TICAD II, and to ensure tangible results by giving particular attention to monitoring the outcome of their efforts. These are all promising signs. Still, from a pragmatic point of view, the decline in Japan's aid to the region in recent years mutes optimism about the achievement of these goals.

On June 30, 1992, Japanese Prime Minister Kiichi Miyazawa announced Japan's ODA charter and identified the following issues as the four principles that would thenceforth inform Japan's ODA allocation to developing countries:

1. Environmental conservation and development should be pursued in tandem.
2. Any use of ODA for military purposes or for the aggravation of international conflict should be avoided.
3. Full attention should be paid to trends in aid recipient countries' military expenditure, their development and production of mass destruction weapons and missiles, and their export and import of arms, so as to maintain and strengthen international peace and stability. In addition, developing countries should place appropriate priorities in the allocation of their resources on their own economic and social development.
4. Full attention should be paid to efforts for promoting democratization and the introduction of a market oriented economy, in tandem with the preservation of basic human rights and freedoms in the recipient countries (Development Cooperation 1996:149-150).

Some of the findings of this research indicate the application of these principles to Japan's allocation of its aid to sub-Saharan Africa. The levels of democratization in the recipient states featured as the most important variable in the explanation of Japanese aid to the region. The positive correlation between this variable, PR (Political Rights) and Japanese ODA ($t = 4.122$) suggests that Japan tends to allocate more aid to those countries with relatively more impressive records on support for periodic elections and other political procedural rights. The regression result also reveals a statistically significant inverse correlation between Japanese ODA and the defense expenditure of the recipient states ($t = -2.967$).

That the principles of the ODA Charter inform the pattern of Japan's ODA to sub-Saharan Africa is further illustrated by Figure 6.1 - a scattergram showing the distribution of Japan's aid to the region in the years 1990-1997.

114 *Contending Theories on Development Aid*

It is evident from this scattergram that in the years preceding the proclamation of its ODA charter (1990-1992), two notoriously authoritarian states – Nigeria (in 1990) and Sudan (in 1991) - were among the five aid recipients in sub-Saharan Africa who received relatively larger volumes of Japanese aid. Beginning from 1993, however, one finds more aid being targeted to countries such as Senegal, Zambia, Kenya, and Ghana - all states with relatively better records of democratization.

Figure 6.1 Scattergram Showing the Favorite Recipients of Japan's Bilateral ODA (1990-1997)

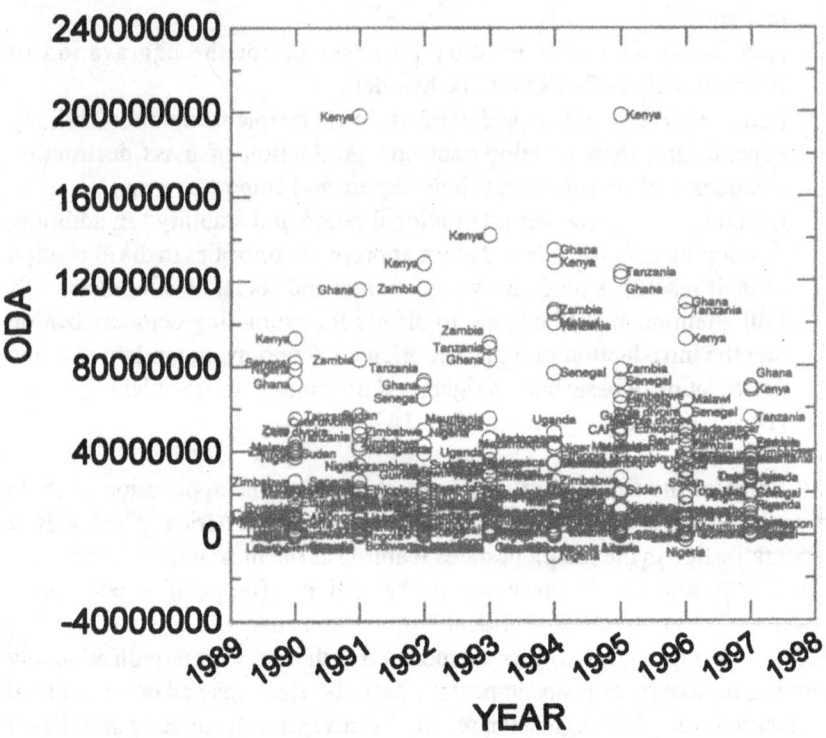

Source: Geographic Distribution of Financial Flows to Aid Recipients, 1960-1997. (CD-ROM). Paris. OECD (1998).

While this finding appears to confirm the propositions of democratic peace theory on the link between democracy and development cooperation, the selective manner in which Japan applies this aid conditionality in other regions of the world calls for a more nuanced interpretation of the democratic peace thesis. As Steven Hook and Guang Zhang[73] observed, Japan applies the levels of democratization metric to sub-Saharan African states and other states of low importance to Japan's trade and investment interests in a punitive way. For example, from 1993 through 1996, Sierra Leone, Nigeria, Somalia, Chad, and Liberia were all punished for their appalling records on democratization. Japan either drastically reduced its aid to these countries (Sierra Leone, Angola and Equatorial Guinea), or it completely cut off aid to them (Nigeria and Somalia). China, Cambodia, Indonesia, and Iran – all states that maintained extensive trade and investment interests with Japan – were, however, not punished even though one of these states (Indonesia) clearly had a worse record on democratization than many sub-Saharan African states.

The size of the population of sub-Saharan African states is another key variable in understanding Japanese aid to the sub-continent in the post-Cold War period ($t = 3.200$). Larger states tend to receive more aid from Japan. Contrary to what the humanitarian thesis of foreign aid would indicate, however, this study found no statistically significant correlation between Japanese aid and the poverty of recipient states. This is not surprising because poverty reduction has never been a prominent feature of Japan's ODA, even though it funds such efforts to some degree in the South Asian region.[74]

Another notable feature of Japanese aid to sub-Saharan Africa relates to the positive correlation between its ODA and recipient states hosting relatively larger values of the stock of the foreign direct investment (FDI) of Japanese national firms ($t = 1.973$). This finding provides some support for the assertion by neorealists that, because aid is used by donors in furtherance of their national interest, they tend to allocate more aid to the countries hosting higher values of the foreign direct investment stock of their national firms. This finding also confirms the observation by Hook and Zhang[75] that the overall pattern of Japanese aid suggests preferential allocation of aid to countries where Japanese firms have higher levels of investment. Pertinently, however, neither Hook and Zhang's finding of a corollary, significant positive relationship between the global allocation of Japanese aid and the value of its aid recipients' trade with Japan for the years 1986-88 and 1993-95, nor the finding by Peter Schraeder, Steven Hook and Bruce Taylor[76] of a similar positive relationship

---

[73] Hook and Zhang, 1998.

[74] Yasutomo, 1990.

[75] Hook and Zhang, op. cit., p. 1060.

[76] Schraeder, Hook and Taylor, 1998.

in the flow of Japanese aid to sub-Saharan Africa during the Cold War era are supported by the results of this study. In fact, in the post-Cold War era, one finds an inverse relationship between Japanese aid and the value of the aid recipient states' imports from Japan, although the coefficients pointing to this inverse relationship are not statistically significant.

An equally notable finding of this study that is, however, problematic for realist theory is the absence of a statistically significant correlation between Japanese aid and the scores of recipient states on the strategic mineral index (SMI).[77] Because of Japan's high dependence on imported minerals (See Appendix III), one would have expected to find (if the proposition of realist theory about the parochial interest motivation behind foreign aid is correct), Japanese aid flowing disproportionately to states like Zaire, Zimbabwe and Botswana which have relatively higher scores on the strategic mineral index. But this is not the case here. My finding, however, confirms the observations reported by other scholars who studied the pattern of Japanese aid during the Cold War era. In particular, Maizels and Nissanke[78] reported the absence of a significant relationship between the global allocation of Japanese aid and the presence of strategic minerals in recipient states. The finding in this present study is remarkable because, by developing the strategic mineral index, I employed a more accurate measure of the influence of strategic minerals on the allocation of foreign aid. It is interesting that, even by this more sophisticated measure, there is an absence of a significant correlation between Japanese ODA and the presence of strategic minerals in the recipient states.

The distribution of aid between former British and French colonies is another interesting dimension of Japanese aid. The addition of these two variables to the calculation of the multiple regression equation, while slightly changing the percentage of the variation in Japanese aid explained by the new combination of variables (R^2 increases to 20 percent), does not affect the direction of the beta coefficients. The new equation reveals positive correlation between Japanese aid and Anglophone and Francophone countries, with the beta weights being stronger for the latter group. The finding of a positive correlation between Japanese aid and former British colonies supports a similar result reported by Schraeder, Hook and Taylor about the pattern of Japanese aid to Africa during the 1980s. Their interpretation of their finding is, however, unsupported by the results of this present study. According to them, "an obvious reason" for Japan's focus on Anglophone countries was the "facility of doing business in a common language (English); Francophone economies, by contrast, were more difficult to penetrate because of powerful French

---

[77] Arase (1995:24) asserts that in Japan, the need to establish sources of raw materials import and export markets gave birth to *Keizai Kyoryoku* (economic cooperation).

[78] Maizels and Nissanke, op. cit.

monopolies that were actively supported by the French government".[79] In contrast to their observation, I found a stronger positive correlation between the allocation of Japanese aid and former French colonies (t =3.789). There are two possible explanations for my finding. The first is that because former French colonies tend to have relatively impressive records of democratization, they tend to attract more aid from Japan. The second reason relates to the tendency of Japan's aid to go to countries where its national firms have relatively high stocks of foreign direct investment – middle income countries like Gabon and Cote d'Ivoire – which are also former French colonies.

Further insights into the nature of Japan's aid to sub-Saharan Africa could be gained by examining the pattern and degree of its concentration, or dispersion. As Figure 6.1 above illustrates, the pattern of Japan's aid reveals a significant level of dispersion. Kenya, Ghana, Zambia, and Tanzania, and Senegal were some of the favorite recipients of Japanese aid during the period covered by this study. Important dimensions of Japanese aid are also revealed in Table 6.1.

Table 6.1 Dimensions of Japan's ODA (1991-1997)

Dimension	1991	1992	1993	1994	1995	1996	1997
Total ODA to All LDCs ($millions)	8860	8388	8044	9558	10419	8207	6552
ODA to SSA as % of ODA to All LDCs	11	10	11	12	12	12	11
ODA to SSA as % of GNP	0.04	0.03	0.04	0.04	0.04	0.04	0.03
% of Concentration on Top Five Recipients in SSA	48	54	50	52	47	42	38

Source: Geographic Distribution of Financial Flows to Aid Recipients, 1960-1997. (CD-ROM). Paris, OECD (1998).

---

[79] Schraeder, Hook and Taylor, op.cit., 313.

118 *Contending Theories on Development Aid*

As the above table amply illustrates, Japan's aid to sub-Saharan Africa represents only about a tenth of its bilateral aid to less developed countries (LDCs), and it takes up a very small proportion of its GNP. Pertinently too, no sub-Saharan African country in either the Cold War period, or the post-Cold War era has attracted up to 2 percent of total Japanese aid to developing countries.[80]

Japan's global aid allocation favors Asian countries. This is evident from examining the countries represented in the list of the top ten recipients of its bilateral aid allocation in 1998.

Table 6.2 Top Ten Recipients of Japan's Global ODA (1998)

Rank	Country	(US$ m)
1	China	1124
2	Indonesia	1114
3	Thailand	712
4	India	711
5	Philippines	648
6	Pakistan	396
7	Malaysia	349
8	Viet Nam	318
9	Bangladesh	302
10	Sri Lanka	227

Source: *The DAC Journal. Development Cooperation, 1999 Report.* Vol.1, No.1. (2000):90.

The income-group and regional focus of Japan's aid also reflects a concentration on lower middle - income countries in Asia and Oceania. The fact is better captured by the pie-charts - Figures 6.2 and 6.3 respectively.

---

[80] Although no sub-Saharan African country received up to two percent of Japan's total aid to all developing countries, the proportions of its total aid to developing countries allocated to the following countries are note worthy: *1970-71*: Nigeira:1.1, Kenya: 0.3, Tanzania: 0.2, Uganda: 0.1, and Ethiopia: 0.1. *1980-81*: Zaire: 1.3, Tanzania: 1.1, Kenya: 0.8 and Zambia: 0.4. *1985-86*: Zambia: 0.9, Kenya: 0.8, Tanzania: 0.6, Sudan: 0.5 and Ghana: 0.5.

Japan 119

Japan's Gross Bilateral ODA Allocation (1998)

Figure 6.2 By Income Group (US$ m)

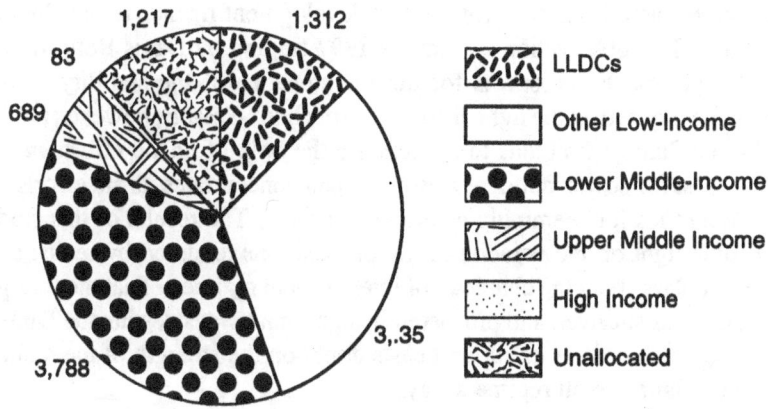

Figure 6.3 By Region (US$ m)

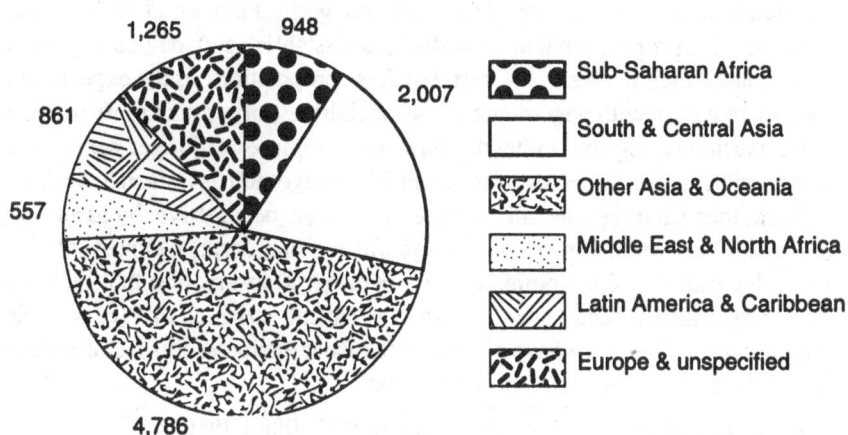

Source: The DAC Journal. Vol. 1, No. 1 (2000): 90

Notwithstanding the small proportion of the variation in Japanese post-Cold War aid explained by the independent variables I employed, the results of this study provide ample support for some important propositions. From a broader perspective, the prediction by hegemonic stability theorists that the decline of the United States will occasion a broad collapse in international system management[81] has not occurred, at least with respect to the foreign aid arena. This condition is attributable, in part, to Japan's increased international activity in the provision of development finance to developing countries. This observation confirms a 1997 finding by Davis Bobrow and Mark Boyer on the prospects for the maintenance of the stability of the international system in the light of American decline. Notably, however, unlike the United States who tends to concentrate the bulk of its aid efforts in the Middle East for power-political reasons, Japan concentrates its aid efforts on Asian countries for seemingly economic reasons. The results of this study shed some light on the veracity of the propositions tendered by realist and liberal scholars about the character of international regimes. That the foreign aid regime has survived and prospered in significant ways despite the United States' retrenchment of its support casts doubt on the strength of the realist/neorealist claims about regime decay.

Regime creation usually occurs at times of "fundamental discontinuities in the international system such as the conclusion of major wars".[82] Neorealists like Kenneth Waltz,[83] accurately observe that there is a high degree of congruity between the distribution of power in the international system and the characteristics of emergent regimes. Robert Gilpin, is equally on the mark in emphasizing that the history of war and change in the international system buttresses his proposition that powerful states establish and maintain regimes that enhance their interests.[84] Central to these propositions, is the expectation that when a state with hegemonic power withdraws, or retrenches its support for a particular regime, either because such regime no longer serves the hegemon's interest, or because the power of the hegemon has began to decline, or both, then such regime will collapse. From this perspective, by assuming the mantel of leadership of the foreign aid regime, Japan has prevented it from degeneration. This point confirms Krasner's observation that regimes do not necessarily decay even though "the causal variables that led to their creation in the first place have altered".[85] Krasner attributes this result to four feedback mechanisms inherent in regimes:

---

[81] See Kindlebeger 1973, 1981, and 1986; Kennedy, 1987; Gilpin, 1981.
[82] Krasner, 1982: 499.
[83] Waltz, 1979.
[84] Gilpin, 1981.
[85] Krasner, 1982: 500.

First, regimes may alter actors' calculations of how to maximize their interests. Second, regimes may alter interests themselves. Third, regimes may become a source of power to which actors can appeal. Fourth, regimes may alter the power capabilities of different actors, including states.[86]

Thus, even though the Cold War has ended, and although the US has retrenched its support, the foreign aid regime has endured because of the above factors, especially the emergence of Japan as a major economic power. As persuasive as Krasner's propositions are, however, a nagging question remains: Why has Japan, rather than some other state elected to fill the position vacated by the United States? *Gaiatsu* (the role of foreign pressure on Japan's policy) has often been reported as one of the forces shaping the trajectory of Japan's aid allocation. There are two strands to the *gaiatsu* proposition. The first relates to the influence which bureaucratic and interest group politics exert on Japan's foreign policy. The second pertains to the concepts of political comparative advantage and division of labor among members of the Western Alliance. Both strands of the *gaiatsu* argument are equally problematic.

With respect to the first strand of the *gaiatsu* argument, K.E. Calder,[87] submits that the susceptibility of Japanese foreign policy to US pressures stems from the influence which internal bureaucratic and interest group politics exerts on Japan's ability to initiate an independent and effective foreign policy path. According to him, Japan is a reactive state - the government consistently demonstrates a reluctance to embark on policy initiatives even when doing so would serve the country's interest – because of strong sectionalism in the bureaucracy. The fragmentation of interests in the Japanese bureaucracy, coupled with the weak authority that the Japanese political leadership has over its bureaucracy, in Calder's view, engender Japanese foreign policies that are readily susceptible to external pressure. A 1999 study by Akitoshi Miyashita has demonstrated, however, that Japan's response to US pressure is a result of choice rather than an inability to act on the part of the Japanese government. Miyashita asserts that in two instances - Japan's resumption of aid to post-Tiananmen–Square China, and its economic assistance to Russia under Yeltsin – Japan's sensitivity to *gaiatsu* stemmed from the asymmetrical power balance between her and the US, and consequently, Japan's desire to avoid major disruptions in its relations with the US.

The second strand of the *gaiatsu* argument is even more problematic. Mark Boyer, advanced the concepts of a division of labor and political comparative advantage to explain the cooperation among members of the

---

[86] Ibid, 503.
[87] Calder, 1988.

Western Alliance in their production of public goods during the Cold War.[88] According to him, during this period, the United States specialized in the production of defense goods because the receptivity of the American public to defense initiatives endowed the US government with a comparative advantage in this area. Similarly, other NATO members such as Japan and Italy lacked a political comparative advantage in the defense sector because of the hostility of their citizens to high defense expenditures. Japan, Italy, and these other members of NATO, however, enjoyed a comparative advantage in the production of public goods like foreign aid because their citizens were more receptive to such initiatives. More importantly, US pressure on these countries served as an additional incentive. Intent on ameliorating the effects of the free riders' problem on the production of public goods within the Western Alliance, the US began to pressure Japan and other countries to specialize in the provision of foreign aid to render burden sharing within the alliance less inequitable. Indeed, during the Cold War, there were many instances of such US pressure on it allies. Carol Lancaster cites as a case in point the pressure that the US exerted on Japan to provide aid to Sudan to reward the Sudanese government for its support of the Camp David accords between Egypt and Israel.[89]

Still, while Boyer's proposition can be persuasively applied to the behavior of US allies during the Cold War era when the common danger confronting the Western Alliance was clear and present, its application to the post-Cold War era is tenuous. If the demise of the Soviet Union has obviated the salience which the logic inherent in the division of labor and specialization in public goods production once held for members of the Western Alliance; if the end of the Cold War has also rendered the political advantage of such specialization slender, why should Japan continue to increase its contribution to the maintenance of the foreign aid regime? Perhaps, the answer to this question lies elsewhere. It calls into sharp relief the behavior of Japan's foreign aid in sub-Saharan Africa.

Since 1989 when Japan's $10.9 billion in global ODA surpassed that of the United States, crowning her as the world's largest donor in absolute amount, scholars and commentators on international affairs, have called attention to Japan's aspiration to the status of a great power.[90] In addition to utilizing its ODA to integrate the Asian pacific region under its suzerainty, Japan has made significant in roads into Africa. The pattern of its aid allocation and the success of the international conferences it has sponsored amply attest to this point.

---

[88] Boyer, 1993.
[89] Lancaster, 1999: 168-169.
[90] See for example, Waltz, 1993.

Japan also appears to be using ODA to open up new markets for Japanese products. This study found a significant, positive correlation between Japan's ODA and the stock of FDI by its national firms in its aid recipient states. This study, however, did not find any significant relationship between its ODA and the value of goods imported from Japan by its aid recipient states. This does not contradict the assertion that Japan employs its ODA to expand the orbit of its economic influence, because of its peculiar practice of untying significant portions of its aid. Japan allows its aid recipients autonomy over the uses to which they employ their aid receipts. Its level of untied aid has consistently been higher than the DAC average. In 1997, the untied portion of Japanese aid stood at 98.9 percent, against the DAC average of 69.7 percent.[91] Steven Hook also observed that, the tendency by Japan to untie large portions of its aid:

> ...reflects the broader Japanese aid strategy: Having constrained its aid recipients through relatively strict terms of aid, it allows them considerable flexibility in the use of their concessional financing.[92]

The pattern of Japanese aid to sub-Saharan Africa, especially the degree of its dispersion, also indicates a foreign aid behavior calculated to maximize its chances of attaining a great power status. Because foreign aid represents one of the leverages of influence a wealthy state could exert over poor states, spreading aid thinly, as Japan tends to do, allows her to maintain an aid presence in many countries. Such aid presence could stand her in good stead as she seeks to pursue an independent foreign policy agenda in the post-Cold War international system.[93]

A more serious concern about the increases in the levels of Japan's economic activities and capabilities to that of a great power is that, such activities thrusts her more deeply into world affairs and elevates their importance to her national interest. This in itself may not pose any threats to the stability of the international system. But if one considers the neorealist reasoning on the subject of anarchy, the implications of Japan's increasing international activities begin to coagulate. According to Kenneth Waltz, the *paterfamilias* of neorealist thought:

---

[91] Development Cooperation Report, 1998.
[92] Hook, 1995: 86.
[93] See Arase, 1995. One area where such leverage could come in handy for Japan relates to the lobbying for votes in international forums like the United Nations General Assembly over such questions as what states should be included in the imminent expansion of the number of permanent members in the Security Council.

In a self help system, the possession of most but not all of the capabilities of a great power leaves a state dependent on others and vulnerable to those who have the instruments that the lesser state lacks.[94]

From the neorealist's vantage point, the question is obvious: Having attained such impressive economic capabilities, will Japan remain contented as a lesser political power? Paul Kennedy's history of the *Rise and Fall of Great Powers* suggests that Japan will not remain contented with economic might alone, because no state having attained economic power has remained satisfied as a lesser political power.[95] Waltz's 1993 article also leaned towards this prediction of Japan's future actions, and added that, because the possession of nuclear weapons is the panoply of a great power, Japan should be expected to traverse the same route that has served the security interest of other great powers.

There are two sets of reasons why in the near future, the Japanese government might be expected to amend the clause in the Japanese constitution, which currently bars the government from military build up. First, the behavior of rival states in Asia provokes anxieties in the minds of Japanese leaders about the country's security. Many examples abound that one should limit citations to the most recent ones. On September 1, 1998, North Korea fired a two-stage ballistic missile over Japan, indicating that it has greatly increased the range of its weapons. North Korea's explanation four days later that the purpose of its deployment of the two-stage rocket was to carry a satellite into orbit did little to soothe Japanese anxieties.[96]

In addition to the threat North Koreas poses to Japan, Japan must also contend with the rising power of China. With the union of Hong Kong and China, the new China now commands a more significant share of global finance capital and market. In addition to its increasing economic power, it has also embarked on actions in the military arena that could only render Japan more nervous. In March 1999, US officials announced that China has made a leap in the miniaturization of its bombs by stealing nuclear secrets from US labs. When one adds to these reports the nuclear arms race between India and Pakistan, the vulnerabilities of a Japan lacking its own nuclear weapons becomes glaring. So far, one of the restraints on Japanese nuclear ambitions has been the security guarantee provided by the United States. But the drawback of American forces in the region, coupled with increasing incidents of economic conflict and verbal sparring between leaders from the two

---

[94] Waltz, 1993: 64.
[95] Kennedy, 1987.
[96] See Kristoff, 1998.

countries do little to assuage Japanese fears. In 1988, then Japanese Prime Minister Takeshita called for a defensive capability matching Japan's economic power. In 1992, an off color remark by Japanese former Prime Minister Miyazawa alleging that Americans lack a decent work ethic drew an equally caustic response from US Senator F. Hollis. Hollis reminded the Japanese that the atomic bomb was made by lazy and illiterate Americans and tested in Japan. Waltz, asserts that incidents such as these magnify the vulnerabilities of Japan and are likely to motivate Japan's leaders to acquire greater military capabilities, even though many Japanese may prefer not to do so.[97]

The second reason why Japan may be expected to join the nuclear club in the near future relates to developments in the country's local politics and the changing attitudes of the Japanese people to the constitutional clause barring the country from such undertakings. In April 1999, Japanese voters humiliated the governing Liberal Democratic Party in a major local election, when they elected a maverick nationalist – Shintaro Ishihara - to the governorship of Tokyo. Although Ishihara's views on the nuclear question are somewhat benign, his nationalist credentials are impeccable.[98] And as a maverick politician, one could expect his views on the nuclear question to move closer toward supporting Japan's ascension to the nuclear power club should Japanese public sentiments lean in that direction. On this score, it is significant that in October of 1999, a senior official of the Japanese Ministry of Defense stated that Japan should abandon its long time renunciation of nuclear weapons.[99] Although this official was promptly relieved of his position by the Japanese government, there are indications that many Japanese do not disagree with him. Rather, they consider his expression of the sentiments felt by many Japanese a little premature. Neorealists assert that it would be naïve to expect the Japanese nuclear inhibitions to last permanently. Waltz reasons that one might expect such inhibitions to expire as generational memories fade in Japan, because:

> ...when a country receives less attention and respect and gets its way less often than it feels it should, internal inhibitions about becoming a great power are likely to turn into public criticisms of the government for not taking its proper place in the world.[100]

---

[97] Waltz, 1993.

[98] In his 1991 book: *The Japan that Can Say No*: Why Japan will Be First Among Equals, Ishihara argues that Japan does not need nuclear weapons to be able to play a major role in nuclear politics. He asserts that because of Japan's technological superiority, if it refused to sell chips to any of the major powers that would alter the nuclear balance in significant ways.

[99] See French, 1999.

[100] Waltz, 1993: 66.

Moreover, the probability of Japan becoming a nuclear power is all the higher because it can easily do so. There is only one nuclear technology, and a country that has so far been able to harness the atom for peaceful purposes can quickly move into the nuclear military business. These are the waves of issues, which the realist/neorealist radar picks up from the rise of Japan to a dominant position in the foreign aid arena. Still, there are counter arguments worth pondering.

Scholars such as Dennis Yasutomo perceive only benign and positive motivations behind Japan's ascension to the status of an aid great power. According to him, while foreign aid improves Japan's economic and national prestige, it provides its government and the Japanese people with a glimpse of a desired future – "a vision of Japan as an activist nonmilitary power contributing in international security and political as well as economic and financial arenas".[101] Similarly, scholars such as Robert Keohane, Joseph Nye, and Neil Richardson argue that increasing trade and other economic ties expand the zone of interdependence between countries.[102] The extension of this reasoning to Japan's relations with its neighbors leads one to expect that the increasing ties between China and Japan in recent years will significantly thaw the ice of mutual suspicion that the Cold War engendered in the relations between the two countries. In addition, there is the consideration that the rise of issues relating to environmental degradation and new strains of microbial diseases – issues which no nation can effectively address by unilateral effort – underscores the necessity of cooperation between Japan, China, North Korea and other states in the Asian region. Thus, because the possession of nuclear weapons is of questionable utility in the resolution of these issues, fears of nuclear blackmail are therefore misplaced.

Essentially too, there is the consideration of the point tendered by John Mueller that, since World War II, war between the major powers has become obsolete not because of the nuclear deterrent, but because substantial agreement has arisen among great power contenders, and developed nations more broadly, that prosperity and economic growth should be their central national goals.[103] From this perspective, wars in particular, and indeed preparations for war are deemed counter productive for achieving national goals. The collapse of the former Soviet Union appears to lend credence to this position.

In addition to the above points, there is the consideration of the African apothegm that, because a tiger need not go about professing its *tigerhood*, it is not necessary for Japan, having attained such impressive economic and

---

[101] Yasutomo, 1990: 502.
[102] See Keohane and Nye, 1989, and Richardson, 1995.
[103] Mueller, 1989.

technological superiority over its neighbors, to take the next step to joining the nuclear club. Moreover, such action would not necessarily enhance its security. On this score, there is much merit to Ishihara's claim that Japan could alter the nuclear balance in its favor without itself acquiring nuclear weapons. Indeed, it could be argued that Japan's economic prosperity and investment abroad builds a web of security against its invasion by any of its neighbors. Such actual or, intended invasion would send shock waves through the global economy to the effect that other major powers would have to deter Japan's potential aggressors, or come to its aid in the event of any invasion, if nothing else, for the preservation of their own prosperity. From this perspective, even if ironically, just as Adam Smith's proverbial consumer expects his dinner, not so much from the benevolence of the butcher, the brewer, or the baker, but from their attention to their own interests, so is Japan rendered secure not so much by the altruism of its major commercial partners, but by their regard to their own prosperity.

Conclusion

Japan has emerged as the foremost aid donor in the post-Cold War world. Although it was only the fourth largest source of aid to sub-Saharan Africa in the period covered by this study, it has expanded its economic activities in the region and taken notable steps to engage the sub-continent in a new development partnership. An examination of the pattern of Japanese aid to the region yields a mixture of motives. On the one hand, its emphasis on democratization and the reduction of expenditures on defense by its aid recipients suggests a link between democracy and development cooperation as an extension of the democratic peace thesis would lead one to expect. It also calls for the adjustment of the realist/neorealist vision. On the other hand, a consideration of other salient issues mutes the optimism inherent in broad declarations about the triumph of liberal principles in the post-Cold War international system. Japan selectively applies the democratization metric to punish errant sub-Saharan African states while some equally problematic states in Asia continue to receive high levels of aid. This observation reinforces claims by realist/neorealists about the parochial national interest motivation behind the foreign aid policies of developed countries.

The emergence of Japan as a foreign aid power, especially the high levels of dispersion evident in the pattern of its aid allocation present additional food for thought. From the realist/neorealist vantage point, this pattern represents notable footprints on the rungs of the great power ladder pointing to an upward climb. And because a country with such expanded global interests cannot be expected to refrain from arming itself with the weapons which "have served as the great deterrent" (Waltz, 1993:64), for similarly positioned powers all through history, it is prudent to keep a wary eye on Japan's future behavior. Liberalism presents an alternative optimistic vision. But as persuasive as that vision might be, several developments in Asia and elsewhere suggest that realism is not yet the anachronism.

7 Norway: The Inexorable Influence of National Role Conception?

Post-Cold War evidence from sub-Saharan Africa demonstrates the influence of national role conception on the behavior of Norway in the foreign aid arena. As a small country with strong commitments to domestic welfare policies, Norway perceives its role in the international system as the moral voice for poor countries on issues of international peace (Stokke, 1989), hence its impressive commitment to development cooperation.[104]

According to Kal Holsti, a national role concept enables the policy makers in a given country to:

> ...define the general kinds of decisions, commitments, rules and actions suitable to their state, and of the function, if any, their state should perform on a continuing basis in the international system or in subordinate regional systems. It is their image of the appropriate orientation or functions of their state towards, or in the external environment (Holsti, 1970:12).

Norway's bilateral assistance is provided exclusively in grant form. About one-third of Norway's bilateral aid is tied, half of which is for technical cooperation. While its capital assistance is untied in principle, the bulk of its commodity assistance is tied to procurements in Norway, provided the prices for such goods are internationally competitive. A scheme of concessionary export credit uses budgeted funds mainly to subsidize the interest rates of

---

[104] The Nordic countries cooperate extensively in the field of development assistance, and coordinate their positions in international organizations. A significant example of Nordic aid cooperation is the Agreement on Expanded Economic and Cultural Cooperation between the Nordic states and the member states of the Southern African Development Cooperation Conference (SADCC), signed in 1986. Under this agreement responsibilities for various areas of cooperation, including individual projects, were distributed among the Nordic countries. A regional Nordic/SADCC Fund (NORSAD) for promoting the establishment of joint Nordic/SADCC ventures was also established (see Development Cooperation, 1994).

export credits, the subsidy amount being reported as ODA and the credits as associated financing.

The independent variables in this study accounts for about 34 percent in the variation of Norwegian aid to sub-Saharan Africa in the post-Cold War era. The direction of the statistically significant coefficients reveals a mixture of humanitarian and selfish motives behind Norwegian aid. The size of the recipient states' population is the most significant variable in the explanation of Norwegian aid to the region. The positive correlation between this variable and ODA (t =3.798) suggests that Norway targets aid to the relatively more populous countries in sub-Saharan Africa.

The scores of the recipient states on the strategic mineral index (SMI) was another significant element in the motivation behind Norwegian aid (t =3.612). On first cut, this finding is at odds with the popular belief about the humanitarian motivation behind Norwegian aid. When Zambia, Zimbabwe, and Botswana - all favorite recipients of Norway's aid with relatively high scores on the SMI - are excluded from the calculation of the multiple regression equation, the statistical significance of the SMI as a predictive variable drops markedly. Nonetheless, this finding lends some credence to the realist proposition about the influence of parochial interests on foreign aid.

The value of goods imported by aid recipient states from Norway is another important variable in understanding the motivations behind Norwegian aid. The correlation between this variable and ODA is positive (t =2.439), indicating that Norwegian aid discriminates in favor of countries importing more goods from Norway. This finding confirms the declared objective of the Norwegian government published in a 1996 report to the *Storting* (Report #19), which articulated Norway's need to use foreign aid to further the country's commercial interests. This finding provides additional support for the realist thesis on foreign aid.

Another notable feature of Norwegian aid is the finding of an inverse relationship between ODA and the value of the stock of the foreign direct investment (FDI) of Norwegian firms in sub-Saharan Africa (t = -3.708). This finding is curious and somewhat problematic because it suggests an irrational behavior on the part of Norway. Upon close inspection, however, the finding is not so strange. For one, while Norwegian aid is concentrated in Eastern and Southern Africa, Norwegian firms tend to invest more in the littoral countries in West Africa such as Senegal, Nigeria, Cote d' Ivoire, and Benin.

The finding of an inverse relationship between Norwegian ODA and the values of Gross Domestic Product (GDP) of the recipient states (t = -2.487) is another significant aspect of the motivation behind Norwegian aid to sub-Saharan Africa. This finding confirms the widely held belief that Norwegian aid, emerging from a Christian tradition, is directed towards the promotion of the principles of humane internationalism. Successive governments and parliaments in Norway have emphasized the altruistic principles motivating Norwegian aid. In 1961, the Engen committee located the origins of this principle in the belief by Norwegians' about the equality of all peoples and their solidarity with all countries and races. In 1975, the labor government stated that the moral obligations to help human beings in distress were the most powerful incentive behind Norwegian aid. Then again in 1984, a coalition government made up of the Center Party, the Christian People Party and the Conservative Party emphasized that Norwegian development assistance was an extension of the humanitarian dimensions of the country's welfare state into the international arena (Stokke 1989:163-170).

The variable - Foreign Military Presence (FMP) also registered as an important predictor of Norwegian aid. Its inverse correlation with ODA (t=-2.935) suggests that Norwegian aid discriminates against countries hosting foreign military troops. This finding is understandable given that the sub-Saharan African countries hosting foreign troops are essentially the former French colonies of Central African Republic, Chad, Cote d' Ivoire, Gabon and Senegal; whereas Norwegian aid is highly concentrated on countries in Southern Africa.

The guideline undergirding the concentration of Norway's aid was established in late the 1960s. The main argument for this was the desire to render aid more effective. As Stokke (1989) notes, Norway's small development assistance had to be concentrated on a few countries (and even in a few sectors) if the reciprocal knowledge between the partners deemed necessary to facilitate effective aid was to be developed. Figure 7.1 illuminates the extent of the concentration of Norwegian aid.

Additional insights into Norwegian aid are gained by examining the trend in its aid allocation to sub-Saharan Africa against the backdrop of its global aid efforts. Norway's global ODA net disbursements rose to $1.2 billion in 1990, a growth of 14 percent in real terms over the 1989 figure. Its bilateral aid to sub-Saharan Africa that year was about $400 million. This increase was due to the 18 and 7 percent rise in bilateral and multilateral aid respectively and resulted in a substantially higher ODA/GNP ratio of 1.17 percent, by far the highest ratio among DAC members for that year.

Historically, until the late 1970s, Norway's ODA favored countries in Asia. But between 1980 and 1989, it gradually shifted the geographical focus of its bilateral aid away from Asia to Southern Africa. Whereas, in 1980 the shares of Norwegian aid to Asia and Southern Africa were 45 percent and 30 percent respectively, by 1990, the shares had been reversed to 20 and 60 percent respectively. Since the end of the Cold War period, some 50 percent of Norwegian aid has been allocated to its designated main partners in these two regions.

132 Contending Theories on Development Aid

Figure 7.1 Scattergram Showing the Favorite Recipients of Norway's Bilateral ODA (1990-1997)

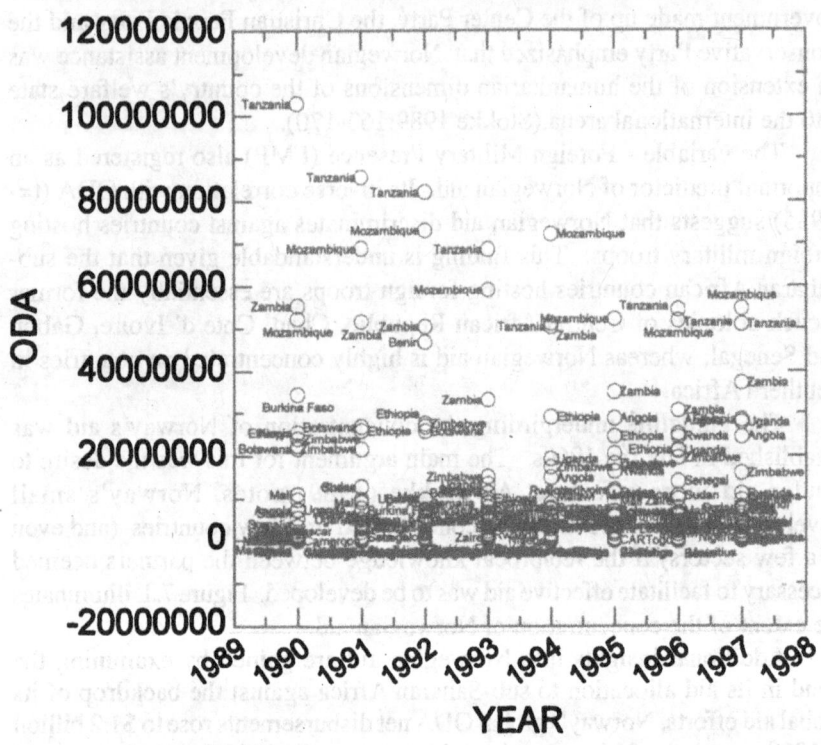

Source: Geographic Distribution of Financial Flows to Aid Recipients, 1960-1997 (CD-ROM). Paris, OECD (1998).

Like other members of the DAC, Norwegian aid has had to face the challenges of the 1990s. In a paper presented to Parliament in 1992 (Report No. 51), the Norwegian government proposed adjusting its aid policies and priorities in light of the problems and opportunities of the 1990s. The ministry of Foreign Affairs began to establish integrated embassies in its major aid recipient countries with a mandate that covered both foreign policy and development cooperation. After virtually no growth in 1991, Norway's global ODA net disbursements increased by 5 percent in real terms in 1992 to $1.3 billion, and its aid to the sub-Saharan states in this study increased from $356 million to $392 million. Also, in 1992, Norway reached an ODA/GNP ratio of 1.16 percent (1.13 percent in 1991), the highest ratio among DAC member countries. Its ODA/GNP ratio for sub-Saharan Africa also increased from 0.49 percent in 1991 to 0.51 percent in 1992. That same year, Norway's bilateral ODA rose by 7 percent in real terms, and its contributions to multilateral institutions increased by 1 percent. Norway's share of multilateral contributions, which represents about one third of its total ODA remains relatively high in comparison to other DAC members like the United States and France.

In 1993, however, Norway's high ODA volume dropped sharply by 11 percent to $1.01 billion, reflecting falls of bilateral and multilateral ODA of 9 and 14 percent respectively. This decline was also reflected in its aid to sub-Saharan Africa, which, at $278 million reached an all time low for the 1990s. This decrease was due in large part to budgetary predictions that had foreseen a less severe slow-down for that year. Still, with an ODA/GNP ratio of 1.10 percent, Norway remained the second highest contributor to development cooperation on this measure of burden sharing among DAC members, next to Denmark, and well above the 0.7 percent established by the United Nations and recommended by the DAC. Norway's official aid to Part II CEECs/NIS countries in 1993, declined marginally to $77 million but rose as a share of its GNP to 0.08 percent. The comparative figures for Norwegian aid to sub-Saharan Africa illustrated by Table 7.1 reveals the proportion of the country's resources that goes to support the development efforts of the states in the region. Both as a percentage of its GDP, and as a percentage of its aid to all LDCs, Norway's contribution to development assistance efforts in sub-Saharan Africa, though concentrated on the countries of eastern and southern Africa, has been quite impressive.

Table 7.1 Dimensions of Norway's ODA (1991-1997)

Dimension	1991	1992	1993	1994	1995	1996	1997
Total ODA to All LDCs ($millions)	734	810	658	828	907	945	916
ODA to SSA as % of ODA to All LDCs	49	48	42	39	36	35	36
ODA to SSA as % of GNP	0.49	0.51	0.31	0.33	0.33	0.29	0.30
% of Concentration on Top Five Recipients in SSA	73	72	68	70	59	56	60

Source: Geographic Distribution of Financial Flows to Aid Recipients, 1960-1997. (CD-ROM). Paris, OECD (1998).

It is evident from the scope and pattern of Norwegian aid that the country's contribution to international development assistance, and indeed, to international affairs belies its power rankings in realist calculations. Because Norway ranks the establishment and reinforcement of peace as an important prerequisite for durable development, in the early 1990s, it took the lead in search for peace in the Middle East between the Israelis and Palestinians. As a follow up to this work, substantial budget appropriations were allocated for rehabilitation activities among Palestinian Communities. Furthermore, in 1993, Norway actively supported the peace process in Mozambique and El Salvador and it also engaged in post-war reconstruction work through government-to-government cooperation in Eritrea and Ethiopia. All these laudable efforts were the continuation of the country's traditional engagement in issues of international cooperation and development. Recall that in 1987, it was Mrs. Gro Harlem Bruntland, who as Prime Minister of Norway, chaired the World Commission on Environment and Development that published the 1987 report titled *Our Common Future* that rekindled the worldwide interest in environmental issues.

Among specialists of international political economy (IPE), there is a consensus that the foreign policies of small AICs differ in several respects from those of large AICs.[105] There is, however, the absence of a consensus among scholars about the factors responsible for such differences. Neorealists, such as Gilpin (1987) and Jervis (1988) underscore differential power capabilities as the most salient factors accounting for their observed differences in state behavior. Other scholars, such as Holsti (1987), draw attention to the influence that national role conception exerts on the behavior of some small states in the international system. With respect to foreign aid policies, Hoadley (1980) tested, albeit with crude instruments, the pattern of behavior exhibited by small states. He tendered the following hypotheses:

1. Small donor aid will tend to be given to a relatively narrower geographic range of recipients.
2. Small donor aid and resource transfers will tend to be more generous.
3. Small donor aid will tend not to be given to the enemies of large states with whom the small donor is allied.
4. Small donor aid will tend to be channeled through multilateral agencies to a greater extent.
5. Small donor aid will tend to achieve internationally accepted norms and targets frequently (Hoadley, 1980:124).

Despite the fact that these hypotheses have the ring of post-facto rationalization to them, and ignoring the fact that his study was based on a single year (1976), Hoadley concluded that his findings pretty much confirmed his hypotheses.

Norway's behavior in the foreign aid arena calls into question, the usefulness of the emphasis that realists place on the proposition that the distribution of national capabilities is the primary determinant of a state's behavior in the anarchic international system. The point here is not to deny the relationship between a state's resources and the type of international action in which it elects to participate. True, there is a threshold of capability a state must attain before it could credibly get itself involved in international actions. But to place undue emphasis on the role of such capability is to under-estimate the influence of national role conception on a state's behavior. The proposition tendered by East (1975), and reiterated by Hoadley (1980:126) that the generosity of small states is simply the demonstration of prudence on their part, "since the military and diplomatic means of statecraft available to and

---

[105] See for examples, Vital (1967), Schou and Bruntland, eds. (1971), East (1973), Plischke (1976), and Stokke, ed. (1989). With respect to foreign conflict, however, Rummel (1968) argued against the conventional wisdom when he demonstrated that size variables have low correlations with foreign conflict behavior.

employed by large states are too risky or ineffectual by small states" understates the humanitarian motivation behind such behavior. The so-called small states do not all behave alike even in an arena such as foreign aid. The foreign aid policies of Portugal, Austria, and New Zealand are both quantitatively and qualitatively different from those of Denmark, Norway, and Sweden. The observation that similarly constrained small states respond in markedly different ways suggests that one must look beyond the conventional notions of capabilities to explain their behavior.

Measured by the conventional attributes of national capability - population, geographic size, percentage of population fit for military service, size of economy, natural resources, and defense expenditures - Norway ranks low among the donors in this study (see Appendix 3 for the ranking of the ten donors on conventional measures of capability). Yet, in terms of relative contribution to development assistance (ODA/GNP ratio) it ranks highest among all members of the DAC. Moreover, while many other donors have been retrenching their foreign aid efforts in sub-Saharan Africa, when measured in current dollars, Norway's aid to the region has actually gone up. Such apparent behavior belies the emphasis on the distribution of capabilities as the primary determinant of a state's conduct in the international system.

In 1994, Norway's global ODA disbursements amounted to $1.4 billion, of which 73 percent was spent under the bilateral program. Compared with 1993, this was an increase of about 11percent in real terms. Its ODA/GNP ratio improved from 1.01 percent to 1.05 percent, again, the highest ratio among DAC countries for that year. Norway's bilateral aid to the sub-Saharan African states in this study for that year amounted to about $318 million, or 38 percent of its total aid to LDCs. As indicated by the strong inverse correlation between the GDP of the recipient states in this study and its ODA, Norwegian aid manifests a commitment to poverty reduction in the region. Norway's strong commitment to the reduction of poverty in Third World countries is reflected in the large size of its aid effort as well as in the general orientation and quality of its development cooperation program. Rating ODA in terms of GNP places Norway at the top among DAC donors. With an ODA/GNP ratio of 0.87 percent in 1995, Norway ranked second (next to Denmark) among DAC members on burden sharing. Norway's commitment to poverty reduction is also manifested in the strong support of the development cause by Norwegian NGOs in areas such as the mobilization of public opinion in favor of development cooperation and concrete aid initiatives in the field.

A comparison of Norway's commitment to poverty reduction with the efforts of other DAC members sheds more light on the orientation of its aid efforts. In 1994, 72 percent of Norwegian bilateral aid was channeled to poorer countries (LLDCs and other LICs), compared to a total DAC share of 60 percent. In addition, as Table 7.2 illustrates, in the post-Cold War period, unlike the foreign aid pattern of wealthier states such as Japan and the United States, Norway has increased the number of poor states in sub-Saharan Africa receiving at least 2 percent of the total of its aid to all LDCs. Tanzania, Mozambique, Uganda, Angola, and Rwanda, who are some of the poorest states in the world have been the primary targets of Norwegian aid.

By the mid-1990s, however, although the volume of Norwegian aid to the sub-Saharan African states in this study did not suffer any serious reversals, the focus of its global bilateral assistance was becoming more nuanced. The hitherto uncritical attitude by the Norwegian public to their country's aid efforts based on the moral argument was being replaced by a questioning of the effectiveness of aid and by demands for more accountability by the government for the use of the tax payer's money.

In tandem with the above point, by the mid-1990s, an unforeseen expansion of aid for emergency and humanitarian purposes and peace building began to change the pattern of Norwegian aid. An indication of this is evident in the fact that the former Yugoslavia, particularly Bosnia, became by 1995, Norway's single largest aid recipient. By the mid 1990s, as the Development Cooperation Report for 1995 notes, Norwegian global aid effort became characterized by four main elements:

Table 7.2 Comparison of Favorite Recipients of Norway's ODA to Sub-Saharan Africa (Cold War Years v Post-Cold War Period)

Cold War Years

1970-71	% of ODA[106]	1980-81	% of ODA	1985-86	% of ODA
Kenya	7.0	Tanzania	8.8	Tanzania	8.5
Tanzania	5.4	Kenya	4.4	Mozambique	3.9
Uganda	2.7	Mozambique	2.4	Kenya	3.8
Zambia	2.1	Botswana	2.3	Zambia	3.3
		Zambia	2.0		

---

[106] This is calculated as the percentage of the donor's total ODA to all developing countries (LDCs).

138 *Contending Theories on Development Aid*

Post-Cold War Period

Year	Recipients	% of ODA
1991	Tanzania	12.0
	Mozambique	9.4
	Zambia	7.0
	Botswana	3.7
	Ethiopia	3.5
	Zimbabwe	3.0
1992	Tanzania	10.0
	Mozambique	9.0
	Zambia	5.0
	Benin	5.8
	Zimbabwe	3.4
	Botswana	3.2
	Ethiopia	3.3
1993	Tanzania	10.4
	Mozambique	9.0
	Zambia	5.0
	Zimbabwe	2.3
	Uganda	2.0
1994	Mozambique	8.7
	Zambia	6.2
	Tanzania	6.1
	Ethiopia	3.5
	Uganda	2.3
	Zimbabwe	2.0
1995	Tanzania	17.3
	Mozambique	16.3
	Zambia	4.2
	Angola	3.5
	Ethiopia	3.0
	Uganda	2.5
	Zimbabwe	2.1
	Rwanda	2.0
1996	Tanzania	5.8
	Mozambique	5.5
	Zambia	3.2
	Angola	2.7
	Rwanda	2.5
	Uganda	2.3
	Zimbabwe	2.1
1997	Mozambique	6.0
	Tanzania	5.6
	Zambia	4.1
	Ethiopia	3.1
	Uganda	3.0
	Angola	2.7

Source: Development Cooperative Report. Paris, OECD (Various Years).

(1) Bilateral cooperation, with policy framework set by the bilateral department of the Ministry of Foreign Affairs (MFA), and implemented by the Norwegian Agency for Development Cooperation (NORAD), both under the responsibility of the Minister for Development Cooperation.
(2) Emergency assistance and political development cooperation with the Political Affairs Department of the MFA responsible for policy design and management.
(3) Cooperation with NGOs, comprising some 80 organizations, a number of which have major human, logistical and financial resources, with funding from both the bilateral system (NORAD) and the emergency system (Political Affairs Department of the MFA).
(4) Multilateral cooperation with policy-making and funding for both Multilateral Development Banks and UN agencies entrusted to the multilateral department of the MFA under the administrative responsibility of the Minister for Development Cooperation.

In 1995, Norway's net ODA amounted to $1.2 billion, a fall of 4 percent in real terms from the previous year. Its aid to sub-Saharan Africa, however, remained steady and even increased a little to about $327 million from $319 million the previous year. Equally worth noting is that Norway was the first OECD country to introduce a new system of National Accounts, which has led to a major upward revision of its GNP estimates. As a result, its ODA/GNP ratio fell from 1.05 percent in 1994 to 0.87 percent in 1995, but remained the second highest ratio, after Denmark, even on this new basis.

In 1996, Norway's global net ODA increased by 5.4 percent to $1.3 billion. There was no significant change in the pattern of its ODA distribution, which concentrated on bilateral assistance and contributions to the United Nations system, although there was some effort to allocate extra funding into the emergency aid sector and into regional funds to support a more flexible approach to bilateral aid. That same year, Norwegian bilateral ODA, which is provided almost entirely in grant form, consisted of three components: financial assistance for investment in development projects and programs (31 percent of total ODA), emergency assistance (15 percent) and technical cooperation (14 percent). In 1996, Norway's aid to sub-Saharan Africa rose slightly to about $332 million.

Essentially, since the end of the Cold War, Norway's aid strategy has been periodically updated to adapt to the changing international situation.

This process involves both government and Parliament in an intensive dialogue based on governmental reports prepared by the MFA. An example of this is the 1996 white paper entitled *A Changing World: Main elements of Norwegian policy towards developing Countries* (Report No. 19 to the Storting, 1995-96). The report emphasized the integration of foreign, trade and aid policies into one policy set, which would not only help to reinforce Norway's engagement in international efforts to promote peace, democracy and the resolution of conflict, but would also further its commercial interests abroad. In 1997, global Norwegian bilateral and multilateral aid increased in real terms by 3 and 13 percent respectively, resulting in an overall increase in total ODA of 6 percent. At 0.86 percent, for that year, its ODA/GNP ratio continued to exceed the UN's 0.7 target. Its aid to the sub-Saharan African states in this study rose slightly to about $333 million, or 36 percent of its aid to all LDCs.

In 1998, while most members of the DAC were retrenching their aid efforts, Norwegian aid increased by 8.4 percent in real terms; and at 0.91 percent, its ODA/GNP ratio continued to exceed the United Nations' 0.7 percent target. Moreover, although Russia and Bosnia-Herzegovina also featured among the top ten recipients of Norwegian aid, sub-Saharan Africa continued to be a priority focus for Norway.

Table 7.3 Top Ten Recipients of Norway's Global ODA (1998)

Rank	Country	(US$ m)
1	Mozambique	52
2	Tanzania	48
3	Palestinian Adm. Areas	41
4	Zambia	35
5	Bosnia and Herzegovina	34
6	Bangladesh	31
7	Russia	31
8	Uganda	30
9	Ethiopia	28
10	Angola	24

Source: *The DAC Journal. Development Cooperation, 1999 Report.* Vol.1, No.1. (2000):96.

Figures 7.2 and 7.3 also underscore Norway's focus on low-income countries and sub-Saharan Africa.

With respect to future trends in Norwegian assistance to sub-Saharan Africa, in its 1999 budget, Parliament adopted a debt relief plan, which lays out how Norway could contribute to an improvement in international debt mechanisms. Such high level discussions of the debt crises confronting many countries in the region could help mobilize concerted international efforts to address the debt problem. Norway is also working actively to improve trade policy framework for developing countries because, according to the Norwegian government, Norway considers the development of a healthy private sector in developing countries as a prerequisite for the eradication of poverty. In 1998, it elaborated an overall strategy for its approach to private sector development. The main thrust of the strategy is that efforts must be based on the interest of developing countries, and not be steered to primarily address the business interest of developed countries. As a consequence of this development, Norway, which has traditionally tied about one third of its bilateral aid to purchases in its home market has begun to untie its aid disbursements. It has also urged other members of the DAC to do the same.

Conclusion

How might one best characterize Norway's aid given the mixture of humanitarian and apparently, parochial interests evident in the pattern of its post-Cold War aid to sub-Saharan Africa? Three essential points recommend an answer: first, in terms of burden sharing of development assistance among DAC members, Norway's contribution has frequently ranked highest. Just as Norway has consistently posed impressive ODA/GNP ratios globally, so has it assumed a considerable share of the development effort in sub-Saharan Africa, even though its aid is highly concentrated on the countries of Eastern and Southern Africa. Secondly, the humanitarian dimension of Norwegian aid is also quite clear. The poorest states in sub-Saharan Africa have consistently attracted the most aid from Norway. Third, there is the unmistakable and expressed intention of the Norwegian government that its aid should also promote its commercial interests. Besides, Norway only recently began to untie substantial parts of its aid. When these points are taken into account, the striking thing that emerges about Norwegian aid is the influence that its national role conception and its domestic economic culture exert on its behavior in the foreign aid arena. As a small country with a rich history of commitment to issues of humane internationalism, Norway has

142 *Contending Theories on Development Aid*

Norway's Gross Bilateral ODA Allocation (1998)

Figure 7.2 By Income Group (US$ m)

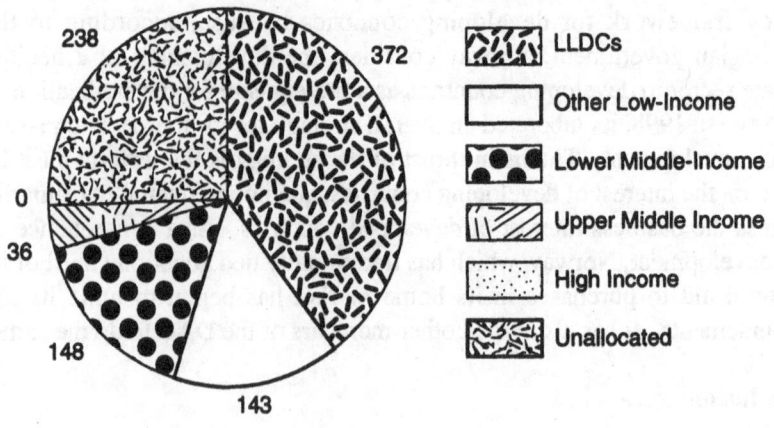

Figure 7.3 By Region (US$ m)

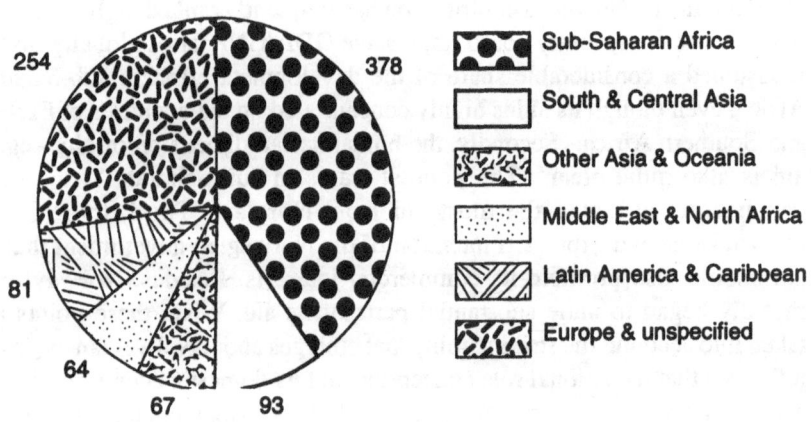

Source: The DAC Journal. Vol. 1, No. 1 (2000): 96

selected the issue of development assistance as an area where it could make significant, positive difference. But its domestic economic culture, straddling welfarism and capitalism as it does, represents two strains that tend to simultaneously propel its aid giving towards humanitarian and parochial interests.

Because of the influence of its welfare culture, Norway is undoubtedly committed to the goal of poverty reduction in sub-Saharan Africa as evident in the countries upon which it concentrates its aid efforts. And because of the influence of the capitalist strain in its economic culture, it also realizes that for its aid programs to continue to enjoy the support of the Norwegian public, especially in times of budgetary difficulties, it must present some tangible commercial gains to the country, hence the articulation of this objective in the Report to the *Storting*, #19.

The finding of a statistically significant positive correlation between Norway's aid to sub-Saharan Africa and (1) the scores of the recipient states on the strategic mineral index, and (2) the value of their imports from Norway, are interesting findings which point to the presence of parochial interests in the mixture of factors driving its aid policies. These observations lend credence to the assertion by realist that aid is employed by donors to service their power-political and economic interests.

Nevertheless, when one locates this finding within the overall context of Norway's behavior in the international system, it becomes evident that the findings also call for a nuanced interpretation.

Norway disburses 100 percent of its ODA to sub-Saharan Africa as grants. Poverty reduction is a prominent feature of its aid program. In addition, it has consistently advocated for more generous aid to Africa within the DAC. And although it has tied its aid to the sub-continent to imports from Norway, it has begun to untie substantial portions of such aid. Taking these factors into consideration suggests that a realist interpretation of Norwegian aid is, at best, incomplete. A more persuasive explanation for Norwegian aid is the country's national role conception in the international system.

True, the conditions of possessing certain levels of national resources "seem to be related to a state's propensity to organize the performance of a task internationally" (Ruggie, 1972:83). Still, the influence that the principles of humane internationalism exert on the national role conception of a country like Norway need not be underestimated.

Norway perceives its role in the international system as both the moral voice for the Christian principles of assisting countries in need (Stokke, 1989), and serving as a bridge between quarrelsome countries. Norway's limited resources account for the high levels of concentration in the pattern of its aid giving, but the influence of its national role conception informs both the type of countries it elects to aid, and the high ODA/GNP ratios of its aid.

8 USA: Simultaneous Tides of Retrenchment and Recommitment

Next to France and Germany, in the post-Cold War period, when measured in absolute dollars, the United States has been the third largest donor of economic assistance to sub-Saharan Africa. Globally, the provision of US aid, according to a DAC peer review report, are directed at the satisfaction of six broad goals: promoting sustainable development; building democracy; promoting peace; providing humanitarian assistance; promoting US prosperity; and advancing its diplomacy.[107]

The variables in this study account for about 23 percent of the variation in US aid to sub-Saharan Africa in the post-Cold War period. Only two variables - GDP and Population - however, had statistically significant correlation with American ODA. The inverse correlation between the GDP of recipient states and ODA (t = -4.441) indicates the poverty amelioration focus of US aid. Lending further credence to this point is the positive correlation between the population of recipient states and the amount of aid they received from the US (t =2.160), suggesting that the US allocates aid disproportionately to poorer states with larger population. A 1995 study of US global aid also reported that US "aid flows are generally concentrated among recipients with lower levels of per capita calorie consumption, an indication of social welfare needs" (Hook, 1995:137).

Notably, because of the way the foreign aid data is collected and reported by the DAC, emergency relief aid is not distinguished from aid for development. This presents some difficulties in the calculation of the development assistance effort of a hegemonic power such as the US, which tends to respond to emergency situations in Africa, only to revert to an approach of benign neglect once such emergencies are reduced to manageable proportions. Pertinently too, many previous studies of US aid, for example,

---

[107] See Development Cooperation, 1996.

Knorr (1973), Vengroff (1982), Maizels and Nissanke (1984), and Kruger, Meernik and Poe (1998) either refute, or seriously question the attribution of humaniarian objectives to American aid.

An interesting finding of this study is that, contrary to suggestions by some scholars about the uses of American aid to promote democratization in sub-Saharan Africa, for example, Lancaster (1999:85-86) there was an absence of a statistically significant correlation in the multiple regression equation between the levels of democratization in aid recipient states and the amount of aid they received from the US. There was, however, a significant bivariate, inverse correlation between the two variables, suggesting that US aid tends to flow disproportionately to less democratic countries. While this finding is problematic for the democratic peace thesis, it is not surprising, given the orientation of American post-Cold War aid to sub-Saharan Africa, which tends to target countries torn by civil strife and ecological disasters. Such countries also tend to be less democratic and to allocate more of their meager resources to the procurement of military weapons.

In this regard, the behavior of US aid in some states in sub-Saharan Africa could be characterized as a fire brigade approach to development assistance. In the event of episodic crises, such as the famine in Ethiopia in the 1980s, the collapse of order in Somalia in the early 1990s, and the genocide in Rwanda in the mid 1990s, the US rushes in with massive amounts of aid; but no sooner do the crises abate than it retreats to its earlier posture of benign indifference. An understanding of the origins of US aid and a comparison of the pattern of its aid to sub-Saharan Africa against the backdrop of its global aid effort should lend useful insights into the nature and motivations behind its post-Cold War foreign aid policy.

Historically, US ODA has strongly concentrated on the Middle East and North Africa. These two regions have perennially received some 40-50 percent of US bilateral ODA. Comparatively, Latin America and sub-Saharan Africa receive about 20 and 15 percent respectively. The United States initiated the provision of aid to sub-Saharan Africa in the early 1960s to serve two objectives - one diplomatic and the other related to development. As many African states became independent in the 1960s, Africa was seen as an arena for the Cold War competition between the former Soviet Union and the Western alliance, and United States officials sought to use aid to encourage the new governments in Africa to support the United States and the West at the United Nations. With the memories of the loss of China to the communist bloc still fresh in the minds of US policy makers, the country was determined to keep Africa within the capitalist ideological fold. Initial concerns in Washington about Soviet incursions into Africa, however, subsided with the overthrow and murder of Patrice Lumunba of the Congo whose communist leaning, especially, his appeal to Moscow for assistance in the wake of the Belgian invasion of his country, had alarmed Washington.

The other impetus for the commencement of US aid to sub-Saharan Africa relates to the optimistic spirit of the American intellectual establishment in the early 1960s. Newly independent Africa, with its abundant natural resources and teething democracies represented the newest development challenge to the US aid community. It was widely believed by influential American scholars and policy makers such as W.W. Rostow that the political and social conditions that made the advancement of the West possible could be replicated in Africa. The intentions were good, but the reasoning was fatally flawed. In particular, such reasoning failed to take into account the effect of the international division of labor, where Africa's role did not transcend the supply of raw materials for the industries of the developed countries, on the perpetuation of under development in the continent.[108] Nonetheless, the progressive administration of President John F. Kennedy initiated the US Peace Corps, identified with the plight of African countries and supported the extension of development assistance to them. Some vocal critics such as General Lucius Clay objected to the expansion of US aid programs into Africa, but by and large, such objections did not significantly affect the emerging consensus on the need to "help poor countries help themselves". Then in the 1970s, the severe occurrence of drought in the Sahelian countries prompted Congress to increase aid to Senegal, Mali, Burkina Faso, Niger, Chad, and Mauritania. With this effort, US aid to the region witnessed a rapid expansion, and shifted decisively towards the goal of poverty reduction. By the early 1990s, the US had a pronounced aid presence in about forty-three African countries, and the United States Agency for international Development (USAID) had a field presence in over thirty countries (Lancaster, 1999).

The financial terms of United States aid are highly concessional, but because of the comparatively low level of its ODA/GNP ratio, the US is not in compliance with the DAC Terms Recommendation. During the decade of the 1980s, its multilateral contribution grew annually by about 25 percent. The US bilateral aid can be grouped into three major headings: The Economic Support Fund (ESF) was for a number of years the largest part of its bilateral aid program. It accounted for roughly 40-50 percent of its bilateral aid in the 1980s. ESF is a source of cash transfer or commodity import programs used to promote economic and political stability in countries where the US has special security interests. In addition to the ESF, the Development Assistance account has represented about 30 percent of bilateral assistance in recent years

---

[108] See Amin (1976) and Frank (1970) for an elaborate discussion of this point.

and is the basic mode of economic assistance to finance development projects. It is divided into seven functional accounts for Agriculture, Population, Child Survival, Education, Private Sector, Environment and Energy. Third, about 15 percent of US bilateral aid are channeled through the Food for Peace program (PL 480) under which food is used both to meet emergency needs and aid in development by alleviating the food problems in recipient states. Notably, some studies of the motivations for the United States' establishment of the PL 480 program during the Cold War, for examples Vengroff (1982) and Vengroff and Tsai (1982) observed that the preservation of the selfish interests of the United States was the primary motivation for the program in sub-Saharan Africa and the larger Third World community.

In 1990, US global net ODA disbursement increased by 42 percent in real terms over the 1989 figure to $11.4 billion, making her clearly the largest donor in absolute terms. Its aid to sub-Saharan Africa that year amounted to about $948 million, and its global ODA/GNP ratio also rose from 0.15 percent in 1989 to 0.19 percent. In 1991, this figure rose to about $11.5 billion, and again increased to $11.7 billion in 1992. By comparison, US aid to sub-Saharan Africa also rose from $922 million in 1991 to $1.11 billion in 1992. The US contribution to multilateral institutions increased by $2 billion to nearly $4 billion in 1992. Most of the increases concerned the World Bank group and regional development banks. That same year, although the US was with Japan at the head of DAC in terms of absolute aid volume, its ODA/GNP ratio of 0.20 percent was the second lowest among DAC countries, and well below the DAC average.

Essentially, it should be noted that the high volume of US aid to sub-Saharan Africa during the early post-Cold War years of 1990-1992 was the result of the campaign on behalf of Africa begun in 1987 by an informal coalition of the Congressional Black Caucus, InterAction (an NGO umbrella group) and some proactive intellectuals. This coalition championed the establishment of a separate Development Fund for Africa (DFA) within the US bilateral aid program. Advocates for the DFA requested the establishment of important safe guards which would at once guarantee the autonomy of the fund and free it from Congressional earmarks which tended to include not only specific provisions aimed at identifying the recipient countries, but also the specification of the uses to which aid money was to be allocated in the identified recipient countries. Congress successfully passed the DFA in 1988. Upon its passage, the DFA came to represent a shift in US approach towards Africa, from the discredited "constructive engagement" that President Ronald Reagan had adopted towards the dismantling of apartheid in South Africa. In 1991, Congress uncharacteristically appropriated $800 million to the DFA, against the $560 million requested by President George Bush's administration.

Such gesture was, however, short lived.

In 1993, net United States ODA declined sharply from $11.7 billion to $9.7 billion – a fall of 19 percent in real terms. Its net bilateral ODA fell by $0.9 billion (13 percent in real terms) while its multilateral ODA fell by $1.1billion (31 percent in real terms). The ODA/GNP ratio for the US also fell from 0.20 percent to 0.16 percent. Its aid to sub-Saharan Africa, however, increased to $1.33 billion. Also, in contrast to its total ODA decline in 1993, US aid to Part II CEECs/NIS rose sharply from $682 million in 1992 to $1.65 billion in 1993, representing 0.03 percent of its GNP.

In 1994, US net ODA disbursements declined by 4.0 percent to $9.93 billion. Its bilateral disbursements also declined by 3 percent to $7.28 billion, and multilateral disbursements by 8 percent to $2.64 billion. In contrast to the broad decline in its global aid effort, US aid to sub-Saharan Africa increased to $1.34 billion. This increase was primarily attributable to its aid to Somalia, Rwanda and Ethiopia. The United States ODA/GNP ratio fell from 0.16 percent in 1993 to 0.15 percent that year. It disbursed $2.42 billion in official aid to countries on Part II of the DAC List, up strongly from the $1.65 billion it disbursed in 1993. 1994 was, however, the last year when US aid to sub-Saharan Africa recorded an increase. Between that year and 1997, US aid to the declined steadily, such that by 1997, its aid to the sub-continent was about half of the 1994 figure.

The United States, who for decades was the world's largest aid-donor has now fallen behind Japan, France and Germany. In particular, its 1996 aid to sub-Saharan Africa, at $518 million was the lowest level in the period covered by this study. Similarly, the US global foreign aid budget at an ODA/GNP ratio of 0.10 percent in 1995, was the lowest among DAC members, and in fact the lowest level in the country's foreign aid history since record keeping began in 1950. Despite these cuts, there are still strong pressures, especially in the US Congress for additional reductions in US aid efforts. A 1996 DAC peer review report on the US aid efforts observed that, it is difficult to know what level of ODA the US will produce because the ODA concept is not taken into account in the preparation of the US budget.

Three main factors account for the reductions in the levels of US aid to sub-Saharan Africa in recent years. The first reason relates to the 1994 election of the first Republican controlled Congress in about four decades. This event altered the American political landscape on issues from welfare policies, through issues of immigration and gays in the military, to foreign policy. With respect to US foreign aid policy toward sub-Saharan Africa, the 1994 election of Newt Gingerich as the Speaker of the House of Representatives was analogous to the emergence of a pharaoh who neither knew nor cared about Joseph. In collaboration with the newly elected, ultra-conservative Republican law makers, often with poor knowledge of foreign policy in general, several chair persons of Congressional sub-committees dealing with foreign aid wondered why with the end of the Cold War the US should continue to provide aid to sub-Saharan Africa, a region many realists consider to be of no intrinsic value to American interests. They then proceeded to cut US aid to the region.

The second factor that influenced the reduction of US aid to sub-Saharan Africa, was the size of the US budget deficit. By the middle of the 1990s, the US budget deficit had grown to record proportions. The interest on the country's public debt alone stood at $343 billion in FY 1996.[109] There was popular consensus among Democrats and Republicans on the need to either take steps to begin reducing the US deficit, or at least halt its growth. But the major items on the budget were related to defense expenditures, the reduction of which would ruffle the feathers of powerful constituencies in the country. Moreover, many policy makers believed that, although the Cold War had just ended, the emerging structure of international politics was still too foggy for the country to begin massive retrenchment in the defense sector. Thus, intent on providing consolation for many of its citizens, some American politicians, with a penchant for playing to the gallery, seized upon foreign aid as a scapegoat.[110]

The third reason that accounts for the decline in US aid to sub-Saharan Africa bears close relation to the second factor discussed above, and is attributable to what appears to be the erosion of the support for aid by the American public. This erosion of the support for aid by the American public is itself the result of (1) damaging misconceptions in the United States about the percentage of the country's budget allocated to foreign aid; and (2) misperceptions about the record of aid effectiveness in regions like sub-Saharan Africa. Many Americans believe that the foreign aid budget is the largest item in the US Federal budget, and that it takes up some 20 percent of total government spending. In reality, however, US global economic and humanitarian assistance has never exceeded 0.35 percent of its budget (Development Cooperation Report, 1998). Moreover, when one considers that

---

[109] See http://home.earth.net/'arison/debt.html for periodic updates on the US national debt.
[110] See, for example, a press briefing by Senator Mitch McConnell on December 13, 1994: *US Information Agency Wireless File,* December 14, 1994.

Table 8.1 Dimensions of US ODA (1991-1997)

Year

Dimension	1991	1992	1993	1994	1995	1996	1997
Total ODA to All LDCs ($millions)	9396	7875	7316	7284	5613	6917	4940
ODA to SSA as % of ODA to All LDCs	10	14	18	18	16	7	13
ODA to SSA as % of GNP	0.02	0.02	0.02	0.02	0.02	0.01	0.007
% of Concentration on Top Five Recipients	39	53	60	60	42	41	41

Source: Geographic Distribution of Financial Flows to Aid Recipients, 1960-19997. (CD-ROM). Paris, OECD (1998).

much of this small proportion of the national budget expended on foreign aid goes to Israel and Egypt, the relative small share of US aid allocated to sub-Saharan Africa comes into sharper relief. Table 8.1, which summarizes essential dimensions of US aid to the region in the post-Cold War period, illustrates this point.

As evident from the above table, between 1991 and 1996, US aid to sub-Saharan Africa as a percentage of US GDP averaged 0.02 percent, but dropped to 0.007 percent in 1997. This steep decline in an already low foreign aid figure stemmed from the impressive growth of the US economy at a time when the country's aid budget suffered severe cut backs. Curiously, when informed about the small size of the US budget that is allocated to foreign aid, about two-thirds of Americans responding to an opinion poll disagreed with cutting the aid budget (Kull, 1995).

Furthermore, it is widely believed in the United States that because of the persistence of challenges to development in sub-Saharan Africa, aid to the region has failed. Until recently, the proliferation of repressive regimes in the sub continent, coupled with anecdotal stories about massive misappropriation and embezzlement of aid funds by government officials contributed to the perception that US aid to Africa is analogous to pouring money down a rat hole. This is unfortunate because, by and large, US aid disbursements to the region that are specifically targeted at development issues have produced impressive results. One such area where US aid has produced laudable and cost effective results relates to the Demographic and Health surveys funded by USAID.

The Kenya fertility studies that were part of this program revealed in the late 1970s that Kenya had the highest fertility rates in the world, with a population annual growth rate of about 4 percent. When these results were presented to the Kenyan government, its factual basis convinced the government about the severity of the population crisis in Kenya. The government was then able to present the results of the studies to its political opponents and muster the political commitment to initiate family planning programs in the country (Dumm, 1992).

Table 8.2 Comparison of Favorite Recipients of US ODA to Sub-Saharan Africa (Cold War Years v Post-Cold War Period)

		Cold War Years			
1970-71	% of ODA[111]	1980-81	% of ODA	1985-86	% of ODA
None		None		Sudan	2.4

	Post-Cold War Period	
Year	Recipients	% of ODA
1991	None	
1992	Somalia	4.0
1993	Somalia	3.7
1994	Somalia	4.8
	Rwanda	2.7
1995	None	
1996	None	
1997	None	

Source: Development Cooperation Report. Paris, OECD. (Various Years).

[111] This is calculated as the percentage of the donor's total ODA to all developing countries (LDCs).

A comparison of the composition of countries in sub-Saharan Africa receiving at least 2 percent of US aid during the Cold War era with that of the post-Cold War period sheds additional light on the nature of US aid to the region.

As Table 8.2 shows, whereas Sudan was the only country to receive more than 2 percent of US aid for development during the 1985-86 period, in the post Cold War era, three states - Somalia, Ethiopia and Rwanda have been favorite recipients of American aid. Other than receiving the largest volume of US aid in 1990, Sudan, since 1992 has fallen out of the circle of US favorite states in the region. Somalia and Ethiopia were, however, recipients of the largest volume of US aid to the sub-continent in 1993 and 1994 (see Figure 8.1) for the amount of aid allocated to these countries.

Figure 8.1 Scattergram Showing the Favorite Recipients of USA's Bilateral ODA (1990-1997)

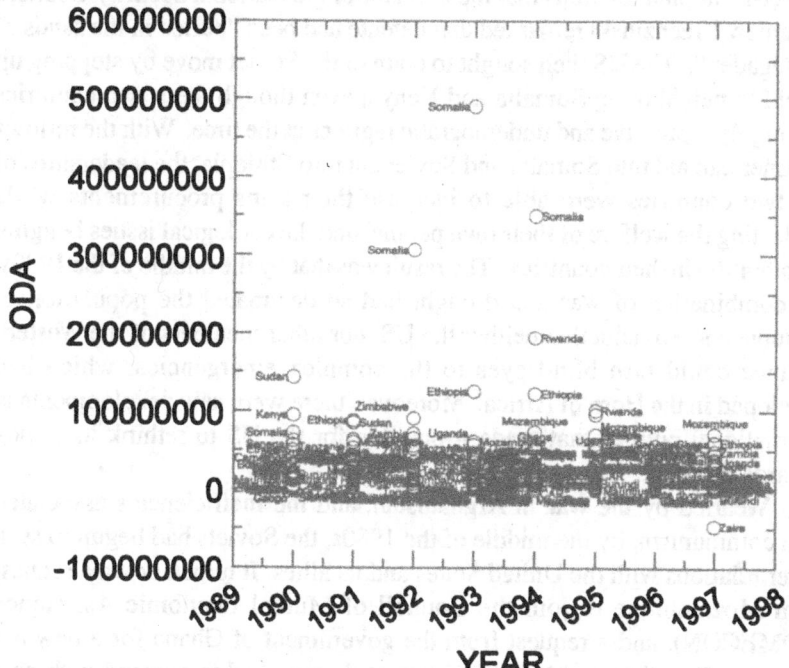

Source: Geographic Distribution of Financial Flows to Aid Recipients, 1960-1997. (CD-ROM). Paris, OECD (1998).

United States aid to Ethiopia and Somalia tells an interesting tale about how foreign aid policies conceived by Cold War imperatives gave birth to support for authoritarian regimes, which nurtured the occurrence of complex emergencies that then assisted in the metamorphosis of Cold War rationality into humanitarian concerns.

In 1974, a group of young military officers led by Megistu Haile Mariam successfully toppled the regime of Emperor Haile Selassie of Ethiopia. In a bid to win popularity both at home and in the Third World community, Megistu assumed a highly critical stance of the United States in particular and the West in general. When neighboring Somalia invaded Ethiopia, however, he did not hesitate to appeal for military aid from Washington. When the US denied his request, he quickly turned to Moscow for help. The Soviets who had long sought a foothold in the Horn of Africa, in part because of Ethiopia's proximity to the Arabian oil fields, and its geo-strategic location along the world's busiest shipping lanes seized the opportunity and readily obliged Megistu's request. This development was occurring at a time when the Nixon-Kissinger's initiatives of 1972 and 1973 had signaled a rapprochement with the Soviet Union. The United States was so offended by the developments in Soviet-Ethiopian relations that the Director of the National Security Council, Zbigniew Brzenzinski remarked that détente had been "buried in the sands of the Ogaden". The US then sought to counter the Soviet move by stepping up its aid to neighboring Somalia and Kenya, even though these two countries had highly repressive and undemocratic regimes at the time. With the inflows of American aid into Somalia and Soviet aid into Ethiopia, the leaderships of the two countries were able to increase their arms procurements while neglecting the welfare of their own people, and the ecological issues begging for attention in their countries. The result was that by the middle of the 1980s, the combination of war and drought had so decimated the population of Ethiopia and Somalia that neither the US, nor other members of the Western alliance could turn blind eyes to the complex emergencies, which had developed in the Horn of Africa. Moreover, there were new developments in international politics that made it possible for the US to rethink its policy towards Ethiopia.

Wearied by the war in Afghanistan, and the inefficiencies associated with communism, by the middle of the 1980s, the Soviets had begun to seek better relations with the United States and its allies. It turned down a request from Mozambique to join the Council of Mutual Economic Assistance (COMECON), and a request from the government of Ghana for a new aid program. Equally too, Megistu's Marxist rhetoric had to contend with new realities. In addition to diminishing financial support from Moscow, the separatist demands by the people of Eritrea for statehood was degenerating into a civil war at a time when famine was increasingly decimating the Ethiopian population. The United States then responded with massive disbursement of aid to Ethiopia and Somalia and persuaded its allies to do the same.

As for the future prospects of American aid, although the decline in its aid volume has raised serious concerns about the broad collapse of the foreign aid regime, reforms in (USAID) have resulted in a redefined mission statement and a reengineered agency. In recent years, USAID has been one of the lead agencies in a government wide program to "reinvent government". The Agency was one of the nearly 200 "Reinvention Labs" in the National Performance Reviews (NPR) of the United States, a major management reform initiative begun by then President Bill Clinton in 1993 and placed under the direction of his Vice President, Albert Gore. The application of the principles of the National performance Review has resulted in extensive reorganization at USAID, including the establishment of the Bureau for Global Programs, Field Support and Research with the aim of making the agency more results oriented. In September 1997, USAID issued a Strategic Plan setting out a mission statement for the Agency and reiterating the six objectives of US aid. Compared to other members of the DAC, by 1998 US aid effort recovered some lost grounds. In that year, the US was the second largest donor in the DAC (next to Japan), and its net global ODA rose by 26.5 percent in real terms to reach $8.8 billion. With respect to its ODA/GNP ratio, however, the US at 0.10 percent posted the lowest ratio among the DAC (DAC Journal: Development Cooperation, 1999 Report). In addition, although Israel and Egypt maintained their favorite positions among the top ten recipients of US global aid effort, South Africa also featured on this list, albeit as the last country.

Table 8.3 Top Ten Recipients of US Global ODA (1998)

Rank	Country	(US$m)
1	Israel	1229
2	Egypt	749
3	Russia	366
4	Bosnia and Herzegovina	201
5	Peru	172
6	India	148
7	Jordan	136
8	Bolivia	128
9	Ukraine	106
10	South Africa	94

Source: The DAC Journal. Development Cooperation, 1999 Report. Vol.1, No.1. (2000):103.

Although Egypt and South Africa are two African countries attracting high volumes of US aid, both countries are the exception rather than the norm. Both countries are excluded from this study for reasons discussed in chapter three. In any case, US aid to Egypt in particular is best understood in the light of US interests in the Middle East. A more accurate picture of the positions of the majority of sub-Saharan African states in the global distribution of US aid is depicted by Figures 8.2 and 8.3.

156 *Contending Theories on Development Aid*

USA's Gross Bilateral ODA Allocation (1998)

Figure 8.2 By Income Group (US$m)

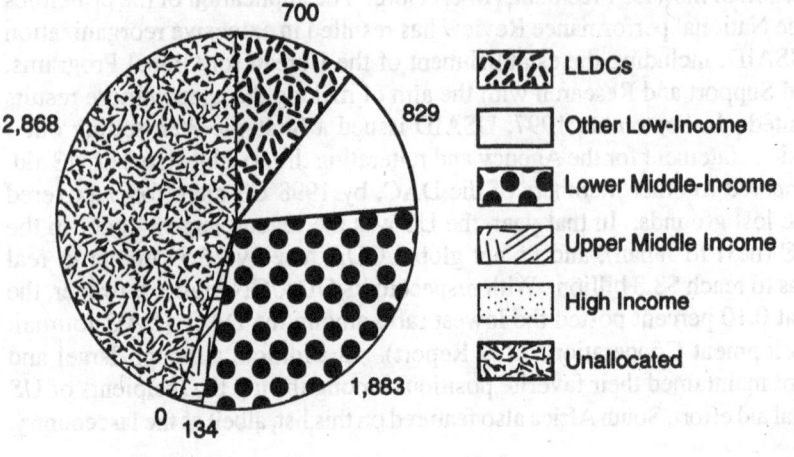

Figure 8.3 By Region (US$ m)

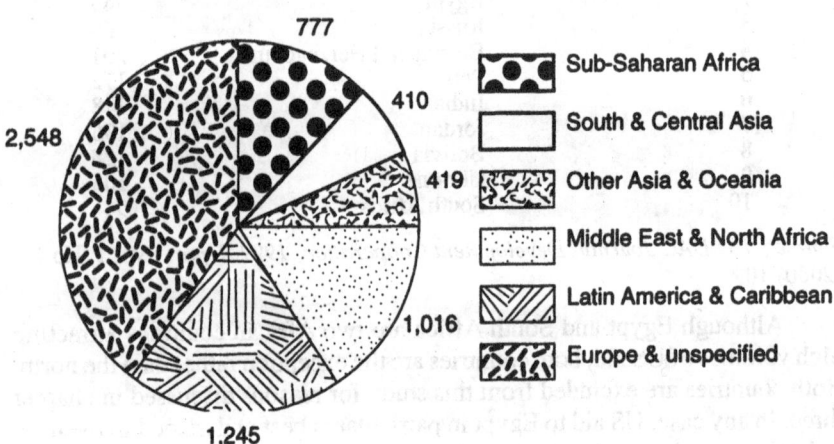

Source: The DAC Journal. Vol. 1, No. 1 (2000): 103

As Figure 8.2 shows, in 1998, US aid to LLDCs - the income group under which most sub-Saharan African states are classified - amounted to $700 million, while US aid to the high-income countries amounted to $2.8 billion. An even clearer picture of the distribution of US global bilateral aid is captured by Figure 8.3 showing the distribution of US aid by region. In 1998, sub-Saharan Africa received a total of $777 million dollars from the United States. This was a significant improvement from the 1997 figure, is probably attributable to the efforts by then President Bill Clinton to reorient the dynamics of US-Africa relations.

In 1996, in a report submitted by his administration to the Congress, then President Bill Clinton initiated an innovative policy designed to reorient US policy toward Africa in the direction of aggressively pursuing new markets in the region.[112]

President Bill Clinton's effort culminated in the passage of the African Growth and Opportunity Act (HR1432/S778) by Congress in 2000. This law promises to engage the US in a more meaningful partnership with the continent. Some of the important aspects of the Act include: (1) the provision of African nations with the necessary tools to sustain long term economic growth and to compete effectively in global markets, (2) the extension of bilateral privileges to eligible African nations through the Generalized Systems of Preferences Program (GSP), (3) the establishment of a non-quota policy for African imports, and (4) the Act also urges aggressive debt relief to African nations instituting economic and political reforms.[113] Indeed, the passage of HR1432 marked an important milestone in US relations to the African continent.

Conclusion

The symbolic highlight of the Clinton administration's policy toward Africa came in 1998 when then President Bill Clinton embarked upon a twelve-day diplomatic tour of the continent. For many Africanists, this was a welcome departure from the benign neglect of Africa by previous US administrations, and a reflection of the new directions in US-Africa relations. With the exception of President Jimmy Carter who paid a four-day visit to Nigeria under the military regime of General Olusegun Obasanjo (March 29-April 2, 1977), and the one-day visit to Somalia by President George Bush (Sr.) in 1993 while in transit to the Middle East, no other seating US president had

---

[112] See "A Comprehensive Trade and Development Policy for the Countries of Africa: A Report submitted by the President of the United States to Congress" US Department of Commerce, February 1996.

[113] See www.USAfrica.org for details about HR1432 and other developments in US-Africa relations.

ever visited Africa. To other skeptical observers of US-Africa relations, however, that Bill Clinton's visit came in the wake of the Monica Lewinsky scandal was more a reflection of the symbolic, Machiavellian attempt by a lame duck president to divert attention from his domestic woes than a meaningful shift in US-Africa relations. Whatever kernel of truth might be found in the latter assertion, there is no denying the fact that more than any other presidential administration, the Clinton presidency spotlighted Africa in positive ways, and it sought to forge a new development partnership with the continent.

The controversial victory of President George Bush (Jr.) in the 2000 US presidential elections was initially greeted with cautious pessimism in the African development community. Recall that during the 2000 presidential election campaign, candidate George Bush, echoing the sentiments of many scholars of the realist persuasion had asserted that Africa did not fit into the strategic interest of the United States. But in the aftermath of the 2000 election debacle, President-elect George Bush, in the announcement of his first cabinet appointment selected General Colin Powell, an African-American as the next US Secretary of State. This bold move left many Africanists wondering if Washington's sun will shine on Africa in the new administration.[114] Soon after his appointment, Secretary Powell met with President Paul Kaga of Rwanda and President Joseph Kabila of the Democratic Republic of Congo, the two leading antagonists in the Congo conflict. Secretary Powell's initiatives have been interpreted as a welcome signal that the new Bush administration intends to play an active role in the resolution of some of the many challenges confronting African states.[115]

In addition to Secretary Powell's initiatives on Africa, there have been other promising signs that the Bush administration might not undo the efforts by its predecessor to foster a more active US interest in Africa. In February, 2001, US trade representatives intimated that the new Bush administration would not reverse a critical US policies begun by the Clinton administration that could affect millions of people suffering from HIV infections in Africa. The Clinton administration had begun a policy of not seeking sanctions against poor nations who attempt to force down the prohibitive price of potential Aids drugs by legalizing the importation or manufacture of generic versions.[116]

The emerging optimism about future US-Africa relations under the Bush administration is, however, muted by recent, crucial developments that bear

---

[114] See Ian Fisher, "Africans Ask if Washington's Sun will shine on Them", New York Times, February 8, 2001.

[115] See "General Powell Engages Africa", New York Times Editorial, February 2, 2001.

[116] See "Bush Keeps Clinton Policy on Poor Land's Need for Aids Drugs", New York Times, February 22, 2001.

directly on US foreign aid policy. First, in the wake of the 2000 US national election results that has given control of the three branches of the US government to conservatives, Republican Senator Jesse Helms of North Carolina, the most powerful critic of foreign aid in Congress, has stated that he would support legislation to abolish USAID, and shift the responsibility for overseeing US foreign aid program to private charity groups.[117]

The second development that does not augur well for Africa in the new Bush administration relates to the US budgetary appropriation for foreign aid. The 2001 US budget allocated $7.7 billion to USAID. This is a decrease of over $100million from the current funding for the agency, and it will further reduce the already low US ODA/GNP ratio.[118] Such substantial retrenchment of US aid effort in the light of what appears to be signs of a recommitment on the part of the Bush administration toward Africa revives pessimism about the prospects of mitigating the marginalization of Africa in the international system under the leadership of the United States.

---

[117] See Eric Schmitt, "Helms Urges Foreign Aid be Handled by Charities", New York Times, January 12, 2001.

[118] See Mark Lacey, "Who Gets What Slice of the President's First Federal Budget Pie", New York Times, April 10, 2001.

9 Rethinking Aid to Sub-Saharan Africa in the New Millennium: Enduring Threats and Opportunities for a New Partnership

The preceding discussion of the cases of France, Japan, Norway, and the United States makes a clean breast of the divergence in the motivations that drive their foreign aid policies toward sub-Saharan Africa. Notwithstanding this point, however, there are some interesting commonalties in their pattern of aid giving. This study found that, with the exception of France, there was a statistically significant inverse correlation between the ODA allocated by these donors and the GDP of the recipient states, suggesting that poorer states tended to receive more aid even from an, allegedly, self interested donor like the United States. Buttressing this point about the poverty alleviation focus of these three donors is the study's corollary finding of a positive correlation between ODA and the size of the population of the recipient states. Both findings bolster the contention by liberal scholars about the humanitarian motivations behind foreign aid. This and other important findings of this study speak, not only to the emergence of a foreign aid regime, but the rise of one that appears to have internalized the important principles which realists do not care to admit. Despite its shortcomings, the many successes of the foreign aid regime have become so commonplace that one might be forgiven for taking them for granted. Recall that in 1972, when members of the DAC, mutually agreed on the need to offer some portion of their development assistance to developing countries without expectation of repayment, the portion of ODA, which they pledged as grant was 25 percent. It is remarkable that in spite of the absence of sanctions attached to this target, members of the DAC not only complied with the goal, but most have exceeded it by wide margins. By the same token, some donors, especially the Nordic countries, have often reported grant elements of 100 percent. The average rate for the DAC in 1996/97 was 92 percent (Development Cooperation Report, 1998). This is one unprecedented achievement in the history of international finance, which fails to register on the realist/neorealist's radar screen programmed to pick up waves of war.

The premise of this study has been the presumption that the transfer of financial resources in the form of foreign aid by advanced-industrial countries (AICs) to sub-Saharan Africa represents a rational decision on the part of the former to incur the opportunity cost that prevents such resources from being allocated to alternative uses. I have sought to argue that a scrutiny of such spending behavior provides valuable insights into the motivation for different donors, and that it allows one to evaluate the positions of rival theories of international relations about these motivations. Just as the neorealist fixation with the influence, which anarchy exerts on state behavior tends to confine considerations of morality to intra-state dynamics, so do their tendency to over-emphasize the role that the asymmetrical distribution of capabilities among states exert on the behavior of states lead them to discount the effect that the principles of humane internationalism have on a small state's conception of its national role in the international system. Evidence from this study challenges the veracity of the neorealist/realist position on these issues. It is remarkable that in spite of the constraints of anarchy, the foreign aid regime has flourished; and to a large extent, the principles of humane internationalism have been important features of the foreign aid programs of most donors. Measured by the conventional indices of power, Denmark, Norway and Sweden rank low among the ten donors in this study (See the Table of Comparative Indicators of Capabilities for All Donors in Appendix II). Yet, measured by the ODA/GNP ratio, these countries have borne relatively larger portions of the burden of providing aid to a poor region such as sub-Saharan Africa.

The aim of the above point is not to deny that the foreign economic policies of the donors in this study have been "affected by both the international economic structure and their positions in it" (Lake, 1983). The point rather is that on an important subject such as international finance, some states do not behave in ways that the propositions of realism would lead one to believe. On this score, the observation tendered by Kegley (1993:138), that "[T]here is less to realism than meets the eye" is persuasively accurate.[119]

---

[119] Even more undermining of the realist thesis on capabilities is the observation that by accepting deep cuts in their strategic arsenals, Russia and the United States continue to violate realism's cardinal commandment that states should "fight rather than fail to increase capabilities" (Kaplan:1957:23).

Still, the symmetry between the finding of this study and the liberal thesis on foreign aid is not without difficulties. Realists may "have been consistently surprised over the past generation as one seemingly immutable tyranny after another has self destructed" (Fukuyama, 1992:24), but the increasing cooperation between relatively more democratic states and aid donors, which the democratic peace thesis leads one to expect has not been evident in the pattern of aid flows from most donors to sub-Saharan Africa in the period covered by this study. Emerging trends in the foreign aid arena, and in the international system more broadly, mute optimism about the triumph of liberal ideas. Evidence supporting the increasing marginalization of sub-Saharan Africa in the international system multiplies in small and large ways. Funding for international research into cures for tropical diseases, such as "sleeping sickness" and malaria, by the major pharmaceutical companies have dwindled in outrageous proportions even as funding for cosmetic ailments in the developed world have increased. The irony is that we appear closer to finding cures for the separation anxiety experienced by some pet animals when their owners go on extended vacations than we are to finding effective treatments for many tropical diseases.

Furthermore, the timing and the degree of cut backs implemented by most donors on their aid budgets to sub-Saharan Africa suggest justifications other than sheer coincidence. In particular, despite the impressive expansion of the US economy since the late 1990s, the US contributions to global ODA, as well as its aid to sub-Saharan Africa have fallen to unprecedented low levels. In addition, Canada, the hitherto, champion of humane internationalism has reordered its aid priorities and began diverting substantial portions of its aid money away from Africa and into other regions. Collectively, these observations provide, if not support for the neorealist position on the salience of relative gains concerns among competitive state actors, then at least a reminder that, contrary to the affirmation by Holsti (1991:84) neorealism is not yet the anachronism. In the remaining portions of this chapter, I turn to a consideration of the overarching paradox revealed by this study, and weigh in on the effectiveness of aid debate.

Parallax Snaps: Marginalization in the Age of Globalization

At the dawn of the 21st century, the provision of development assistance to sub-Saharan Africa presents an interesting paradox. On the one hand, the end of the Cold War has liberated thinking about issues of development from the constraints of competing ideologies and world views, and removed most of the non-developmental objectives that once informed aid allocations to the sub continent, albeit the "peace dividend" that many observers anticipated would ensue are yet to materialize. On the other hand, against a backdrop of globalization and the triumph of liberal ideas, we are witnessing the increasing marginalization on sub-Saharan Africa. Sub-Saharan Africa has largely been excluded from the gains of globalization. While the West has made many successful trips to other planets and back, the African is still struggling to make it to the next village. It is estimated that in the decade of the 1990s, sub-Saharan Africa accounted for only about 1 percent of total world trade (Gilpin, 2000:21). Worse still, in the West, the political support for foreign aid is increasingly being eroded by misperceptions about the effectiveness of aid. Aid is widely believed to have failed despite impressive records achieved by many states in the region in the expansion of social services in education and health care.[120] This has prompted some scholars and aid administrators to tender proposals whose implications would eliminate, or further reduce the volume of aid to the region.[121]

Given the above scenario, what directions ought to be taken in the allocation of aid to the region in the years ahead? And for that matter, how accurate is the popular perception that because many states in the region have failed to record appreciable levels of economic growth despite receiving huge volumes of aid, then aid does not work? Or, is it that the challenges to development in sub-Saharan Africa are so "unique" that approaches to development, which have proven successful in other regions of the world are destined to fail? These are some of the nagging questions to which this chapter hopes to provide some insights.

To facilitate the coherent discussion of these issues, I have divided the remaining portion of this discussion into three sections. In section one, I address the issues relating to the volume of aid to sub-Saharan Africa, the question of whether aid to the region has indeed been ineffective, and if so why. In section two, I examine some of the enduring threats to the continuation of development assistance to the region in the years ahead, and offer some suggestions for overcoming these threats. Then in a final section, I provide a discussion of how well meaning donors might engage the states in

---

[120] Acknowledging the success of development efforts in this area as "real and even spectacular", in the early 1990s, scholars such as Lancaster (1992:66) expressed fears that the structural adjustment programs, which many countries have embarked upon since the 1980s could erode such achievements.

[121] See the recommendations for better aid effectiveness in Graham and O'Hanlon (1997), and Hancock (1991). Hancock (1991:190), went as far as calling for the elimination of aid on the grounds that "most poor people in most poor countries most of the time never receive or even make contact with aid in any tangible shape or form: whether it is present or absent, increased or decreased, are thus issues that are simply irrelevant to the ways in which they conduct their daily lives". This assertion is a gross distortion of the effect of aid in many countries.

the sub-continent in an effective and mutually beneficial partnership.

So Much Aid, but So Little Development?

In terms of volume, the almost forty years history of aid allocation to sub-Saharan Africa has been a checkered one where periods of high volumes to countries like Cote d'Ivoire have been succeeded by periods of low volumes to others like Nigeria, while a few others, such as Tanzania and Mozambique, have received steady and high volumes of aid flows in recent times. With respect to the continent as a whole, during the 1960-64 period, a few countries North of the Sahara received fifteen percent more aid than all of the other countries combined. Beginning in 1965, however, the balance in aid receipt shifted decisively in favor of the sub-Saharan countries. Cumulatively speaking, during the period 1960-1997, countries south of the Sahara received about $170 billion in official development assistance. This figure accounts for about 30 percent of the total aid to all developing regions of the world, and more than 70 percent of total aid to the African continent from all the members of the Development Assistance Committee (DAC) combined (see Table 9.1).

Rethinking Aid to Sub-Saharan Africa in the New Millennium 165

Table 9.1 Geographic Distribution of Financial Flows (Total ODA net) from DAC Donors by Region (1960-1997)

Year	1960	1961	1962	1963	1964
Recipient					
Total, Africa	1,006.0	1,255.8	1,303.2	1,205.5	1,446.6
Total, North of Sahara	708.5	788.2	756.0	679.2	638.8
Total, South of Sahara	297.6	466.6	545.2	521.2	794.5
Total, Americas	278.2	816.7	787.4	810.3	681.2
Total, N. & C. America	89.9	188.7	140.8	139.1	101.5
Total, South America	146.9	578.1	573.1	573.0	422.1
Total, Asia	2,144.8	2,089.5	2,185.5	2,530.6	2,628.7
Total, Middle East	253.9	349.4	257.2	227.3	192.1
Total, South & Central Asia	1,059.2	948.0	1,109.7	1,489.0	1,698.7
Total, Far East	831.7	792.1	806.6	797.3	721.1
Total, Oceania	23.2	25.9	40.7	43.3	42.3

Year	1965	1966	1967	1968	1969
Recipient					
Total, Africa	1,331.6	1,258.9	1,167.1	1,170.0	1,180.4
Total, North of Sahara	455.0	342.9	289.0	303.4	300.3
Total, South of Sahara	852.8	873.3	855.4	844.8	854.5
Total, Americas	837.4	888.0	747.7	813.9	696.0
Total, N. & C. America	279.3	213.1	221.3	202.9	194.3
Total, South America	452.6	639.5	496.8	582.6	478.3
Total, Asia	2,770.7	2,780.3	3,155.8	2,845.1	2,715.7
Total, Middle East	232.7	208.8	158.5	110.2	101.7
Total, South & Central Asia	1,637.5	1,497.8	1,702.9	1,438.2	1,190.3
Total, Far East	890.6	1,053.7	1,277.1	1,279.6	1,405.1
Total, Oceania	148.7	149.3	161.9	194.0	220.7

Year	1970	1971	1972	1973	1974
Recipient					
Total, Africa	1,186.1	1,332.9	1,364.9	1,607.4	1,963.5
Total, North of Sahara	314.8	328.6	290.3	309.6	438.8
Total, South of Sahara	847.2	972.8	1,045.3	1,255.0	1,478.5
Total, Americas	708.7	629.5	627.3	655.5	711.3
Total, N. & C. America	221.5	207.6	206.5	202.3	233.3
Total, South America	455.3	383.7	384.7	390.7	410.7
Total, Asia	2,815.2	3,219.2	3,162.7	3,277.0	3,761.8
Total, Middle East	120.3	147.5	213.5	290.2	235.9
Total, South & Central Asia	1,249.1	1,412.9	1,128.6	1,175.9	1,392.1
Total, Far East	1,427.1	1,626.7	1,791.9	1,787.2	2,108.9
Total, Oceania	257.7	275.4	372.8	432.7	502.3

166 Contending Theories on Development Aid

Table 9.1 Geographic Distribution of Financial Flows (Total ODA net) from DAC Donors by Region (1960-1997)

Year	1975	1976	1977	1978	1979
Recipient					
Total, Africa	2,588.9	2,832.1	3,257.0	4,343.4	5,242.1
Total, North of Sahara	647.2	867.4	1,064.1	1,424.3	1,446.3
Total, South of Sahara	1,901.6	1,922.8	2,121.8	2,823.6	3,681.4
Total, Americas	843.6	837.4	779.9	968.6	1,197.8
Total, N. & C. America	292.3	363.8	348.8	455.5	583.5
Total, South America	485.5	420.3	382.0	459.8	554.2
Total, Asia	4,278.5	3,698.4	3,683.5	4,810.6	5,731.1
Total, Middle East	651.8	837.3	1,133.7	1,283.9	1,499.3
Total, South & Central Asia	2,109.1	1,633.5	1,428.7	2,166.5	2,587.6
Total, Far East	1,488.2	1,187.2	1,105.7	1,134.6	1,586.8
Total, Oceania	597.0	551.4	593.3	733.8	844.1

Year	1980	1981	1982	1983	1984
Recipient					
Total, Africa	6,241.7	6,227.4	6,595.9	6,424.0	7,127.6
Total, North of Sahara	1,663.0	1,624.3	1,759.9	1,715.4	2,156.0
Total, South of Sahara	4,436.4	4,474.3	4,703.5	4,576.3	4,827.8
Total, Americas	1,322.5	1,627.7	1,881.4	2,072.4	2,192.2
Total, N. & C. America	711.6	797.8	1,077.4	1,306.5	1,407.7
Total, South America	550.7	756.2	725.9	658.8	708.6
Total, Asia	5,567.5	5,921.3	5,641.9	6,191.7	5,979.7
Total, Middle East	1,217.8	1,151.0	1,216.7	1,747.2	1,537.1
Total, South & Central Asia	2,447.2	2,599.6	2,324.9	2,271.2	2,184.2
Total, Far East	1,841.3	2,131.6	2,046.9	2,092.8	2,205.2
Total, Oceania	948.2	900.6	937.8	923.9	912.4

Year	1985	1986	1987	1988	1989
Recipient					
Total, Africa	8,063.4	9,328.4	10,686.8	11,984.2	12,139.1
Total, North of Sahara	2,278.9	2,132.9	2,289.9	2,212.1	2,113.7
Total, South of Sahara	5,597.2	7,033.4	8,196.0	9,569.4	9,679.2
Total, Americas	2,607.8	2,862.3	3,420.3	3,340.7	3,788.8
Total, N. & C. America	1,756.6	1,860.3	2,049.2	1,975.7	2,088.7
Total, South America	759.3	893.0	1,198.5	1,195.0	1,463.5
Total, Asia	6,889.2	8,617.1	8,901.1	10,365.1	10,648.6
Total, Middle East	2,302.0	2,372.9	2,043.1	1,913.9	1,808.0
Total, South & Central Asia	2,300.5	3,278.3	3,137.6	3,991.2	3,676.6
Total, Far East	2,229.4	2,885.1	3,658.1	4,346.0	5,089.2
Total, Oceania	851.0	1,098.7	1,251.0	1,291.3	1,273.6

Table 9.1 Geographic Distribution of Financial Flows (Total ODA net) from DAC Donors by Region (1960-1997)

Year	1990	1991	1992	1993	1994
Recipient					
Total, Africa	15,958.5	16,686.5	16,335.8	13,556.9	14,553.2
Total, North of Sahara	4,225.3	5,347.3	4,410.5	2,643.1	3,084.3
Total, South of Sahara	11,454.9	10,950.0	11,539.8	10,647.4	10,870.3
Total, Americas	4,188.4	4,856.7	4,293.7	4,263.9	4,550.0
Total, N. & C. America	2,361.4	2,529.9	2,386.7	1,937.6	2,486.3
Total, South America	1,588.5	2,119.4	1,715.7	2,104.9	1,727.7
Total, Asia	11,402.7	13,349.3	13,602.8	12,176.0	13,910.3
Total, Middle East	2,211.6	3,783.4	2,871.8	2,086.8	3,061.8
Total, South & Central Asia	3,369.3	4,183.6	3,356.5	3,110.4	4,118.9
Total, Far East	5,719.3	5,242.6	7,235.1	6,831.6	6,623.3
Total, Oceania	1,214.7	1,212.9	1,315.1	1,444.6	1,666.0

Year	1995	1996	1997
Recipient			
Total, Africa	13,231.5	12,828.1	11,378.1
Total, North of Sahara	2,405.8	2,643.3	1,987.9
Total, South of Sahara	10,391.8	9,688.5	8,598.8
Total, Americas	4,798.7	5,757.4	3,920.9
Total, N. & C. America	2,532.9	2,134.4	1,540.3
Total, South America	2,037.8	2,007.1	1,897.1
Total, Asia	12,481.7	11,975.1	8,119.9
Total, Middle East	1,715.3	3,597.5	1,355.3
Total, South & Central Asia	3,551.6	3,297.2	2,669.5
Total, Far East	6,917.0	4,782.5	3,981.7
Total, Oceania	1,710.9	1,698.3	1,433.0

Source: Geographic Distribution of Financial Flows to Aid Recipients, 1960-1997. (CD-ROM). Paris, OECD (1998).

As Table 9.1 makes manifest, total global ODA allocated by the members of the DAC increased by about 48 percent in real terms between 1970 and 1980. It also increased by about 32 percent in the decade of the 1980s. In the first half of the 1990s, however, global ODA plunged by 13 percent, and it has been declining ever since. During the period of the record growth of ODA flows, aid to sub-Saharan Africa was also quite substantial in absolute volume. Given this fact, it is therefore legitimate to ask whether aid has been effective, and if the answer is not in the affirmative, proper to ask why? Besides, the end of the Cold War and the attendant scarcity of aid resources have generated a lot of emphasis on aid effectiveness.[122]

There are no generally accepted methods for evaluating the effectiveness of aid. Some scholars, for example Chenery and Strout (1966), focus on the impact of aid on economic growth, but as Riddell (1995) and Lancaster (1999) accurately observe, it is difficult to establish this relationship because of the role that other social, political and economic variables play in the achievement of economic growth. Other approaches to the evaluation of the effectiveness of aid focus narrowly on the extent to which aid projects/programs have achieved their stated objectives and sustained those achievements. There are, however, constraints stemming from the peculiar problems of data gathering and analysis in a developing region like sub-Saharan Africa, which makes it difficult to accurately gauge the impact of aid even by this modest criterion. Moreover, assessments of aid effectiveness "must often rely on "plausible attribution" rather than scientifically established causality" (DAC Journal, 2000:128). Still, for understandable reasons, the evaluation of the effectiveness of aid in the recipient countries has moved increasingly towards the center of the debate about development assistance. Many well-meaning citizens in donor countries whose taxes underwrite the aid efforts of their countries legitimately seek to find meaningful results that would justify their endeavors. Other skeptical citizens who are ill disposed to aid in the first place, readily point at the substantial media coverage of failed programs as evidence for why aid should be abolished.

Despite the difficulty of measuring the effectiveness of aid, empirical findings from several studies done in the last decade, often with sophisticated measurement tools do not support the assertion tendered by the skeptics that aid has been largely ineffective. Table 9.2 presents a representative sample of the findings by empirical studies on the effectiveness of aid in sub-Saharan Africa.

---

[122] Aid effectiveness is often defined by evaluation specialists as a measure of the extent to which a policy program, or project achieves its objectives. See the Evaluation Group homepage at www.oecd.org/dac.

Rethinking Aid to Sub-Saharan Africa in the New Millennium 169

Table 9.2 Results from a Sample of Scholarly Studies Measuring the Effectiveness of Aid[123]

Author (s)	Publication Ref.	Period of Study	% of African States in Study	Research Method	Findings
Burnside, C. & Dollar, D.	Finance & Development Vol. 34, No.4 (1997):4-7	1970-1993	38%	OLS 2SLS Six 4-Year periods	Foreign aid accelerates growth in developing countries that pursue sound economic policies.
Hansen, H. & Tarp, F.	Journal of Development Economics, Vol. 64, No. 2 (2001): 547-570	1970-1993	38%	OLS 2SLS Six 4-Year periods	Aid in all likelihood increases the growth rate. This result is not conditional on good policy. There are, however, decreasing returns to aid, and the estimated effectiveness of aid is highly sensitive to the choice of estimators and the control of variables.
Lensik, R. & Morrissey, O.	Journal of Development Studies, Vol. 36, No. 3 (2000):31-49	1970-1995	48%	Cross-Country Regression	The impact of aid on growth is a function of the effects of aid on investment levels. The finding that uncertainty reduces aid is robust.
Boone, P.	European Review Vol.4, No.2 (1996): 289-317	1972-1990	37%	OLS Pooled	Measured by human development, aid does not significantly increase investment, nor benefit the poor. But other things

[123] Where African states represent at least 20 percent of the sample population.

					being equal, liberal regimes and democracies have on average, a 30% lower infant mortality than the least free regimes.
Ghura, D. & Hadjimichael, M.T.	IMF Staff Paperws, Vol. 43, No. 3 (1996): 605-619.	1981-1992	100%	GLS/OLS Panel Data	Increases in private investment has relatively large positive impact on growth. Growth is stimulated by public policies that lower the budget deficit, reduce inflation, maintain external competitiveness, promote structural reforms, encourage human capital development, and slow population growth.
Feyzioglu, T., Swaroop, V. & Zhu, M.	The World Bank Economic Review, Vol. 12, No. 1 (1998): 29-44	1971-1990	21%	OLS (Pooled) Panel Data	Aid has positive and significant impact on public investment. Because most aid appears to be fungible, the rate of return on specific donor-funded project tells little about impact of that assistance. A better approach may be tie aid to an overall public expenditure program.

Moreover, where aid has failed in sub-Saharan Africa, the reasons are attributable as much to the misappropriation of development funds by government officials in the recipient states, as the motivations behind the donors' allocation of aid together with the absence, or paucity of other sources of development finance.

The Link Between the Motivations Behind Donors' Aid Allocation and Poor Aid Performance

The poor performance of aid in many sub-Saharan African countries stems in large part from the factors motivating different donors to allocate aid. As the preceding chapters in this study have made manifest, there are divergences in the motivations that drive the aid allocations of the donors. It is, however, interesting that the recipient states where aid is widely believed to have been effective in the satisfaction of basic needs and the prevention of further deterioration of impoverished conditions (such as Tanzania, Mozambique, and Zambia), have all been states upon which the Nordic donors concentrate their aid efforts. Equally notable is the observation that United States has reduced the amount of aid it allocates to the region in the post-Cold War era, although its aid effort now appears to have a poverty reduction focus. Previous studies have made a strong link between the Cold War and the high volumes of aid allocated by the US to some states in sub-Saharan Africa. For example, Schraeder, Hook and Taylor, (1998) reported that those sub-Saharan African states that maintained security alliance with the US received more generous provision of foreign aid. According to them, the most notable example of this point was the effect that the United States' successful negotiation of military base access arrangements with Kenya, Somalia and the Sudan in the 1970s had on their receipt of higher volumes of aid than other countries in the region.

The non-developmental motive behind a donor's foreign aid policy exerts a double negative impact on the performance of aid. First, donors who are motivated by non-developmental concerns lack the practical and moral incentives to hold recipients accountable for the non-developmental uses to which aid funds are directed. The effect of this is that when in some sub-Saharan African countries, for examples Rwanda, and Zaire under the late President Sese Sekou Mobutu, instances of the gross embezzlement and misappropriation of aid funds come to the fore, such donors generally look the other way, or at best issue weak statements condemning such abuses.[124]

Second, the non-developmental motives behind the aid programs of some

---

[124] See Uvin (1998) for a discussion of how the failure by donors like the United States to hold the Rwanda government accountable for the diversion of aid funds into non-developmental objectives encouraged the latter occurrence of the Rwandan genocide.

donors militate against the development of joint efforts by all DAC members that could render aid more effective. Frustrated by the non-developmental objectives of their peers, other donors with genuine concerns for the correct uses of aid funds become reluctant to engage such donors in joint efforts that could promote the genuine development goals.

Since the end of the Cold War, however, there have been some encouraging developments on the motivation issue. For one, whereas in the Cold War era, the goal of poverty alleviation was more pronounced only in the aid policies of Canada, the Nordic countries, and a few other donors, it is now an essential feature of the aid policies of the United States, Germany, the United Kingdom, Italy, and Japan. Also, for France who now provides the most amount of aid to the region (in absolute terms), although the traditional, multifaceted motives evident in its aid policies - the promotion of the *rayonnement* of French culture, and the interests of its national-firms - remain important features of its aid policies, its debt cancellation efforts are also notable. The coincidence between the shift from security interests to poverty alleviation in the factors motivating donors to allocate aid, and the increasing emphasis on aid performance lend credence to the point that the blame for poor aid performance can neither be leveled on the recipient states alone, nor can the broad assertion that aid does not work be readily substantiated. Aid works when it is designed to work. And it will fare poorly if donors use it as a facade for the pursuit of other non-developmental objectives.

The Paucity of Other Financial Flows as a Cause of Poor Aid Performance

The other reason for the poor performance of aid in sub-Saharan Africa is attributable to the paucity of other financial flows into the region. Unlike developing states in regions such as East Asia and Latin America, where aid has succeeded in promoting appreciable development, in many sub-Saharan African countries, aid has been employed as the *only* source of development finance. Table 9.3 illustrates this point.

Table 9.3 Geographic Distribution of Financial Flows (Direct Investment) from DAC Donors by Region (1960-1997)

Year	1960	1961	1962	1963	1964
Recipient					
Total, Africa	-	-	-	-	-
Total, North of Sahara	-	-	-	-	-
Total, South of Sahara	-	-	-	-	-
Total, Americas	-	-	-	-	-
Total, N. & C. America	-	-	-	-	-
Total, South America	-	-	-	-	-
Total, Asia	-	-	-	-	-
Total, Middle East	-	-	-	-	-
Total, South & Central Asia	-	-	-	-	-
Total, Far East	-	-	-	-	-
Total, Oceania	-	-	-	-	-
Year	**1965**	**1966**	**1967**	**1968**	**1969**
Recipient					
Total, Africa	-	-	-	654.2	611.6
Total, North of Sahara	-	-	-	310.1	240.1
Total, South of Sahara	-	-	-	169.2	279.4
Total, Americas	-	-	-	1,349.6	1,160.8
Total, N. & C. America	-	-	-	560.2	525.8
Total, South America	-	-	-	583.8	444.8
Total, Asia	-	-	-	446.5	522.1
Total, Middle East	-	-	-	91.6	43.0
Total, South & Central Asia	-	-	-	61.1	47.6
Total, Far East	-	-	-	112.5	232.2
Total, Oceania	-	-	-	22.3	45.3
Year	**1970**	**1971**	**1972**	**1973**	**1974**
Recipient					
Total, Africa	810.0	547.6	634.3	-27.8	230.4
Total, North of Sahara	414.5	165.5	238.2	-105.9	29.6
Total, South of Sahara	198.6	266.5	333.5	62.9	160.3
Total, Americas	1,539.8	1,421.0	1,596.8	3,156.5	4,809.2
Total, N. & C. America	684.3	470.6	498.4	1375	2,768.5
Total, South America	489.7	570.8	626.5	1,386.8	1,658.5
Total, Asia	689.0	660.9	954.6	831.8	-4,885.3
Total, Middle East	54.8	-126.9	111.8	-912.3	-6,512.7
Total, South & Central Asia	48.7	47.9	17.1	39.9	72.2
Total, Far East	362.5	450.8	516.3	1,351.0	792.1
Total, Oceania	132.2	49.0	90.3	127.1	84.8

174 Contending Theories on Development Aid

Table 9.3 Geographic Distribution of Financial Flows (Direct Investment) from DAC Donors by Region (1960-1997)

Year	1975	1976	1977	1978	1979
Recipient					
Total, Africa	751.6	1,191.1	885.3	1,236.5	1,151.4
Total, North of Sahara	-516.8	302.9	55.5	157.9	268.0
Total, South of Sahara	851.4	490.9	790.1	451.3	415.9
Total, Americas	4,225.5	2,969.1	5,130.9	6,304.8	6,199.2
Total, N. & C. America	1,674.9	1,096.7	950.9	1,678.9	2,743.8
Total, South America	2,058.2	1,545.0	2,672.0	2,427.7	2,911.7
Total, Asia	4,894.3	3,015.7	2,385.9	2,662.2	4,212.0
Total, Middle East	2,467.3	1,328.8	1,048.6	1,070.9	2,164.8
Total, South & Central Asia	64.0	41.9	-10.0	42.8	67.5
Total, Far East	1,844.1	1,327.2	513.3	1,232.5	824.4
Total, Oceania	-0.7	86.5	40.6	59.1	47.9

Year	1980	1981	1982	1983	1984
Recipient					
Total, Africa	1,433.0	1,983.0	2,447.7	978.4	-35.9
Total, North of Sahara	404.2	152.6	160.4	605.8	249.1
Total, South of Sahara	994.7	1,808.9	2,239.5	337.1	-290.2
Total, Americas	7,269.0	6,243.6	5,887.2	3,776.3	5,868.7
Total, N. & C. America	4,687.9	2,781.6	2,001.2	2,709.4	3,811.9
Total, South America	2,352.0	3,119.4	3,463.3	680.9	1,760.1
Total, Asia	-660.5	6,504.8	2,459.0	3,412.4	4,687.8
Total, Middle East	-2,844.0	390.6	860.5	586.6	784.4
Total, South & Central Asia	129.9	142.9	97.1	71.3	115.0
Total, Far East	1,885.2	5,691.2	1,573.0	2,314.0	3,371.9
Total, Oceania	59.0	-14.2	105.6	14.5	103.8

Year	1985	1986	1987	1988	1989
Recipient					
Total, Africa	491.5	481.7	443.9	1,219.4	2,848.8
Total, North of Sahara	789.5	-181.2	-82.7	259.0	253.4
Total, South of Sahara	-218.3	609.3	1,174.2	522.9	2,518.0
Total, Americas	5,000.9	5,901.6	8,781.5	9,736.9	9,740.8
Total, N. & C. America	3,789.0	4,093.7	7,302.6	6,091.9	4,716.8
Total, South America	758.5	1,350.8	1,595.5	2,178.8	3,805.0
Total, Asia	655.6	3,026.4	8,211.8	7,687.3	10,060.6
Total, Middle East	162.6	875.5	-95.9	325.0	87.3
Total, South & Central Asia	122.5	99.8	255.8	145.3	290.8
Total, Far East	130.4	1,984.9	7,609.5	6,648.8	9,659.4
Total, Oceania	60.6	67.1	141.8	483.6	444.7

Table 9.3 Geographic Distribution of Financial Flows (Direct Investment) from DAC Donors by Region (1960-1997)

Year	1990	1991	1992	1993	1994
Recipient					
Total, Africa	606.1	1,383.7	-378.6	1,550.6	1,141.6
Total, North of Sahara	-102.3	111.9	-275.7	155.3	350.4
Total, South of Sahara	660.2	1,214.8	351.9	745.7	495.5
Total, Americas	9,509.3	9,966.5	13,617.8	18,543.6	23,718.8
Total, N. & C. America	3,812.3	5,934.7	7,576.8	11,077.1	10,422.3
Total, South America	2,931.7	4,023.9	5,982.1	6,669.2	11,810.6
Total, Asia	11,430.3	9,296.6	12,148.3	16,058.9	21,210.7
Total, Middle East	724.5	1,724.9	1,594.6	1,585.2	608.2
Total, South & Central Asia	448.0	78.7	320.7	714.0	588.6
Total, Far East	10,315.6	7,434.2	10,204.9	12,077.6	19,014.1
Total, Oceania	1,135.4	533.7	391.5	139.7	26.0

Year	1995	1996	1997
Recipient			
Total, Africa	2,913.4	3,704.7	5,728.1
Total, North of Sahara	148.7	1,136.2	1,137.2
Total, South of Sahara	2,425.9	2,118.6	4,432.0
Total, Americas	24,245.1	31,320.5	45,975.2
Total, N. & C. America	6,633.2	14,155.7	14,461.3
Total, South America	15,599.7	13,556.3	26,474.6
Total, Asia	22,985.1	22,576.2	17,207.1
Total, Middle East	1,920.4	145.4	1,246.9
Total, South & Central Asia	797.9	1,115.9	2,339.8
Total, Far East	19,868.7	20,873.9	13,191.3
Total, Oceania	46.0	-3.3	193.3

Source: Geographic Distribution of Financial Flows to Aid Recipients, 1960-1997. (CD-ROM). Paris, OECD (1998).

As Table 9.3 shows, in comparison to other regions of the world, during the 1960-1997 period, sub-Saharan Africa received only 5 percent of the total direct investment by DAC members. When one considers this paucity of FDI flows to the region, together with how the non-developmental motivations behind donors' aid allocations depreciate aid performance, the reasons why high volumes of aid have not produced significant economic development in sub-Saharan Africa becomes less mysterious. Equally evident is the need to identify and address the primary sources of threats to the continuation of development assistance to the region, the subject of the following section.

Sources of Threats to the Continuation of Aid to Sub-Saharan Africa

In the early years of new century, there are at least four primary sources of threat to the continuation of development assistance to sub-Saharan Africa. These include the erosion of the political support for aid in donor countries, the perception of a divergence of interest between the developed democracies and the people of sub-Saharan Africa, the budgetary constraints in donor countries, and the shift in regional preferences of many donors occasioned by the end of the Cold War.

The Erosion of the Political Support for Aid in Donor Countries

Between 1989 and 1992, the volume of aid to many sub-Saharan African states reached an all time high. Beginning in 1993, however, this began to decline progressively such that by 1997, total aid as a percentage of donor's GNP reached rock bottom for most donors. The reason for this decline was due in part to the erosion of the political support for aid in many donor countries. This erosion of political support for aid in donor countries is itself a consequence of the popular perception in many of these countries that the pace of development in a majority of sub-Saharan African states does not justify the continuation of aid. Aid is widely believed to have been ineffective. Reports about the embezzlement of aid funds by government officials in recipient countries contribute significantly to this perception.

True, the gross abuses to which aid funds are sometimes subjected by government officials in some recipient states is vexing and ought to provoke indignation in the citizens of the developed democracies whose taxes go to support such aid efforts. One particularly egregious example of the misappropriation of aid funds by recipient states is the story of a central government official in one state who purchased a gold bed with aid funds even though his people lacked access to the basic necessities of food and shelter (Svendson, 1989). The offensive thing about such actions by recipient government officials, aside from its depravity is that it communicates to the donors a lack of commitment by government officials in the recipient states to the development effort. Thus, the actions of a few officials, in a few states come to have a magnified negative effect on the general commitment of the people of sub-Saharan Africa to development. Worse still, aid comes to be viewed as having uniformly failed in the region even though this is not the case. The example of cases like Botswana, where aid has promoted appreciable development gets subsumed by the record of poor aid performance in a few countries.

At its independence in 1966, Botswana was one of the poorest countries in the world. It relied primarily on grant-in-aid from Britain to finance its imports and government expenditures. In subsequent decades, due in part to significant inflows of foreign aid, and its mineral reserves, particularly diamonds, it is now a middle income country with per capita income well over $2000 dollars. Generalizations of aid failure crowds out this type of significant achievement.

Another reason for the erosion of political support for aid to sub-Saharan Africa has been the revelations of massive corruption in the aid agencies of some donor countries. The case of the Italian Fund for Development is one example. In the early 1980s, Italian aid agencies enjoyed broad support from a diverse spectrum of the Italian society. This support was concretized in a 1987 Italian aid legislation (Public Law 99), that allowed the government to allocate huge amounts of money to aid agencies for disbursements to sub-Saharan African countries, although about 50 percent of this effort was concentrated on Somalia and Ethiopia. Then, in 1992, a wide spread political scandal revealed the extent of corrupt practices about how the aid agencies administered aid funds for development. It was revealed that Italian firms frequently over priced the value of goods and services rendered to aid recipient countries, and in some cases, the services that were charged to the aid budget were never rendered at all. Not surprisingly, support for aid by the Italian public began to evaporate such that by 1997, Italian aid to sub-Saharan Africa declined consistently from about $1.3 billion in 1990 to about $263 million by 1997.

In addition to the above points, public misperceptions in donor countries about the proportion of the national budget that is allocated to foreign aid contribute to the negative public opinion about aid. For example, in the United States, whereas the percentage of the gross national product (GNP) that is allocated as aid to all developing countries has never reached the OECD average of 0.35 percent, many Americans erroneously believe that between 5 to 20 percent of their country's GNP is allocated as foreign aid. Thus, when the news media report impressionistic stories of abuses of aid funds, such news immediately rev up the ire of the American taxpayer who then perceives foreign aid as analogous to pouring so much money down a rat hole.

Budgetary Constraints in Donor Countries

Another principal source of threat to the continuation of aid to sub-Saharan Africa relates to the budgetary constraints facing many members of the DAC. The 1996 report of the DAC showed that aid to developing countries in general have fallen fastest in those DAC member states that have been running the largest fiscal deficits. In contrast, the DAC members with the smallest fiscal deficits were able to increase their aid in real terms for the 1995/96 period (Development Cooperation, 1997:55).

Several factors account for the huge budget deficits of OECD members in recent years. First, there is the ageing problem - the graying of the population – that is most acute in a country like Japan. This has dramatically increased the share of the pensions and health care components of Japan's national budget. Second, labor and product market rigidities have made it difficult for some countries to adapt to rapid technological and structural changes in the economy, with the result that some governments have had to allocate greater percentages of their national budgets to increased expenditures on unemployment benefits and retraining programs. The United States has been the clear exception in this regard. The US has successfully harnessed new technologies in computer information and biological sciences with other sectors of its economy to promote record economic growth while at the same time managing to keep wages up, and the interest rate and inflation down. The retrenchment of Canada's aid effort in recent years, and the shift from its traditional policy of humane internationalism to an emphasis on narrow economic and trading interests amply illustrate the effect of budgetary constraints on aid policies.

In 1993, the Canadian government announced deep cuts to the budget of the Canadian International Development Agency (CIDA) and indicated that it would drop seven sub-Saharan African countries from its bilateral aid program Since then, the government has progressively implemented cuts to CIDA's budget. With respect to regional focus, Canada's aid is now primarily oriented towards Latin America and the former Soviet bloc, especially Poland. While the shift in regional focus in favor of Latin America is partially informed by the principles of the North American Free Trade Agreement (NAFTA), the reorientation of Canadian aid towards Poland and other countries in the former Soviet bloc at the expense of its traditional aid recipients in sub-Saharan Africa is best explained by the desire to employ aid in the service of Canada's economic interests (Pratt, 1994). Canada's aid to sub-Saharan Africa has dropped by more than 50 percent in seven years, from over $410 million in 1990 to under $200 million by 1997. Like Canada, other members of the DAC also attribute the reductions in their respective aid allocation to sub-Saharan Africa to budget stringency, and some, like Sweden and Japan, stressing that the reductions have not been disproportionate when compared to other government programs, have promised a return to earlier high levels as soon as their budgetary situation improves (Development Cooperation, 1998 Report).

In addition to its impact on aid volumes, the budgetary constraints on many donors have increasingly made it difficult for them to maintain a field presence in their program/project countries at a time when such presence could most contribute to aid effectiveness. Thus, many donors have had to delegate responsibilities to recipient states with few trained officials who are already overwhelmed by the demands of monitoring other projects.

It is pertinent to observe that, while fiscal stringency might be a persuasive explanation for the decline in the aid volume of other DAC members, it does not justify the retrenchment in development assistance efforts on the part of the United States. It is ironic that at a time when the US economy is enjoying record growth, the country has become more miserly in its allocation of aid to sub-Saharan Africa. Indeed, the pattern of United States' allocation of aid to sub-Saharan Africa could be likened to a fire brigade approach to development assistance. In the event of episodic crises, for examples, the Ethiopian famine of the 1980s, the regime crisis in Somalia in the early 1990s and the genocide in Rwanda in the mid 1990s, the US rushes in with massive amounts of aid, but as soon as the crisis is circumscribed to manageable proportions, it retreats to its earlier minimal effort or benign indifference. Such approach to development assistance is disturbing for several reasons. First, it produces a vicious circle whereby the earlier allocation of inadequate resources to effectively address issues of sustainable development nurtures the occurrence of complex emergencies, which then require massive input of resources to address. Second, such vicious circle engenders disappointment over the ability of aid to serve as a catalyst to development, and it diminishes confidence in the prospects of the region or the seriousness of the people to confront the challenges of development.

Moreover, the effects of such a pattern of aid giving provides cover for those who seek to argue that sub-continent is inhospitable to "western style development". The fact of the matter is that although there are several challenges to development in the region, these challenges are not so different that the combination of generous aid, foreign investment, and determination on the part of recipients that have produced impressive results in East Asia would not successfully address.

Perceptions of a Divergence of Interest Between Donors and Recipients

Even though advances in transport and communication technologies have combined to harness the world into the now fabled global village, other than paying lip service to the processes of globalization, policy makers in many DAC countries still perceive a divergence of interest between their people and the people of sub-Saharan Africa. This perception of a divergence of interest is evident at two levels: (1) in their definition of security, and (2) in their implementation of aid projects and programs.

Despite the end of the Cold War and the emergence of new sources of threats to international security, many policy makers in countries like the United States and Britain continue to view issues of international security and the relevance of sub-Saharan Africa through the same old prism offered by the realist paradigm. The expansion of the definition of security that recent developments, such as the threats posed by the emergence of new strains of microbial diseases, call for is either poorly understood, or else policy makers have taken refuge in the false hope that the spread of such diseases could be easily contained. Lost to such illusions is the fact that global interdependence, modern transport and trade have rendered distinctions between domestic and international health obsolete.[125] The genetic variability of HIV, for example, requires that any effort to produce a vaccine for the disease take into consideration the worldwide family of viruses (Shope, 1992). Furthermore, the relative speed with which the recent outbreak of food and mouth disease spread over Europe ought to alert us to the danger inherent in the narrow definition of national security. The continuation of severe poverty in sub-Saharan Africa renders the region propitious to the rise of new diseases that could easily spread to the developed world, notwithstanding concerted efforts to restrict migrants from the sub continent. It is also worth recalling that the number of battlefield deaths in World War I for example, was easily outstripped by the number of deaths in the major influenza epidemic that originated in Kansas in 1918, but quickly spread within the US military. Conservative estimates peg the number of lives lost to the influenza virus at 25 million

---

[125] See "Aids in the Global Village: Why US Physicians Should Care About HIV Outside the United States", JAMA, December 16, 1992 – Vol 268, No. 23 (pp. 3368-3369).

people. Given the ease with which viruses migrate from one continent to the other in the contemporary world, plus the speed at which viruses now mutate, one shudders to think of the human and material losses that would result from a major epidemic outbreak of a 21st century virus. The development aspirations of sub-Saharan Africans cannot be safely ignored. To do so is not only unethical; it is foolhardy.

Besides, there are tangible benefits that could accrue to developed countries, even if medium and long term, of investment in sub-Saharan Africa. Such benefits include the externalities that the elevation of about ten percent of the world's population from a primary preoccupation with the fulfillment of the most basic human needs could generate for the global economy, knowledge and culture. Increased development in sub-Saharan Africa could translate into increased effective demand for global consumer products, expanded markets and increased profits for the goods produced by the agricultural, manufacturing, and service-oriented firms in developed countries. The liberation of a majority of sub-Saharan Africans from impoverishment means the expansion of the pool of contributors to the advancement of human knowledge, and the enrichment of world culture. Development assistance is a positive-sum rather than a zero sum game. Essentially too, even if somewhat mundane, the American, Japanese, or European who loves to travel but must eliminate from his/her list of destinations, visits to many countries in sub-Saharan Africa because of security fears not unrelated to the poor pace of the region's development, is as much deprived of his/her liberty as if Congress, or the Diet, or Parliament promulgated a decree forbidding travel to Orlando, or Osaka, or Oslo.

With respect to the implementation of aid projects and programs, even though donors and recipient states acknowledge the value of local ownership of aid projects and programs, the pattern of recipient-passivism that is encouraged by the failure of donors to actively engage them in a mutual partnership nurtures the perception of a divergence of interest between donors and recipients. Aid recipients come to interpret such attitude to mean that otherwise well-meaning donors have different agendas from their own. Such relationship fosters distrust between donors and recipients, and it more to paternalism than relations of mutual partnership.

In addition, while many donors emphasize the importance of consistency in policies aimed at the pursuit of sustainable development in sub-Saharan Africa, the implementation of severe cuts to their already reduced development assistance budgets, coupled with the disarticulation of their other economic policies toward the region do not reflect perceptions of mutual interest. It hurts the credibility of donors when they extol the virtues of free trade, claim to be concerned with African development, and yet implement trade policies that marginalize the region's participation in the global economy. Practices like tied aid, common among many members of the DAC, continue despite its inefficiency and corrosive effect on the principles of free trade. The incoherence of the economic policies that many donors implement toward states in the region impact aid-program outcomes in negative ways. The case of French aid in Burkina Faso illustrates this point.

Premised on the assumption that specialization in the production of cotton would allow Burkina Faso to channel its meager resources into more efficient use, French aid to that country favored the cotton sector over all other agricultural and industrial sectors. In the 1980s, however, when in response to the giddy swings of the international commodity trade the price of cotton fell drastically, France failed to provide the shelter for Burkina Faso's cotton production that it had indicated it could while steering the country towards specialization. France also failed to provide incentives for French businesses that would have encouraged them to invest in potentially lucrative areas in Burkina Faso. Thus the collapse of the cotton trade had a devastating effect on the economy of that country (Gabas, Faure, and Sindzinger, 1997).

The Impact of the End of the Cold War on Aid to Sub-Saharan Africa

Although the end of the Cold War and the triumph of liberal ideas have liberated discussions of African development from the dominance of unproductive debates about whether socialism or capitalism offers the surest path to development, it has also given rise to new threats to the continuation of aid flows to the region. Now, more than what obtained during the Cold War, members of the DAC have become more selective about the recipients of their aid. With the addition of Part II Central and Eastern European Countries and the Newly Independent States of the former Soviet Union (CEECs/NIS) to the DAC list of aid recipients in 1994, sub-Saharan African states must now compete for aid funds with these countries at a time when many donors have implemented severe cut backs in their overall aid efforts.

The ends of the Cold War has had a negative impact on the allocation of aid to sub-Saharan Africa in another curious regard. It has deprived some people who empathize with the plight of the region a useful justification for aid to the region. During the Cold War, there were some supporters of Africa, especially in the United States and Britain, who never believed in the credibility of the communist threat in the region but who, nonetheless, skillfully used such arguments to convince the Conservatives of the need to provide aid to the region. Now with the end of the Cold War, such effective justification for aid to sub-Saharan Africa has evaporated. It is also curious that African studies now attract fewer graduate students in the United States, and that some scholars are seeking to write their way out of the region.

Towards a New Donor-Recipient Development Partnership

The threats to the continuation of development assistance to sub-Saharan Africa discussed above are indeed serious. It is also ironic that they have emerged at a time when many of the factors that once militated against the effectiveness of aid - authoritarian leadership, weak mass participation in politics, and competing ideological paradigms on development issues - are being dismantled. Still, the challenges posed by these threats present opportunities for the cultivation of a new partnership between donors whose efforts have institutionalized the aid regime. True, the historical record on the progress of different countries from a predominantly traditional society to a rapidly developing nation-state demonstrates that the efforts of the people to help themselves are the main ingredients for their success.[126] The contemporary historical record on the flow of international finance (from the Marshall Plan to the current efforts by the DAC) also demonstrates, however, that development assistance has been an essential, complementary factor in many achievements. The following discussion underscores suggestions for addressing the threats to the continuation of development assistance to sub-Saharan Africa. It also examines some proposals for a new and effective donor-recipient aid partnership.

Halting the Erosion of the Political Support for Aid

As I have stated earlier, the erosion of the political support for aid to sub-Saharan Africa represents the most potent threat to the continuation of meaningful aid allocation to the region. This erosion of political support for aid stems largely from misperceptions about the effectiveness of aid to produce target economic and social development. It bears reiterating that even though there have been instances where aid funds were misappropriated, or put to ineffective use in sub-Saharan Africa, by and large, the allocation of aid has made a lot of positive difference in the states receiving them. One recoils from the thought of what would have happened to the millions of people in Tanzania, Zambia, Mozambique, Mali, Senegal, Ethiopia, Somalia and a host

---

[126] See Development Cooperation 1996 Report, "Shaping the 21st Century: The Challenge of Development Cooperation".

of other countries had they not received foreign aid, as marginal as the amounts were sometimes. For many countries in sub-Saharan Africa, foreign aid has meant the difference between life and death for a lot of people. The principal problem, however; the reason why aid is often perceived to have failed, is the ascription to aid alone the catalyst-to-development role which aid is most effective at producing, but only in complement with other resources. In the more than half a century history of development assistance, no country has attained appreciable levels of economic and social development in the absence of other financial flows. While determination, discipline, and industry played significant roles in the levels of economic growth achieved by countries like South Korea, Singapore, Taiwan, Hong Kong, Brazil, and Argentina, the infusion of Japanese, American and European direct investment played vital roles in their rapid development. A review of the flow of external resources to sub-Saharan Africa indicates that although the sub continent has received a considerable amount of aid funds, unlike East Asia and Latin America, it has received only marginal amounts of direct investment. Moreover, when one discounts the reported net aid to the region by the overpriced and sometimes irrelevant goods that must be bought in donor countries, and is filtered again in the deep pockets of thousands of foreign experts and aid agency staff as Hancock (1990:190) suggests, to expect aid to produce economic and social development reveals a faith in magic that is bound to produce disappointment.

Several strategies have been suggested for halting the erosion of political support for aid to developing countries in general. Many of these suggestions bear particular relevance to sub-Saharan Africa.[127] First, it is imperative that development practitioners, especially those in recipient states demonstrate that they are responsible stewards of public resources with a strong, transparent commitment to the welfare of their own people. This calls for transformations in how aid resources are allocated, and how the procedures for monitoring results and outcomes are established.

Second, the aid effort must be expanded to include the active participation of civil society, including business leaders in donor countries to demonstrate that there is an active constituency for development progress. In recipient states where civil society is either weak, or absent, steps should be taken to cultivate and encourage its development. The stake of business leaders in donor countries in development assistance should be stoked to motivate them to put pressure on their governments to open up aid procurement to competitive bidding and end the practice of tied aid. It is hypocritical to extol the virtues of free trade while at the same time encouraging the tying of aid to purchases

---

[127] See Development Cooperation: Efforts and Policies of the Members of the Development Assistance Committee, 1998 Report. Paris, OECD 1999:14-16 for a full discussion of these strategies.

in donor countries.

Third, the role of the media in the promotion of accurate perception of aid effectiveness cannot be over emphasized. Although the results have not been dramatic, aid has made it possible to increase life expectancy, decrease infant mortality, and promote literacy and gender equality in many sub-Saharan African countries. This fact does not often register on the radar screen of many Western news media chiefly concerned with sensational and negative news. In this regard, advocates of development assistance to sub-Saharan Africa must do a better job of publicizing the many cases where aid has made a qualitative difference, even if such progress have fallen short of being spectacular.

An additional dimension to halting the erosion of political support for aid relates to the role that education can play in shaping the discourse on development issues and values. A great deal of this currently obtains in undergraduate curricular in the social sciences in American colleges. There is a need, however, to broaden these efforts to include middle and high school students and familiarize them with issues of development. One laudable program along these lines is the Connecticut Project in International Negotiation (CPIN) at the University of Connecticut, which engages middle and high school students in simulation and discussion excises on issues of international relations including the subject of foreign aid. This program, however, currently runs in a few schools. There is a need to extend the benefits of the program to broader range of schools, and perhaps too, internationalize the effort by linking participants from different countries.

Finally, a significant responsibility for the encouragement of public understanding of development assistance in donor countries lies with the DAC, the few government officials and aid administrators whose courageous leadership have so far kept aid allocation to sub-Saharan Africa alive. The establishment of the DAC's web site is a laudable step in availing to the public studies that document the usefulness and success of development assistance. It would be prudent, however, to add creative and user friendly pictorial demonstrations of the progress that aid has made possible in many developing countries on the web site. Adding a few web-pages for overseas development games for young people could be one useful way of engaging their attention, and through them the attention of their parents who would otherwise remain indifferent to the concerns of the people of remote regions like sub-Saharan Africa.

Linking ODA with Other Development Assistance Instruments

The primary responsibility for the development of any country falls squarely on the inhabitants of that country, for it is they who must wrestle with the frustrations and successes of efforts to bring about the improvement of the material conditions of their societies. External financial assistance, however, when provided in appropriate levels, and absent the strings of non-developmental objectives, can provide a needed complement to local resources, knowledge and effort. The DAC articulated this point succinctly when it observed:

> Development progress in any country is achieved by the people of that country, with the external factors playing a secondary, if important, role. Among those external factors, development assistance, or "aid" is again, less important than access to markets, capital and technology, but it can serve as a key strategic catalyst to help foster such an enabling environment. And it can help to make the most of progress toward such an environment (Development Cooperation 1994 Report, p.9).

Case studies of the performance of aid in sub-Saharan Africa lend credence to the importance of other sources of finance in bringing about success. In cases like Burkina Faso and Rwanda where aid is deemed to have failed, such failures are attributable in large part to the absence, or paucity of other sources of development finance that would have complemented ODA. In contrast, in countries where aid is widely believed to have succeeded in promoting economic and social development, such as Botswana (high success) and Ghana (moderate success), success stemmed in large part from the availability of other sources of finance. The rise in the value of direct investment received by Ghana correlates positively with the growth of the country's economy and the expansion of social and health services to the Ghanaian people[128] (Aryeetey and Cox, 1997).

Furthermore, the World Bank has reported the existence of a strong correlation between the integration of a country's economy into the global markets and the attainment of economic development by such country.[129] All these points suggest that to achieve better aid performance, it is imperative that donor countries support their ODA disbursements to sub-Saharan Africa with trade policies aimed at reversing the marginalization of the region from the global economy. In this regard, recent efforts by Japan who has hosted two conferences on African development, the Tokyo International Conference on African Development (TICAD I&II), and the United States who organized the Summit on Africa in 2000 are welcome developments. Equally

---

[128] Direct investment in Ghana increased from $2.5 million in 1981-86, to $4.7 million in 1987, $15 million in 1989, and $22.5 in 1992, Aryeetey and Cox (1997:71-72).

[129] See the discussion of trade and liberalization in "Global Economic Prospects and Developing Countries", World Bank 1997 Report.

encouraging is the final communiqué of the Group of Eight summit meeting in Denver in 1997, in which the group promised to provide support for African countries to participate fully in the expansion of global prosperity. Previous inconsistencies stemming from the official pronouncements of many donors about their support for African development and their implementation of other economic polices that tend to undercut such pronouncements, however, weaken their claims of commitment to African development. This reality calls for cautious optimism with respect to the otherwise encouraging developments mentioned above.[130]

Better Donor-Recipient Participation in the Design and Implementation of Aid Programs/Projects

One of the criticisms frequently leveled at the administration of ODA by members of the DAC involves the low levels of participation by the recipients of aid in the design and implementation of funded projects and programs. Where donors endeavor to engage local participants in the aid effort, such engagements frequently entail working with central government officials. There are two major drawbacks with such approach to participatory management. First, it does not foster the sense of ownership that is cardinal to the sustenance of funded projects and programs because the majority of the people who are the target of such programs have been deprived of the opportunity to participate in them. Second, from an administrative point of view, the concentration of donor-recipient dialogue on central government officials encourages the sense of "bigmanship" on the part of such officials with the attendant problems of turf protection, inefficiency and ineptitude that such personalization of official business engenders. The engagement of a broad section of civil society is a necessary antidote to such aid management problems. There is, however, the consideration that in many countries in sub-Saharan Africa, the near absence of a dynamic and active civil society suggests that the conditions are not propitious for the immediate exercise of a leading role by participants other than central government officials. In such instances, part of the aid effort should be the cultivation of an active civil society, because it is often in countries with minimal participation by the citizens that the effectiveness of aid is most endangered. As the DAC has acknowledged, one of the lessons about development assistance is that donor driven initiatives rarely take root hence it is imperative that developing countries and their

---

[130] See Kruger (1993) for a cogent analysis of how US trade and investment policies undercut its development assistance efforts in developing countries.

people must be at the center of an effective system.

A People Centered and Results Oriented Partnership

The most relevant measurement of whether aid has succeeded is the extent to which it has engendered noticeable progress in the lives of the common folks in the recipient states who are the target of such aid. For an impoverished region such as sub-Saharan Africa, progress is invariably measured by the degree to which aid facilitates the satisfaction of the basic needs of the people and the sustainability and security of their environment. The three broad goals of a basic needs approach to measuring aid success are economic well-being, social development, and environmental sustainability. If international conferences were effective spurs to donors' actions, and the collective goals agreed upon by participants were readily implemented, the plight of the people of sub-Saharan Africa, and indeed the people of most developing countries would have received urgent, practical attention by now. In the 1990s alone, there were at least eight major international conferences with a primary focus on issues of development.[131] While such international conferences often come up with laudable declarations and objectives, the post-conference practices of the sponsors often belie their declared goals.

With respect to economic well being, the goal specified by the DAC is to reduce by at least one half by 2015, the proportion of people living in extreme poverty in developing countries. The DAC calculated that based on a standard $370 per capita annual income, about 30 percent of the world's people, or more than 1.3 billion people live in extreme poverty. A significant proportion of this number lives in sub-Saharan Africa. With respect to social development, the DAC identified four areas in need of urgent assistance – primary education, gender equality, basic health care, and family planning. These four areas were derived from commitments reached at the 1994 Cairo conference on population and development, the 1995 Copenhagen summit on social development, and the 1995 Beijing conference on women. The target dates which have been set for the accomplishment of these goals include: (1) universal primary education in all countries by 2015; (2) the elimination of gender disparity in all countries by 2005; (3) the reduction of infant and child mortality rates by two thirds the 1990 level, and the reduction of maternal mortality rates by three fourths the 1990 level by 2015; and (4) the provision of access through the primary health care system to reproductive health services for all individuals of appropriate ages, including safe and reliable family

---

[131] The list of conference themes includes: Education (Jomthien, 1990), Children (New York, 1990), the Environment (Rio de Janeiro,1992), Human Rights (Vienna, 1993), Population (Cairo, 1994), Social Development (Copenhagen, 1995), and Women (Beijing, 1996).

planning methods by 2015.[132]

These goals have particular relevance for sub-Saharan Africa, because the problems of infant mortality, adult illiteracy, poor access to health care and gender disparity are most acute in the region. It is indeed heartbreaking that at the beginning of the 21st century, Africa - continent which anthropologists have widely acknowledged as the original home of humankind - is the most hostile continent for human habitation. The DAC's specification of a timetable for the accomplishments of the above objectives is a useful step to ensuring their realization. It also represents an important milestone in the DAC's approach to development, and a useful complement to the efforts of the United Nation's Development Program. They are commendable proposals. With strong and coherent commitment on the part of donors and recipients, the recruitment of the active participation of the private sectors in the developed countries, remarkable progress toward their accomplishment could be achieved. Still, recent decreases in the aid budget of many DAC member states, and trends in the concentration of direct investment in Asia and Latin-America cast aspersions on the seriousness of the commitments to the accomplishment of these goals. If this trend is not reversed, these goals would lose credibility, and by the time the fast approaching target points come to pass, an opportunity to engage sub-Saharan Africa in a meaningful development partnership would have been lost. That would indeed be unfortunate.

Coordination of Donors' Efforts

One serious flaw in the traditional practice of aid administration by donor countries has been the absence of a coordinated approach to the implementation of aid programs and projects. This, despite the establishment of an institution that provides donors with the opportunities to compare notes, understand the needs of recipient countries and provide a coherent approach to development assistance. Frequently in sub-Saharan Africa, it is not uncommon to find a proliferation of donor projects that tend to overwhelm the capacity of the recipient states to participate effectively in the aid effort. As a corrective to such practice, the establishment of joint donor missions has been suggested (Lancaster, 1999: 235-238). Under this proposal, donor agencies would not have authority over the use of their aid to these missions; rather, they would invest their representatives in the joint-mission with the authority to commit aid funds to agreed activities so long as those activities accorded with the broad policies and regulatory requirements of their agencies. The principal

---

[132] See *Shaping the 21st Century: The Contribution of Development Assistance*, op. cit.

advantage of this strategy, in addition to the better management of aid programs and projects that it would make possible is that it would allow donors to specialize in the delivery of those services over which they have a comparative advantage (Dewald and Welder, 1996). Such suggested specialization has worked well in a country like Botswana. There, US assistance was sought in the agricultural sector because of American expertise on agricultural production and the similarity, which Botswana has with the American Southwest. And German assistance with vocational training was sought because of the German expertise in that area (Maipose, Somolekae and Johnston, 1997: 25).

The adoption of a joint-donor aid mission approach to aid giving has the added advantage of enabling donors to coordinate the timing of their intervention as well as facilitate the rapid dispatch of evaluation missions to the field. This would also curb the overwhelming effect which many separate donor visits tend to have on the staffing levels of many recipient states. There are, however, some challenges to this proposal. As Lancaster, (1999), accurately observes, it must contend with the possible reluctance of some donors to cede a substantial amount of the responsibility for the design and implementation of their aid to the oversight of other donors. This point is all the more cogent, given the non-developmental motivations behind the allocation of aid by such donors. The hope, however, is that the end of the Cold War has weakened the many non-developmental objectives behind the aid policies of countries like the US and Japan. The time is propitious for the implementation of fresh ideas.

The other consideration is that donor coordination could lead to further decreases in the amount of aid to the region. This need not be the case. Increases in the amount of aid and recommendations for donor coordination ought not to be mutually exclusive, or have an inversely proportional relationship. If the concerns are that government officials would embezzle aid funds, an effective monitoring process, such as the creation or involvement of non-governmental organizations in the process could effectively curtail this problem. There is a lot of work to be done in the region if the goals outlined by the DAC are to be accomplished. What are needed are honest efforts that would address these goals, without providing cover for the continuation of the policies of benign neglect. It would indeed be sad if efforts aimed at the realization of more effective management of aid wins the trust of the people of sub-Saharan Africa, only to give rise to further retrenchment in the provision of financial assistance to the region.[133]

---

[133] On this subject, while I agree with Lancaster (1999:237) that "the level of aid to African countries is not as important as what aid accomplishes", given the needs of the region, it is quite doubtful that any proposal which results in further reductions in the already declining levels of aid to the region would result in significant improvements in the economic and social conditions of the people of the region.

Appendices

APPENDIX 1

A Mathematical Formulation of the Strategic Mineral Index

I have developed the strategic mineral index (SMI) an independent variable to tap into the concept of national interest that is at the core of realist theory. It captures the variation in the strategic value of ODA recipient countries to the donor countries with respect to the latter's quest for access to key minerals and metals. Since World War II strategic minerals and metals have become major factors in every serious conflict. More recently, the technological revolution in the communications, electronics and manufacturing industries has increased the demand for such minerals and metals as chromium, manganese, titanium, aluminum, copper and cobalt because of their crucial uses in the production of military and consumer goods. (Hargreaves and Fromson, 1985:3) Because of this development, the African countries where these minerals and metals are found in significant quantities assume more strategic importance to the national interest of advance-industrialized countries than others who are not so endowed.

The construction of the strategic mineral index (SMI) has several steps. The first step is the identification of thirty-seven minerals that are considered strategic and the determination of the mineral risk assessment for each of them based on their score on seven categories of evaluation.[134] These categories are:
1. Existing Capacity
2. Range of Primary Supply Sources
3. Time Lag for New Supplies
4. Availability of Substitutes
5. Longer Term Substitutability
6. Effect on Key Industries
7. Total Economic Impact.

According to Hargreaves and Fromson, they considered several questions in their development of the assessment indicators for each of the above

---

[134]See Hargreaves and Fromson (1985:5-14) for the methodology for this assessment.

categories. For example, in their determination of the score of each mineral on the "Total Economic Impact" category, they asked two important questions: (1) "Is the metal or mineral used in large weights or volumes worldwide?" (2) "What is its market size?". Based on these questions, they surmised that "it is not surprising that iron, copper and aluminum score highly due to the large tonnage used in almost every type of industry, whilst zirconium, the rare earths, gallium and others score low" (p.11).

Proceeding from this type of assessment, which was done for every one of the seven categories in the mineral risk assessment table, Zambia, for example, has a cumulative Mineral Risk Assessment Score (MRAS) of 28:

Available Strategic Minerals	Mineral Risk Assessment Score
Cobalt	44
Copper	50
Gold	42
Selenium	24
Silver	21
Tellurium	20
Uranium	27
Total	228

The second step in the construction of the SMI is the assignment of points to each ODA recipient country based on its score on the percentage of the minerals' world's total reserve score. There are three sub-steps in the calculation of this score. The first is the determination of the percentage of the world's total reserve of each of the strategic minerals and metals available in a particular ODA recipient country. These figures were derived from *Minerals Handbook 1996-1997,* by Phillip Crowson. Second, points were assigned on a scale of 10-100 to every country for the percentage of the world's total reserve of each of the thirty-seven strategic minerals available in its territory. (See the notes on Appendix II for how points were allocated to each percentage category). Third, the sum of each country's points was then calculated based on the cumulative number of strategic minerals it has and the percentages of the world's total reserve it commands for each mineral. Again, a look at how this was done for Zambia illustrates the point:

Available Minerals	% of World's Total Reserve	Allocated Points
Cobalt	9.1	40
Copper	4.0	30
Gold	< 0.1	10
Selenium	4.3	30
Silver	< 0.1	10
Tellurium	10.1	50
Uranium	< 0.1	10

Zambia's World's Total Resource Score (WTRS) = 180

The first procedure of the final step in the construction of the Strategic Mineral Index (SMI) is to determine the maximum and minimum values for the two strategic mineral indicators – MRAS (variable X_1) and the WTRS (variable X_2) given their actual values.

Next, each strategic mineral indicator then places a country in the range of zero to one as defined by the difference between the maximum and the minimum values. Thus, I_{ij} is the strategic mineral indicator for the jth country with respect to the ith variable, and it is defined as:

$$I_{ij} = \frac{\left(\max_j X_{ij} - X_{ij}\right)}{\left(\max_j X_{ij} - \min_j X_{ij}\right)}$$

The second procedure is to define an average strategic mineral value. This is done by taking a simple average of the two indicators – the MRAS indicator and the WTRS indicator:

$$I_j = \sum_{i=1}^{2} I_{ij}$$

The third procedure is to measure the SMI as one minus the average strategic mineral value:

$$(SMI)_j = (1 - I_j)$$

To illustrate, the application of this formula to Zambia is as follows:

Maximum MRAS = Log of 1225
(Sum of scores for all minerals in the assessment table) =3.09
Minimum MRAS = Log of 15 (Lowest value for one mineral) =1.18
Maximum WTRS = Log of 3700
(Total Number of Minerals (37) x Maximum Possible Points (100)) =3.57
Minimum WTRS = Log of 10 (Value of one mineral x Lowest points) = 1.00

Zambia MRAS = Log of 228 =2.35
Zambia WTRS = Log of 180 =2.26

Zambia's MRAS Indicator
= (3.09 − 2.35) / (3.09 − 1.18) =0.387

Zambia's WTRS Indicator
= (3.57 − 2.26) / (3.57 − 1.00) =0.510

Zambia's average strategic mineral value = (0.387 + 0.510) / 2 =0.449

Zambia's Strategic Mineral Index (SMI) = 1 − 0.449 =0.551

APPENDIX 2

Mineral Risk Assessment Table

#	Name of Mineral	Existing Capacity	Range of Primary Supply	Time Lag for New Supplies	Availability of Substitute	Longer Term Substitutability	Effect on Key Industries	Total Economic Impact	Score
1	Aluminum	1	5	8	9	8	9	10	50
2	Antimony	1	5	4	3	3	3	1	20
3	Beryllium	5	6	6	9	9	7	1	43
4	Bismuth	2	2	2	2	2	3	2	15
5	Cadmium	2	1	1	4	3	5	3	19
6	Chromium	3	9	9	10	8	7	7	53
7	Cobalt	1	8	8	7	7	9	4	44
8	Columbium/Niobium	2	8	5	5	5	6	4	35
9	Copper	2	6	8	9	8	7	10	50
10	Diamond	1	4	6	7	4	8	1	31

11	Gallium	1	2	4	6	6	8	1	28
12	Germanium	5	8	1	9	9	9	1	42
13	Gold	1	10	10	6	6	8	1	42
14	Indium	3	7	7	7	6	9	1	40
15	Iron	1	1	1	10	1	3	10	27
16	Lead	1	2	4	5	5	4	7	28
17	Lithium	1	2	1	4	3	4	2	17
18	Magnesium	1	3	3	6	4	7	4	28
19	Manganese	2	8	6	9	9	7	8	49
20	Mercury	1	3	2	6	5	3	2	22
21	Molybdenum	1	5	8	9	8	9	5	45
22	Nickel	1	1	7	6	6	8	6	35
23	Platinum Gp	1	8	8	5	6	7	2	37
24	Rare Earths	2	4	6	8	6	8	1	35

Appendices 197

25	Rhenium	1	2	7	1	3	6	1	21
26	Selenium	1	1	6	3	4	7	2	24
27	Silicon	1	1	1	6	6	2	10	27
28	Silver	1	1	3	5	5	4	2	21
29	Tantalum	1	7	8	6	7	8	1	38
30	Tellurium	1	3	4	3	3	5	1	20
31	Tin	1	7	7	3	3	5	6	32
32	Titanium	1	7	7	8	8	10	6	47
33	Tungsten	1	6	5	6	6	7	5	36
34	Uranium	1	2	4	7	3	7	3	27
35	Vanadium	1	7	9	7	6	6	4	40
36	Zinc	1	3	4	5	5	5	7	30
37	Zirconium	2	4	5	5	4	3	4	27

Source: D. Hargreaves and S. Fromson: World Index of Strategic Minerals: Production, Exploitation and Risk. New York: Facts on File, Inc. 1985.

Notes

Hargreaves and Fromson utilized 13 categories in their calculation of the overall risk assessment for each mineral. Six of these categories – violent conflict (which measured the extent of violent conflict in a mineral producing country), labor disputes, primary and secondary transportation risks, collusive price agreements, and embargoes – have been omitted from consideration in the above table for two reasons: first, Hargreaves and Fromson's ratings for such categories as violent conflict, primary and secondary transportation risks are neither current, nor do they do have the level of importance which they had when they were first used more than a decade ago. Second, in tandem with the forgoing point, categories like embargoes, and to a lesser extent, labor disputes have declined in importance since the end of Cold War because of the transformation in US-Russian relations from confrontation and competition to accommodation and cooperation.

PERCENTAGE OF WORLD'S MINERALS TOTAL RESERVE SCALE

PERCENTAGE (%)	POINTS
- 0.9	10
1-2	20
3-5	30
6-9	40
10-13	50
14-17	60
18-21	70
22-25	80
26-29	90
30 and Above	100

Notes

The assignment of points to each percentage category in this table follows an ascending order whereby higher percentage figures for a country's mineral reserve corresponds to higher points until the 30 percent cut off point. The rationale for choosing 30 percent as the cut off point for maximum points is two fold: first, in practical terms, a country rarely commands more than 30 percent of the world's known reserve for any mineral. Second, even in those rare cases where a country commands more than 30 percent, but less than 75 percent of the world's known reserve for a particular mineral, that fact does not significantly confer additional premium on such country as it would if it commands only 30 percent of such natural resource. There appears to be a law of diminishing marginal utility between the 30 and 75 percentage points. The exception that would require the allocation of higher points is if a particular country enjoyed a virtual monopoly (above 75 percent) in the possession of a particular mineral, such as Zimbabwe and South Africa combined have in chromite reserves. With respect to the For the African countries in this study, however, none alone enjoys such monopoly over any strategic mineral.

Appendix 3
Table of Comparative Indicators of Capabilities for All Donors (1994)

	Canada	Denmark	France	Germany	Italy
Population (million)	28.4	5.2	58	81.3	58.2
Geographic Size (Total Area: sq km)	9,976,140	43,070	547,030	356,910	301,230
Comparative Area	Slightly larger than the US	About twice the size of Massachusetts	About twice the size of Colorado	Slightly smaller than Montana	Slightly larger than Arizona
GDP (1994)	639.8 ($billion)	103 ($billion)	1.08 ($trillion)	1.3 ($trillion)	998.9 ($billion)
Per Capita GDP	$22,760	$19,860	$18,670	$16,580	$17,980
Defense Expenditure ($billion)	9.0	2.7	47.1	40	21.5
Males fit for military service (million)	6.5	1.3	12.2	17.4	12

	Japan	Norway	Sweden	United Kingdom	United States
Population (million)	125.5	4.3	8.8	58.2	263.8
Geographic (Total Area:sq km)	377,835	324,220	449,964	244,280	9,372,610
Comparative Area	Slightly smaller than California	Slightly larger than New Mexico	Slightly smaller than California	Slightly smaller than Oregon	Two and one half times the size of Western Europe
GDP (1994)	2.5 ($trillion)	95.7 ($billion)	163.1 ($billion)	1.4 ($trillion)	6.7 ($trillion)
Per Capita GDP	$20,200	$22,170	$18,580	$17,980	$25,850
Defense Expenditure ($billion)	47.2	3.4	5.4	35.1	284.4
Males fit for military service (million)	27.4	928,774	1.8	12	N/A

Source: CIA World Fact Book, 1995

Appendix 4
Table of Minerals Import Dependence 1994 (In Percentages)
Import as a Percentage of Domestic Consumption plus Exports

	United Kingdom	European Union	Japan	United States
Aluminium	74	70	77	63
Antimony	100	100	100	100
Beryllium	100	100	100	23
Bismuth	100	N/A	46	94
Cadmium	100	19	58	29
Chromium	100	99	99	100
Cobalt	100	100	100	100
Copper	67	69	94	22
Gallium	N/A	N/A	N/A	N/A
Germanium	100	N/A	N/A	N/A
Indium	N/A	N/A	62	100
Iron Ore	100	94	100	23
Lead	59	32	78	13
Lithium	100	100	100	22
Magnesium	100	100	59	10
Manganese	100	100	100	100
Mercury	100	N/A	N/A	14
Molybdenum	100	100	100	-
Nickel	100	91	92	84
Niobium	100	100	100	100
Platinum Group	100	100	100	64
Rare Earths	100	100	100	-
Rhenium	100	100	100	-
Selenium	100	100	5	51
Silicon	100	74	100	39
Silver	75	79	71	42
Tantalum	100	100	100	100
Tellurium	100	N/A	N/A	N/A
Tin	100	80	96	88
Titanium	100	100	100	66
Tungsten	100	99	100	76
Uranium	100	85	100	N/A
Vanadium	100	100	92	68
Zinc	100	91	75	52
Zirconium	100	100	100	48

Source: Crowson, Phillip. Minerals Handbook, 1996-97. New York: Van Norstrand Reinhold (1997).

Bibliography

Amin, Samir. (1976), *Unequal Development*. New York: Monthly Press Review.

Ampiah, Kweku. (1996), "Japanese Aid to Tanzania: A Study of the Political Marketing of Japan in Africa." *African Affairs*, 95, pp. 107-124.

Arase, David. (1995), *Buying Power: The Political Economy of Japan's Foreign Aid*. London: Lynne Reinner.

Aron, Raymond. (1967), "What is a Theory of International Politics?" *Journal of International Affairs*, 21, pp.185-206.

Aryeetey, Ernest and Aidan Cox. (1997), "Aid Effectiveness in Ghana," in Jerker Carlsson, Gloria Somolekae and Nicholas Van de Walle (eds), *Foreign Aid in Africa: Learning From Country Experiences*. Uppsala, Sweden: Nordiska Afrikaininstutet.

Ashley, Richard K. (1984), "The Poverty of Neorealism." *International Organization*, 38, pp.255-286.

Babst, Dean V. (1964), "Elective Governments—A Force for Peace." *The Wisconsin Sociologist*, 3:1 pp. 9-14.

Baldwin, David. (1966), "Analytical Notes on Foreign Aid and Politics." *Background*, 10 pp. 66-90. *Economic Statecraft*. Princeton, NJ: University Press. (1985).

Ball, George W. and Douglas B. Ball. (1992), *The Passionate Attachment: America's Involvement With Israel, 1947 to the Present*. New York: W.W.Norton & Company.

Barbieri, Katherine. (1996), "Economic Interdependence: A Pathway to Peace or a Source of Interstate Conflict?" *Journal of Peace Research*, 33:1, pp. 29-49.

Bates, Robert. (1981), *Markets and States in Tropical Africa: The Political Basis of Agricultural Policies*. Berkeley: University of California Press.

Bauer, Peter T. (1972), *Dissent on Development*. Cambridge, MA: Harvard University Press.

(1984), *Reality and Rhetoric: Studies in the Economics of Development*. Cambridge, MA: Harvard University Press.

Bauer, Peter T. and Bail S. Yamey. (1983), "Foreign Aid: What is at Stake?" in W.S. Thompson (ed.), *The Third World: Premises of US Policy*. San Francisco: Institute for Contemporary Studies, pp. 75-115.

Beck, Nathaniel and Jonathan N. Katz. (1995), "What to do (And not do) With Time Series Cross Section Data." *American Political Science Review*, 89:3, pp. 634-647.

Bencivenga, Valerie R. (1984), "An Economic Model of the Geographic Distribution of Foreign Aid." Ph.D. Dissertation, University of Toronto.

(1985), "Explaining the Foreign Aid Policies of the OECD Donors." *Working Papers in Economics*, No. 257, Santa Barbara: University of California.

Bennett, James and Walter Williams. (1981), *Strategic Minerals: The Economic Impact of Supply Disruptions*. Washington, DC: The Heritage Foundation.

Biersteker, Thomas. (1993), "Evolving Perspectives on International Political Economy: Twentieth Century Contexts and Discontinuities." *International Political Science Review*, Vol.4, No.1, pp.17-33.

Bobrow, Davis and Mark A. Boyer. (1996), "Bilateral and Multilateral Foreign Aid: Japan's Approach in Comparative Perspective." *Review of International Political Economy*, Vol.3, No.1, pp.95-121.

(1997), "Maintaining System Stability: International Cooperation in the Foreign Aid Arena." *Journal of International Relations*, Vol.1, No.4, pp.84-111.

(1998), "International System Stability and American Decline: A Case for Muted Optimism." *International Journal*, Vol.53, No.2, pp.285-305.

Bollini, Paola and Michael Reich. (1994), "Italian Fight Against World Hunger. A Critical Analysis of Italian Aid for Development in the 1980s." *Social Science and Medicine*, Vol.39, No.5, pp.607-620.

Boone, Peter. (1996), "Politics and Effectiveness of Aid." *European Economic Review*, Vol. 40, No. 2, pp. 289-317.

Boyd, J. Barron. (1982), "France and the Third World: The African Connection," in Taylor and Gregory A. Raymonds (eds), *Third World Policies of Industrialized Nations*. Westport, CT: Greenwood Press.

Boyer, Mark A. (1989), "Trading Public Goods in the Western Alliance System." *Journal of Conflict Resolution*, Vol.33, No.4, pp. 700-727.

(1993), *International Cooperation and Public Goods: Opportunities for the Western Alliance*. Baltimore: Johns Hopkins University Press.

Brandt Commission. (1980), North-South: *A Program for Survival: Independent Commission on International Development Issues under the Chairmanship of Willie Brandt*. Cambridge, MA: The MIT Press.

Bremer, Stuart. (1992), "Dangerous Dyads: Conditions Affecting the Likelihood of Interstate War (1816-1965)." *Journal of Conflict Resolution*, Vol.36, No.2, pp.309-344.

Breuning, Marijke. (1995), "Words and Deeds: Foreign Assistance Rhetoric and Policy Behavior in the Netherlands, Belgium, and the United Kingdom." *International Studies Quarterly*, Vol.39, pp.235-254.

Browne, Stephen. (1990), *Foreign Aid in Practice*, New York: New York University Press.

Burnside, Craig and David Dollar. (1997), "Aid Spurs Growth in a Sound Policy Environment." *Finance and Development*, Vol.34, No.4, pp.4-7.

Butterfield, Herbert. (1966), "The Balance of Power," in Herbert Butterfield and Martin Wight (eds), *Diplomatic Investigations*. London: George Allen and Unwin.

Buzan, Barry, Charles Jones, and Richard Little. (1993), *The Logic of Anarchy*:

Rethinking Neorealism. New York: Columbia University Press.

Calder, K.E. (1998), "Japan's Foreign Policy Formation: Explaining the 'Reactive State'." *World Politics*, Vol.40, pp.517-541.

Caprioli, Mary. (1999), *Predicting Bellicosity: The Role of Democracy, Equality, and Economics.* Ph.D. Dissertation. University of Connecticut.

Carr, Edward Halett. (1951), *The Twenty Years' Crisis 1919-1939: An Introduction to the Study of International Relations.* London: Macmillan.

Cerny, Phillip G. (1995), Globalization and the Changing Logic of Collective Action." *International Organization*, Vol.49, No.4, pp.595-625.

Chan, Steve. (1984), "Mirror, Mirror on the Wall ... Are the Freer Countries More Pacific?" *Journal of Conflict Resolution*, Vol.28, No.4, pp.617-648.

Chenery, Hollis and Allan Strout. (1966), "Foreign Assistance and Economic Development." *American Economic Review*, Vol.56, No.4, pp.679-733.

Chow, Jack. (1996), "Health and International Security." *The Washington Quarterly* Vol.19, No.2, pp.63-77.

Christensen, Thomas J. and Jack Snyder. (1990), "Chain Gangs and Passed Bucks: Predicting Alliance Pattern in Multipolarity." *International Organization*, Vol.44, pp.137-68.

Cohen, Mark. (1995), *United States: The Reality of Aid.* London: Earthscan Publications, Limited/Actionaid.

Coleman, J.S. and C.G. Rosberg. (1970), *Political Parties and National Integration in Tropical Africa.* Berkeley: University of California Press.

Copeson, Raymond, Theodore Galdi and Larry Nowels. (1986), The US Aid to Africa: *The Record, the Rationale, and the Challenge.* Congressional Research Service, Library of Congress.

Crowson, Phillip. (1997), *Minerals Handbook* (1996-97). New York: Van Norstrand Reinhold.

Cumming, Gordon. (1995), "French Development Assistance to Africa: Towards a New Agenda?" *African Affairs*, Vol.94, pp.383-398.

Dahrendorf, Ralf. (1959), *Class and Class Conflict in Industrial Society.* Stanford: Stanford University Press.

Davenport, M. (1970), "The Allocation of Foreign Aid: A Cross-Section Study." *Yorkshire Bulletin of Economic and Social Research*, Vol.22, No.1, pp.26-41.

David, Steven R. (1989), "Why the Third World Matters." *International Security*, Vol.14, No.1, pp.50-85.

——— (1993), "Why the Third World Still Matters." *International Security*, Vol.17, No.3, pp.127-159.

Desch, C. Michael. (1989), "The Keys that Lock Up the World: Identifying American Interests in the Periphery." *International Security*, Vol.14, No.1, pp.86-122.

——— (1996), "Why Realists Disagree about the Third World (And Why They Shouldn't)," in Benjamin Frankel (ed.), *Realism: Restatements and Renewals.* London: Frank Cass.

Dewald Michael and Rolf Weder. (1996), "Comparative Advantage and Bilateral Foreign Aid Policy." *World Development,* Vol.24, No.3, pp.549-556.

Dixon, William. (1994), "Democracy and the Peaceful Settlement of International Conflict." *American Political Science Review,* Vol.88, No.1, pp.14-32.

Dougherty, James E. and Robert L. Pfaltzgraff Jr. (1990), *Contending Theories of International Relations,* 3rd ed. New York: Harper and Row.

Doyle, Michael W. (1996), "Kant, Liberal Legacies and Foreign Affairs," in Miller E. Brown, Sean M. Jones and Steven Miller (eds), *Debating the Democratic Peace: An International Security Reader.* Cambridge, Massachusetts and London, England: The MIT Press.

(1997), *Ways of War and Peace: Realism, Liberalism and Socialism.* New York: Norton Press.

Dudley, Leonard and Claude Monmarquette. (1978), *The Supply of Canadian Foreign Aid: Explanation and Evaluation.* Ottawa: Economic Council of Canada.

Dumm, John, et al. (1992), *Evaluation of Aid Family Planning Programs: Kenya Case Studies. Technical Report 3.* Washington, D.C.: Center for Development Information and Evaluation, USAID.

East, Maurice. A. (1973), "Size and Foreign Policy Behavior: A Test of Two Models." *World Politics* XXXV, pp.556-576.

Eberstadt, Nicholas. (1988), *American Foreign Aid and American Purpose.* Washington, D.C.: American Enterprise Institute for Public Policy Research.

Elman, Colin. (1996), "Horses for Courses: Why not Neorealist Theories of Foreign Policy." *Security Studies,* Vol.6, pp. 7-53.

Elman, Colin and Miriam Fendius Elman. (1995), "Correspondence: History vs. Neorealism: A Second Look." *International Security,* Vol.20, pp.182-93.

(1997), "Lakatos and Neorealism: A Reply to Vasquez." *American Political Science Review,* Vol.91, No.4, pp.923-26.

Evans, Graham and Jefrey Newnham. (1998), *Dictionary of International Relations.* New York: Penguin Putnam, Inc.

Evans, Howard. (1989), "France and the Third World: Cooperation or Dependence?" in Robert Aldrich and John Connell (eds), *France in World Politics.* London: Routledge.

Feyzioglu, Tarhan, Vinaya Swaroop, and Min Zhu. (1998), A Panel Data Analysis of the Fungibility of Foreign Aid", *The World Bank Economic Review,* Vol.12, No.1, pp.29-44.

Forde, Steven. (1995), "International Realism and the Science of Politics: Thucydides, Machiavelli, and Neorealism." *International Studies Quarterly,* 39, pp.141-160.

Frank, Andre Gunder. (1970), *Latin America: Underdevelopment or Revolution.* New York: Monthly Review Press.

Frank, Charles R. and Mary Baird. (1975), "Foreign Aid: Its Speckled Past and Future Prospects." *International Organization,* Vol.29, No.1, pp.133-167.

Freedom House. *Freedom in the World,* Lanham, MD University Press of America.

(Various Years).

French, Howard. "Furor in Japan as Military Official Advocates Nuclear Weapon," *New York Times*, October 21, 1999.

Fukuyama, Francis. (1990), "The End of History?" *The National Interest*, 16 (Summer, 1990): 3-18.

Gabas, Jean-Jacques, Yves A. Faure, and Alice Sindzinger. (1997), "The Effectiveness of French Aid in Burkina Faso," in Jerker Carlesson, Gloria Somolekae and Nicholas Van de Walle (eds), Uppsala, Sweden: *Foreign Aid in Africa: Learning From Country Experiences. Nordiska Afrikaininstutet*.

Geddis, John Lewis. (1982), *Strategies of Containment: A Critical Appraisal of Postwar American National Security Policies*. Oxford: Oxford University Press.

Gilpin, Robert. (1981), *War and Change in World Politics*. Cambridge: Cambridge University Press.

(1987), *The Political Economy of International Relations*. Princeton, NJ: Princeton University Press.

(1996), "No One Loves a Political Realist," in Benjamin Frankel (ed.), *Realism: Restatement and Renewal*. London: Frank Cass.

(2000), *The Challenge of Global Capitalism: The World Economy in the 21st Century*, Princeton: Princeton University Press.

Glaser, Charles. (1995), "Realists as Optimists: Cooperation as Self Help." *International Security*, Vol.19, No.3, pp.50-90.

Gleditsch, Nils Peter. (1992), "Democracy and Peace." *Journal of Peace Research*, Vol.29, No.4.

Graham, Carol and Michael O'Harlon. (1997), "Making Foreign Aid Work." *Foreign Affairs*, Vol.76, No.4, pp.96-104.

Grieco, Joseph M. (1995), "Anarchy and the Limits of Cooperation: A Realist Critique of the Newest Liberal Institutionalism," in Charles W. Kegley (ed.), *Controversies in International Relations Theory: Realism and the Neoliberal Challenge*. New York: St. Martin's Press.

Griffiths, Martin. (1992), "Order and International Society: The Real Realism?" *Review of International Studies*, Vol.18, pp.217-240.

Grunbaum, Adolf. (1976), "Can a Theory Answer More Questions than One of its Rivals?" *British Journal for the Philosophy of Science*, Vol.27, pp.1-23.

Gyimah-Brempong, Kwabena. (1992), "Aid and Economic Growth in LDCs: Evidence From Sub-Saharan Africa." *The Review of Black Political Economy*, Winter, pp. 31-52.

Hancock, Graham. (1989), Lords of Poverty: *The Power, Prestige, and Corruption of the International Aid Business*. New York: Atlantic Monthly Press.

Handwerker, W. Penn and Stephen P. Borgatti. (1998), "Reasoning With Numbers," in H. Russell Bernard (ed.), *Handbook of Methods in Cultural Anthropology*. London: Altamira Press.

Hansen, Henrik and Finn Tarp. (2000), "Aid and the Growth Regression", *Journal of*

Development Economics, Vol.64, No.2, pp.547-570.

Hargreaves, D. and S. Fromson. (1985), *World Index of Strategic Minerals: Production, Exploitation and Risk*. New York: Facts On File, Inc.

Hayter, Theresa. (1971), *Aid as Imperialism*. Harmondsworth, Middlesex: Penguin.

——— (1981), *The Creation of Poverty*. London: Pluto Press.

——— (1966), *French Aid*. London: Overseas Development Institute.

Healey, John. (1996), "The Management of British Bilateral Aid and its Effectiveness." *Working Paper No.10*. Maastricht, European Center for Development Policy Management.

Heilbroner, Robert. (1989), The Worldly Philosophers: *The Lives, Times and Ideas of the Great Economic Thinkers*. New York: Simon & Schuster.

Helleiner, Gerald K. (1984), *Canada, the Developing Countries and the International Economy: What Next?* Working Paper No. B.5, Development Studies Program, University of Toronto.

Henderson, P.D. (1971), "The Distribution of Official Development Assistance Commitments by Recipients and Sources." *Oxford Bulletin of Economics and Statistics*, Vol.31, No.1

Hoadley, Stephen. J. (1980), "Small States as Aid Donors." *International Organization*, Vol.34, No.1, pp.121-137.

Hobbes, Thomas. (1968), *Leviathan*. C.B. Macpherson, ed., Harmondsworth, U.K: Penguin Books.

Holsti, K.J. (1987), "Toward a Theory of Foreign Policy: Making the Case for Role Analysis," in Stephen G. Walker (ed.), *Role Theory in Foreign Policy Analysis*. Durham, NC: Duke University Press.

——— (1991), "International Systems, Systems Change, and Foreign Policy." *Diplomatic History*, Vol.15, pp.83-89.

Hook, Steven W. (1995), *National Interest and Foreign Aid*. Boulder, CO: Lynne Reinner Publishers.

——— (1996) (ed.), *Foreign Aid Toward the Millennium*. Boulder, CO: Lynne Reinner.

Hook, Steven and Guang Zhang. (1998), "Japan's Policy Since the Cold War: Rhetoric or Reality." *Asian Survey*, Vol.XXXVIII, No.11, pp.1051-1067.

Howard, Michael. (1978), *War and the Liberal Conscience*. London: Temple Smith.

Huntington, Samuel P. (1991), *The Third Wave: Democratization in the Late Twentieth Century*. Norman, OK: Oklahoma University Press.

——— (1996), *The Clash of Civilizations and the Remaking of World Order*. New York: Simon & Schuster.

International Monetary Fund. *Direction of Trade Statistics Yearbook*, Washington, D.C. (Various Years).

Ishihara, Shintaro. (1991), *The Japan that Can Say No*. New York: Simon & Schuster.

Janoski, Thomas and Larry Isaac. (1994), "Introduction to Time Series Analysis," in Thomas Janoski and Alexander Hicks (eds), *The Comparative Political Economy of the Welfare State.* New York: Cambridge University Press.

Jervis, Robert. (1978), "Cooperation Under the Security Dilemma." *World Politics*, Vol.30, pp.167-214.

Kaplan, Morton. (1957), *System and Process in International Politics.* New York: Wiley.

Karre, Bo and Bengt Svensson. (1989), "The Determinants of Swedish Aid Policy," in Olav Stokke (ed.), *Western Middle Powers and Global Poverty: Determinants of the Aid Policies of Canada, Denmark, the Netherlands, Norway, and Sweden.* Uppsala: Scandinavian Institute of African Studies.

Kegley, W. Charles. (1995) (ed.), *Controversies in International Relations Theory: Realism and the Neoliberal Challenge.* New York: St. Martin's Press, 1995.

——— (1993), "The Neoidealist Moment in International Studies? Realist Myths and the New International Realities." *International Studies Quarterly*, Vol.37, pp.131-46.

——— (1994), "How Did the Cold War Die? Principles for an Autopsy." *International Studies Review*, Vol.38, Supplement 1, pp. 11-14.

Kennedy, Paul. (1987), *The Rise and Fall of the Great Powers.* New York: Random House.

Keohane, Robert O. (1984), *After Hegemony: Cooperation and Discord in the World Political Economy.* Princeton, NJ: Princeton University Press.

——— (1990), "International Liberalism Reconsidered," in John Dunn (ed.), *The Economic Limits of Modern Politics.* Cambridge: Cambridge University Press.

Keohane, Robert O. and Joseph S. Nye. (2001), *Power and Interdependence.* 3rd Edition, New York: Longman.

King, Gary, Robert Keohane, and Sidney Verba. (1994), *Designing Social Inquiry: Scientific Inference in Qualitative Research.* Princeton, New Jersey: Princeton University Press.

Knorr, Klaus. (1973), *Power and Wealth: The Political Economy of International Power.* New York: Basic Books.

Kolodziej, Edward A. (1974), *French Foreign Policy Under De Gaulle and Pompidou: The Politics of Grandeur.* Ithaca, NY: Cornell University Press.

Krasner, Stephen D. (1978), *Defending the National Interest: Raw Materials Investments and US Foreign Policy.* Princeton, NJ: Princeton University Press.

——— (1983) (ed.), *International Regimes.* Ithaca, NY: Cornell University Press.

——— "Structural Causes and Regime Consequences: Regimes as Intervening Variables." *International Organization*, Vol. 36, pp.185-206.

Kratochwil, Friedrich. (1982), "On the Notion of 'Interest' in International Relations." *International Organization*, Vol.36, pp.1-30.

——— (1993), "The Embarrassment of Changes: Neorealism as the Science of Realpolitik Without Politics." *Review of International Studies*, Vol.19, pp. 63-80.

Kristoff, Nicholas. "National Critical of US Base is Elected Governor of Tokyo," New York Times, August 26, 1999.

Kruger, Ann. (1993), *Economic Policies at Cross-Purposes: The US and Developing Countries*. Washington, D.C.: The Brookings Institute.

Kuhn, Thomas. (1970), *The Structure of Scientific Revolutions*. Chicago: University of Chicago Press.

——— (1970), "Reflections on My Critics," in Imre Lakatos and Alan Musgrave (eds), *Criticism and the Growth of Knowledge: Proceedings of the International Colloquium in the Philosophy of Science*. London, 1965, Vol.4. Cambridge University Press.

Kull, Steven. (1995), *Americans and Foreign Aid*. Program on International Policy Attitudes, School of Public Affairs, University of Maryland.

Kuznets, Simon. (1995), "Economic Growth and Income Inequality." *American Economic Review*, Vol.45, No.1, pp.1-29.

Lakatos, Imre. "Falsification and the Methodology of Scientific Research Programs," in Imre Lakatos and Alan Musgrave (eds.) *Criticism and the Growth of Knowledge: Proceedings of the International Colloquium in the Philosophy of Science, London, 1965*, Vol.4. Cambridge University Press.

Lake, David A. (1983), "International Economic Structures and American Foreign Economic Policy, 1887-1934." *World Politics*, Vol.36, pp.517-543.

Lancaster, Carol. (1991), "The New Politics of US Aid to Africa." *Africa Notes, CSIS*.

——— (1992), "New Directions For US Foreign Aid." *Trans Africa Forum*, pp.53-67.

——— (1999), *Aid to Africa: So Much to do, So Little Done*. Chicago: University of Chicago Press.

Lavergne, Real P. (1987), *Canadian Development Assistance to Senegal*. Ottawa: North-South Institute.

——— (1989), "Determinants of Canadian Aid Policy," in Olav Stokke (ed.), *Western Middle Powers and Global Poverty: Determinants of the Aid Policies of Canada, Denmark, the Netherlands, Norway, and Sweden*. Uppsala: Scandinavian Institute of African Studies.

Layne, Christopher. (1993), "The Unipolar Illusion: Why Great Powers Will Rise." *International Security*, Vol.17, No.4, pp.5-51.

——— (1996), "Kant or Cant: The Myth of the Democratic Peace," in Michael E. Brown, Sean M. Lynn-Jones and Steven Miller (eds.) *Debating the Democratic Peace: An International Security Reader*. Cambridge, Massachusetts and London, England: The MIT Press.

Lederberg, Joshua. (1996), "Infectious Disease: A Threat to Global Health and Security." *JAMA*, Vol.276, No.5, pp.417-419.

Lederberg, Joshua, R.E. Shope and S. C. Oaks. (eds.) (1992), *Emerging Infections: Microbial Threats to Health in the United States*. Washington, DC. National Academy Press.

Lefebvre, Jeffrey. (1993), *Arms For the Horn: US Security Policy in Ethiopia and Somalia (1953-1991)* Pittsburgh, PA: University of Pittsburgh Press.

Lensik, Robert and Oliver Morrissey. (2000), "Aid Instability as a Measure of Uncertainty, and the Positive Impact of Aid on Growth" *The Journal of Development Studies*, Vol.29, No.1, pp.31-49.

Levy, Jack. (1989), "Domestic Politics and War," in Robert I. Rothberg and Theodore K. Rabb, *The Origins and the Prevention of Major Wars*. New York: Cambridge University Press.

Loriaux, Michael. (1992). "The Realists and Saint Augustine: Skepticism, Psychology and Moral Action in International Relations Thought." *International Studies Quarterly*, Vol.36, pp. 401-420.

Lumsdaine, David Halloran. (1993), *Moral Visions in International Politics: The Foreign Aid Regime 1949-1989*. Princeton, NJ: Princeton University Press.

Machiavelli, Niccolo. (1950), *The Prince and the Discourses*. New York: Random House.

Maipose, Gervse, Gloria Somolekae and Timothy Johnston. (1997), "Effective Aid Management: The Case of Botswana," in Jerker Carlsson, Gloria Somolekae and Nicholas Van de Walle (eds.), *Foreign Aid in Africa: Learning From Country Experiences*. Uppsala, Sweden: Nordiska Afrikaininstutet.

Maizels, Alfred and Machiko K. Nissanke. (1984), "Motivations for Aid to Developing Countries." *World Development*, Vol.12, pp.879-900.

Mansour, Camille. (1994), *Beyond Alliance: Israel and U.S. Foreign Policy*. New York: Columbia University Press.

Maoz, Zeev and Nasrin Abdolali. (1989), "Regime Types and International Conflict, 1816-1976." *Journal of Conflict Resolution*, Vol.33, No.1, pp.3-35.

Maoz, Zeev and Bruce Russett. (1993), "Normative and Structural Causes of Democratic Peace, 1946-1980." *American Political Science Review*, Vol.87, No. 3, pp.624-638.

McGillivray, Mark. (1989) "The Allocation of Aid Among Developing Countries: A Multidonor Analysis Using a Per Capita Aid Index." *World Development*, Vol.17, pp. 561-568.

McKinlay, R. D. (1979), "The Aid Relationship: A Foreign Policy Model and Interpretation of the Distributions of Official Bilateral Economic Aid of the United States, the United Kingdom, France, and Germany 1960-1970." *Comparative Political Studies*, Vol.11, No.4, pp.411-463.

McKinlay, R.D. and R.D. Little. (1977), "A Foreign Policy Model of US Bilateral Aid Allocation." *World Politics*, XXX:1.

(1978a), "The French Aid Relationship: A Foreign Policy Model of the Distribution of French Bilateral Aid, 1964-1970." *Development and Change*, Vol.9.

(1978b), "A Foreign Policy Model of British Bilateral Aid, 1960-1970." *British Journal of Political Science*.

(1979), "The US Aid Relationship: A Test of the Recipient Need and Donor Interest Models." *Political Studies*, Vol.27, pp.236-250.

Measheimer, John. (1990), "Back to the Future: Instability in Europe After the Cold

War." *International Security*, Vol.15, pp.5-56.

(1995), "The False Promise of International Institutions." *International Security*, Vol.19, No.3, pp.5-49.

(1995), "A Realist Reply." *International Security*, Vol.21, pp.82-93.

Meernik, James, Eric L. Krueger, and Steven C. Poe. (1998), "Testing Models of US Foreign Policy: Foreign Aid During and After the Cold War." *The Journal of Politics*, Vol.60, No.1, pp.63-85.

Miyashita, Akitoshi (1999), "Gaiatsu and Japan's Foreign Aid: Rethinking the Reactive – Proactive Debate." *International Studies Quarterly*, Vol.43, No.4, pp. 695-731.

Morgenthau, Hans J. (1973), *Politics Among Nations: The Struggle for Power and Peace*, 5th Edition. New York: Knopf.

(1952), "Another 'Great Debate': The National Interest of the United States." *American Political Science Review*, Vol.XLVI, No.4, pp.961-988.

(1962), "A Political Theory of Foreign Aid." *American Political Science Review*, Vol.56, pp.301-309.

Morrison, Donald G., Robert Cameron Mitchell and John Naber Padden. (1989), Black Africa: *A Comparative Handbook*, 2nd Edition. New York: Irvington.

Mosley, Paul. (1985), "The Political Economy of Foreign Aid: A Model of the Market for a Public Good." *Economic Development and Cultural Change*, Vol.33, No.2, pp.373-394.

(1987), *Foreign Aid: Its Defense and Reform*. Lexington, KY: University of Kentucky Press.

Moss, Johanna, and John Ravenhill. (1989), "Trade Diversification in Black Africa." *Journal of Modern African Studies*, Vol.27.

Mueller, John. (1989), *Retreat from Doomsday: The Obsolescence of Major War*. New York: Basic Books.

(1995), *Quiet Cataclysm: Reflections on the Recent Transformation of World Politics*, New York: Harper Collins.

Nelson, J.M. (1968), *Aid, Influence and Foreign Policy*. New York: Macmillan.

New York Times. "Excerpts From President Clinton's State of the Union Message." (January 26, 1994): A,17.

Noel, Alain and Jean-Philippe Theiren. (1995), "From Domestic to International Justice: The Welfare State and Foreign Aid." *International Organization*, Vol.49, No.3, pp.523-53.

Norusis, Marija. (1997), SPSS: *Guide to Data Analysis*. New Jersey: Prentice Hall.

Nunan, Richard. (1984), "Novel Facts, Bayesian Rationality, and the History of Continental Drift." *Studies in History and Philosophy of Science*, Vol.15, No.4 pp.267-307.

OECD. *Development Cooperation*. (Various Years) Paris: OECD.

Olsen, Gorm-Rye. (1996), "Do Ethics Matter in International Relations?: A Discussion of Ethics as a Determinant of European Aid to Sub-Saharan Africa in the Post Cold

War Era." *Journal of Developing Societies*, Vol.XII, No.2, pp.232-253.

O'Neal, John. R., Francis H. O'Neal, Zeev Maoz and Bruce Russett. (1996) "The Liberal Peace: Interdependence, Democracy and International Conflict, 1950-85." *Journal of Peace Research*, 33:1 (1996): 11-28.

Opeskin, B.R. (1996), "The Moral Foundations of Aid." *World Development*, Vol.24, No.1, pp.21- 44.

Organski, A. F. K. (1990), *The $36 Billion Bargain: Strategy and Politics in US Assistance to Israel*. New York: Columbia University Press.

Ostrom, Charles, Jr. (1978), *Time Series Analysis: Regression Techniques*. Beverly Hills, CA: Sage Publications.

Owen, John. M. (1996), "How Liberalism Produces Democratic Peace," in Michael E. Brown, Sean M. Lynn-Jones and Steven Miller (eds), *Debating the Democratic Peace: An International Security Reader*. Cambridge, Massachusetts and London, England: The MIT Press.

Oye, Kenneth A. (1992), "Beyond Postwar Order and New World Order: American Foreign Policy in Transition," in Oye, Kenneth A., Robert J. Leiber and Donald Rothschild (eds.), *Eagle in a New World*. New York: Harper Collins.

Packenham, R.A (1976), "Trends in Brazilian National Dependency Since 1964," in Riodan Roett (ed.), *Brazil in the Seventies*. Washington, D.C.: American Enterprise Institute.

Paone, Michael Rocco. (1992), *Strategic Non-Fuel Minerals and Western Security*. Laham, MD: University Press of America.

Patterson, Rubin. (1997), *Foreign Aid After the Cold War: The Dynamics of Multipolar Economic Competition*. Trenton, NJ: Africa World Press, Inc.

Pearson, Lester B. (1969), *Partners in Development: Report of the Commission on International Development*. New York: Praeger.

Pincus, J.A. (1967), *Trade, Aid and Development*. New York: McGraw-Hill.

Pirages, Dennis. (1995), "Micro security: Disease Organisms and Human Well-being." *Washington Quarterly*, Vol.18, No.4, pp.5-12.

Plischke, Elmer. (1976), "Microstates in World Affairs: Policy, Problems, and Choices," Washington, D.C.: *American Enterprise Institute*.

Poe, Steven C. (1991), "US Economic Aid Allocation: The Quest for Cumulation." *International Interactions*, Vol.16, pp.295-316.

Poe, Steven C. and James Meernik. (1995), "US Aid in the 80s: A Global Analysis." *The Journal of Peace Research*, Vol.32, pp.399-412.

Poe, Steven C., Suzanne Pilatovsky, Brian Miller and Ayo Ogundele. (1994), "Human Rights and US Foreign Aid Revisited: The Latin American Region." *Human Rights Quarterly*, Vol.16, pp.539-558.

Poe, Steven C. and Rangsima Sirirangsi. (1994), "Human Rights and US Economic Aid During the Reagan Years." *Social Science Quarterly*, Vol.75, pp.494-509.

Polanyi, Karl. (1957), *The Great Transformation: The Political and Economic Origins of Our Time*. Boston: Beacon Press.

Porter, Gareth. (1995), "Environmental Security as a National Security Issue." *Current History*, pp.218-222.

Pratt, Crawford. (1982), "Canadian Foreign Policy: Bias to Business." *International Perspectives*, Vol.3, No.6.

——— (1993), "Canada's Development Assistance: Some Lessons From the Last Review." *International Journal*, Vol. XLIX.

Przerworski, Adam and Henry Teune. (1967), "Equivalence in Cross-National Research." *Public Opinion Quarterly*, Vol.30.

Redtzki, Mariam. (1991), "Swedish Aid to Kenya and Tanzania: Its Effect on Rural Development, 1970-84," in Uma Lele (ed.), *Aid to African Agriculture: Lessons from Two Decades of Donors' Experience*. Baltimore: Johns Hopkins University Press.

Richardson, Neil. (1995), "International Trade as a Force for Peace," in Charles W. Kegley (ed.), *Controversies in International Relations Theory: Realism and the Neoliberal Challenge*. New York: St. Martin's Press.

Riddell, Roger C. (1987), *Foreign Aid Reconsidered*. Baltimore: Johns Hopkins University Press.

——— (1993), "European Aid to Sub-Saharan Africa: Performance in the 1980s and Future Prospects." *European Journal of Economic Development*, Vol.4, No.1.

Robinson, Mark. (1993), "Aid, Democracy and Political Conditionality in Sub-Saharan Africa." *European Journal of Development Research*, Vol. 5, No.1, pp.85-99.

Rosecrance, Richard and Zara Steiner. (1993), "British Grand Strategy and the Origins of World War II," in Richard Rosecrance and Arthur Stein (eds), *The Domestic Bases of Grand Strategy*. Ithaca, NY: Cornell University Press.

Rosenau, James. (1990), *Turbulence in World Politics: A Theory of Change and Continuity*. Princeton: Princeton University Press.

Rosenberg, Alexander. (1986), "Lakatosian Consolations for Economics." *Economics and Philosophy*, Vol.2, pp.127-39.

Rostow, W.W. (1960), *The Stages of Economic Growth: A Non-Communist Manifesto*. Cambridge: Cambridge University Press.

Rubin, S.J. (1966), *The Conscience of the Rich Nations*. New York: Harper and Row.

Ruggie, John Gerard. (1995), "The False Premise of Realism." *International Security*, Vol.20, No.1, pp.62-70.

Rummel, R.J. (1968), "The Relationship Between National Attributes and Foreign Conflict Behavior," in J. David Singer (ed.), *Quantitative International Politics: Insights and Evidence*, New York: The Free Press.

Russett, Bruce. (1996), "Why Democratic Peace," in Michael E. Brown, Sean M. Lynn-Jones, and Steven Miller (eds), *Debating the Democratic Peace: An International Security Reader*. Cambridge, Massachusetts and London, England: The MIT Press.

Ruttan, Vernon W. (1989),"Why Foreign Economic Assistance." *Economic*

Development and Cultural Change, Vol.37, No.2, pp.411-424.

Sayrs, W. Lois. (1989), *Pooled Time Series Analysis. Sage University Paper 70*: London: Sage Publications.

Schou, August, and Arne Olav Bruntland (eds) (1971), *Small States in International Relations*, Stockholm: Almqvist and Wiksell.

Schraeder, Peter J. (1995), "From Berlin 1884 to 1989: Foreign Assistance and French, American, and Japanese Competition in Francophone Africa." *Journal of Modern African Studies*, Vol.33, No.4, pp.539-567.

Schraeder, Peter J., Steven W. Hook and Bruce Taylor. (1998), "Clarifying the Foreign Aid Puzzle: A Comparison of American, Japanese, French, and Swedish Aid Flows." *World Politics*, Vol.50, No.2, pp.294-323.

Schroeder, Paul W. (1994), *The Transformation of European Politics*, 1763-1848. Oxford: Clarendon Press.

——— (1994), "Historical Reality vs. Neorealist Theory." *International Security*, Vol.19, pp.108-48.

Schweller, Randall L. (1994), "Bandwagoning for Profit: Bringing the Revisionist State Back In." *International Security*, Vol.19, pp.72-107.

Sirleaf, Ellen Johnson. (1996), "Rethinking Aid to Africa." *Development*, No.2, pp.59-63.

Small, Melvin and J. David Singer. (1976), "The War Proneness of Democratic Regimes." *Jerusalem Journal of International Relations*, Vol.1, No.4, pp.50-69.

Snidal, Duncan. (1991), "Relative Gains and the Pattern of International Cooperation." *American Political Science Review*, Vol.85, No.3, pp.702-726.

——— (1991), "International Cooperation Among Relative Gains Maximizers." *International Studies Quarterly*, No.35, pp.387-402.

Sorensen, Georg. (1992), "Kant and the Processes of Democratization: Consequences for Neorealist Thought." *Journal of Peace Research*, Vol.29, No.4, pp.397-414.

Spiro, E. David. (1996), "The Insignificance of the Liberal Peace," in Michael E. Brown, Sean M. Lynn-Jones and Steven Miller (eds.), *Debating the Democratic Peace: An International Security Reader*. Cambridge, Massachusetts and London, England: The MIT Press.

Stein, Arthur. (1990), *Why Nations Cooperate: Circumstance and Choice in International Relations*. Ithaca, NY: Cornell University Press.

Sterling-Folker, Jennifer (1997), "Realist Environment, Liberal Process, and Domestic-Level Variables." *International Studies Quarterly*, No. 41, pp.1-25.

Stokke, Olav. (1989), "The Determinants of Aid Policies: General Introduction," in Olav Stokke (ed.), *Western Middle Powers and Global Poverty: Determinants of the Aid Policies of Canada, Denmark, the Netherlands, Norway, and Sweden*. Uppsala: Scandinavian Institute of African Studies.

——— (1989), "The Determinants of Norwegian Aid Policy," in Olav Stokke (ed.), *Western Middle Powers and Global Poverty: Determinants of the Aid Policies of Canada, Denmark, the Netherlands, Norway, and Sweden*. Uppsala: Scandinavian Institute of African Studies.

(1991), "Policies, Performance, Trends and Challenges in Aid Evaluation," in Olav Stokke (ed.), *Evaluating Development Assistance: Policies and Performance*. London: Frank Cass.

(1996), "Foreign Aid: What Now?" in Olav Stokke (ed.), *Foreign Aid Towards the Year 2000: Experiences and Challenges*. London: Frank Cass.

Stopford, John, Susan Strange, and John S. Henley. (1991), *Rival States, Rival Firms: Competition for World Market Shares*. Cambridge: Cambridge University Press.

Suganami, Hidemi. (1983), "A Normative Enquiry in International Relations: The Case of 'Pacta Sunt Servanda'," *Review of International Studies*, No.9, pp.35-54.

Svedson, Knud Erik. (1989), "Danish Aid," in Olav Stokke (ed.), *Western Middle Powers and Global Poverty: Determinants of the Aid Policies of Canada, Denmark, the Netherlands, Norway, and Sweden*. Uppsala: Scandinavian Institute of African Studies.

Therien, Jean-Philippe and Alain Noel. (1994), "Welfare Institutions and Foreign Aid: Domestic foundations of Canadian Foreign Policy." *Canadian Journal of Political Science*, Vol.XXVII, No.3, pp.529-558.

Thompson, William. R. (1996), "Democracy and Peace: Putting the Cart Before the Horse?" *International Organization*, Vol.50, No.1, pp.141-74.

Thucydides. (1954), *The Peloponnesian War*. Translated by Rex Warner. Harmondsworth, UK: Penguin Books.

Tickner, Ann. (1991), "Hans Morgenthau's Principles of Political Realism: A Feminist Reformulation," in R. Grant and K. Newland (eds.), *Gender and International Relations*. Bloomington: Indiana University Press.

Tisch, Sarah J. and Michael B. Wallace. (1994), *The Dilemmas of Development Assistance: The What, Why, and Who of Foreign Aid*. Boulder, CO: Westview Press.

Tsoutsoplides, Constantine. (1991), "The Determinants of the Geographical Allocation of EC Aid to Developing Countries." *Applied Economics*, Vol.23, No.4a, pp.647-568.

United Nations Development Program. *Human Development Report*. New York: Oxford University Press. (Various Years)

United Nations Development Program. *World Table of Economic and Social Indicators*. Washington, D.C. (Various Years).

Uvin, Peter. (1998), *Aiding Violence: The Development Enterprise in Rwanda*. Hartford, CT: Kumarian Press (1998).

Van Evera, Stephen. (1984), "The Cult of the Offensive and the Origins of the First World War." *International Security*, No.9, pp.58-107.

(1991), "Primed for Peace: Europe After the Cold War." *International Security*, No.15, pp.7-57.

(1990), "Why Europe Matters, Why the Third World Doesn't: American Grand Strategy After the Cold War." *The Journal of Strategic Studies*, Vol.13, No.2, pp.1-51.

Vasquez, John A. (1997), "The Realist Paradigm and Degenerative versus Progressive Research Programs: An Appraisal of Nontraditional Research on Waltz's Balancing Proposition." *American Political Science Review*, No.91, pp.899-912.

Vengroff, Richard. (1982), "Food and Dependency: P.L. 480 Aid to Black Africa." *Journal of Modern African Studies*, Vol.20, No.1, pp.27-43.

Vengroff Richard and Yung Mei Tsai. (1982), "Food, Hunger, and Dependency: PL 480 Aid to the Third World." *Journal of Asian and African Studies*, Vol.XVII, No.3-4 pp.250-265.

Vital, David. (1967), "The Inequality of States: A Study of the Small Powers," in *International Relations*, London: Oxford University Press.

Walker, Stephen G. (1987), "Role Theory and the International System: A Postscript to Waltz's Theory of International Politics?" in Stephen G. Walker (ed.), *Role Theory and Foreign Policy Analysis*. Durham: NC Duke University Press.

Wallerstein, Immanuel. (1974), *The Modern World System: Capitalist Agriculture and the Origins of the European World Economy in the Sixteenth Century*. London: Academic Press.

Walt, Steven M. (1987), *The Origin of Alliances*. Ithaca, NY: Cornell University Press.

——— (1997), "The Progressive Power of Realism." *American Political Science Review*, Vol.91, No.4, pp.931-35.

Waltz, Kenneth N. (1979), *Theory of International Politics*. Reading, Massachusetts: Addison Wesley.

——— (1970), "The Myth of National Interdependence," in Charles Kindleberger, (ed.), *The International Corporation*. Cambridge, Massachusetts: MIT Press.

——— "The Spread of Nuclear Weapons: More May Be Better." *Adelphi Papers*, No.171.

——— (1986), "Reflections on Theory of International Politics: A Response to My Critics," in Robert O. Keohane (ed.), *Neorealism and its Critics*. New York: Columbia University Press.

——— (1993), "The Emerging Structure of the International System." *International Security*, Vol.18, No.2, pp.44-79.

——— (1995), "Realist Thought and Neorealist Theory," in Charles W. Kegley (ed.), *Controversies in International Relations Theory: Realism and the Neoliberal Challenge*. New York: St. Martin's Press.

——— (1997), "Evaluating Theories." *American Political Science Review*, Vol. 91, No.4, pp.913-17.

Weede, Erich. (1983), "Extended Deterrence and Super Power Alliance." *Journal of Conflict Resolution*, 27:2 (June, 1983): 231-253.

——— (1984), "Democracy and War Involvement." *Journal of Conflict Resolution*, Vol.28, No.4, pp.649-664.

——— (1989), "Extended Deterrence, Super Power Control, and Militarized Interstate Disputes." *Journal of Peace Research*, Vol.26, No.1, pp.7-17.

——— (1992), "Some Simple Calculations on Democracy and War Involvement." *Journal of Peace Research*, Vol.29, No.4, pp.377-383.

Weinstein, Brian. (1976), Francophonie: A Language Based Movement in World Politics." *International Organization*, Vol.29, No.1, pp.133-167.

Wendt, Alexander. (1992), "Anarchy is What States Make of it: The Social Construction of Power Politics." *International Organization*, No.46, pp.391-426.

Whiteman, Kaye. (1983), "President Mitterrand and Africa." *African Affairs*, No.82:328, pp.329-45.

Wittkopf, Eugene R. (1992), *Western Bilateral Aid Allocations: A Comparative Study of Recipient State Attributes and Aid Received*. Beverly Hills, CA: Sage.

Wofson, D.J. (1979), *Public Finance and Development Strategy*. Baltimore: Johns Hopkins University Press.

Wood, Robert E. (1986), *From the Marshall Plan to the Debt Crisis: Foreign Aid and Development Choices in the World Economy*. Berkeley, CA: University of California Press.

Young, Crawford. (1991), "Democratization and Structural Adjustment: A Political Overview," in Lulal Dang, Markus Kostner and Crawford Young (eds), *Democratization and Structural Adjustment in Africa in the 1990s*. Madison: University of Wisconsin, African Studies Program.

Zacher, Mark W. and Richard A. Matthew. "Liberal International Theory: Common Threads, Divergent Strands," in Charles W. Kegley (ed.), *Controversies in International Relations Theory: Realism and the Neoliberal Challenge*. New York: St. Martin's Press.

Zakaria, Fareed. (1997), "The Rise of Illiberal Democracy." *Foreign Affairs*, (November/December), pp.22-43.

(1993), "Is Realism Finished?" *The National Interest*, No.30.

Index

Abelin Report 87
Afghanistan 154
African Financial Community (CFA) 94
African Growth and Opportunity Act 157
AICs 6, 38, 48, 68, 74, 78, 134, 161
aid conditionality: Japan 113, 115
Algeria 75
American food aid 17
American-British war 45
Ampiah, Kweku 4, 109
anarchy 29
Anglophone 16, 116
Angola 39, 63, 140
Argentina 184
Aron, Raymond 28
Arusha Declaration 59
Asia 7, 59
Asia-Africa Cooperation 113
assimilation policy 89
Austria 136
Awolowo, Obafemi 108

balance of power 29, 35
Balladur, Edouard 95
bandwagon 34, 80
Bauer, Peter 32
Beijing conference 188
Benin 39, 89, 130
Berlin Wall 1
besoin de rayonnement 91
Beta 51-54
Biersteker, Thomas 24

bipolarity 77
Blair, Tony 71
BMZ 61
Bobrow, Davis 42, 50, 120
Boigny, Houphouet 95
Bosnia 137
Botswana 39, 130
Boyer, Mark 2, 42, 50, 78, 120, 121
Brazil 23, 61, 184
Britain 14, 15
British NGOs 70
British ODA 69
British white paper 69, 71
Bruntland, Gro Harlem 134
Brzenzinski, Zbigniew 154
buck-passing 35
budgetary constraints 178
Burkina Faso 39, 59, 147, 186
Burundi 12, 39, 91
Bush, George 1, 157
Bush, George (Jr.) 158

Cairo 66
Cairo: Population Conference 188
Cambodia 115
Cameroon 39, 89, 94, 101, 105
Camp David accords 122
Canada 8, 38, 48, 50, 55, 75, 78
Canadian ODA 55
Caprioli, Mary 5
Carr, Edward Hallet 10
Carter, Jimmy 157
CEECs/NIS 68, 70, 71, 94, 182
Center Party 131
Central African Republic 39, 131

Index

CFA 94, 105
CFA Franc 92, 104
Chad 39, 115, 131, 147
chain ganging 35
China 61, 115, 121, 124, 126, 146
Christian Democrats 63
Christian People Party 131
CIDA 178
Clinton, William 45, 155, 157, 158
Cold War 1, 2, 92
Colombo Plan 107
colonial ties 43, 69
COMECON 154
Commonwealth 57
communism 2
Comparison of Favorite Recipients of France's ODA 100
Comparison of Favorite Recipients of Norway's ODA 137-138
competitive security 77
Congo 39, 63, 146
Congressional Black Caucus 148
Connecticut Project in International Negotiation 185
Conservative Party 131
Copenhagen summit 188
Cote d'Ivoire 39, 69, 94, 101, 105, 117, 130, 131, 164
Cuban missile crisis 90
cultural similarity 20

DAC 2, 4, 7, 8, 10, 21, 22, 44, 50, 56, 59, 64, 65, 68, 70, 72, 82, 91, 96, 106, 110, 111, 133, 145, 160, 164-167, 180, 186, 188
Dahrendrof, Ralf 28
Danish Law on international development cooperation 58
Danish ODA 58
Darwinian Process 23, 24, 26
Davenport, M. 11, 12, 15
de Gaulle, Charles 84

defense 40
    expenditure as aid conditionality 40, 63, 113
democracy 44
democratic peace 4
democratization as aid conditionality 2, 114
Denmark 8, 9, 19, 48, 50, 57, 79, 80
dependency 23
dependent variable 38
Desch, Michael 32
development 66
DFID 71
Dien Bien Phu 90
Dimensions of France's ODA 102
Dimensions of Japan's ODA 117
Dimensions of Norway's ODA 134
Dimensions of US ODA 151
donors 48

Eberstadt, Nicholas 32
Economic Support Fund (ESF) 147
economic variables 42
effectiveness of aid 168-170
Egypt 61, 94, 122, 155
El Salvador 134
Engels, Friedrich 25
Engen committee 131
Ethiopia 39, 61, 63, 64, 75, 146, 149, 153, 183
European Community 18
European Union 6

FDI 43, 65, 74, 115, 123, 130
flying geese pattern of aid 110
FMP 40, 65, 69, 131
foreign investment 4
France 7, 15, 38, 50, 75, 78, 80, 82, 87-105
Freedom House 45

G7 countries 38, 80, 104

Gabon 39, 69, 75, 101, 105, 117, 131
Gaiatsu 121
GDP 41
generalized least square error component (GLSE) 47
genocide in Rwanda 146
Germany 2, 14, 15, 38, 48, 53, 60, 62, 75, 76, 78, 172
Ghana 39, 59, 61, 72, 114, 117, 154, 186
Gilpin, Robert 5, 19, 23, 24, 25, 30, 31, 120, 163
Gingrich, Newt 149
Global Coalition for Africa 112
globalization 31
GNP 64
Gorbachev, Mikhail 1
Gore, Albert 152
Grieco, Joseph 5
Group of Eight 187
Guinea 39, 90

Handwerker, Penn 46
Heilbroner, Robert 25
Helms, Jesse 159
Henderson, P. D. 11, 12, 13, 15
Hiroshima 107
HIV 158, 180
Hoadley, Stephen J. 132
Hong Kong 23, 124, 184
Hook, Steven 17, 19, 20, 21, 43, 77
human rights as aid conditionality 113
humanitarian aid 63
    basis 19
    concerns 150
    motivation 79, 127
    need 19, 41
Hungary 78

IBRD 49
ideological stance 20
IMF 50
import-substitution industrialization (ISI) 23
independent variables 39, 51
India 61, 124
Indonesia 61, 115
InterAction 148
International Monetary Fund (IMF) 43
investment interest 43, 115
Iran 115
Ishihara, Shintaro 125
Italian Fund for Development 177
Italian ODA 75
Italy 7, 38, 48, 53, 62, 76, 78, 172

Janoski, Thomas 46
Japan 7, 8, 9, 38, 53, 79, 82, 106-128
Jeanneney Report 87
Joint Funding Scheme (IFS) 70

Kabila, Joseph 158
Kant, Immanuel 8
Kegley, Charles 1, 4, 82, 161
Kennedy, John F. 147
Kenya 39, 59, 109, 114, 154, 171
    fertility studies 152
Krueger, Ann 22
Kuhn, Thomas 11

La Baule Summit 88
La Francophonie 55, 90, 104
La Rochefoucauld 80
Lakatos, Imre 26
Lakatosian model 36
Latin America 7, 23, 59, 64, 172, 184
Layne, Christopher 5, 78
LDCs 18, 48, 70, 71, 118, 133, 136
Lesotho 39
Lewinsky, Monica 158
Liberal Democratic Party 125
liberal theory 30
liberalism 23

liberalism/neoliberalism 32
Liberia 39, 115
Little, R. 15, 17, 18, 22,
LLDCs 22, 93, 98, 111, 157
Lumsdaine, David 7, 17, 19, 32, 41
  46, 49, 79, 81
Lumunba, Patrice 146

Maastricht 62
Machiavelli, Niccolo 30
Madagascar 39, 101
Maizels, Alfred 17, 18, 46, 116
Malawi 2, 39
Mali 39, 147, 183
marginalization 3, 6, 7, 73, 162
Marshall, George C. 49
Marshall plan 50
Marx, Karl 25
Mathematical Formulation of the
  Strategic Mineral (SMI) 191-194
Matthew, Richard 30, 33
Mauritania 39, 147
Mauritius 39
McKinlay, R. D. 15, 17, 18, 19, 22
methodological issues 15
methodology 45-46
Mikesell, Raymond 21
Ministry of Foreign Affairs (MFA)
  65, 139
Mitterrand, Francois 88, 91
Miyazawa, Kiichi 113, 125
Mobutu, Sese Sekou 75, 171
Modern World Systems (MWS) Theory
  24
Morgenthau, Hans 5, 29, 32, 74
Mozambique 39, 61, 63, 64,
  71, 134, 140, 164, 183
Mueller, John 5, 126

NAFTA 178
Nagasaki 107
national interest 28

national role conception 129
NATO 6, 122
Nelson, Joan M. 14
New Caledonia 94
New Zealand 136
NGOs 38, 66
Niger 39, 59, 88, 147
Nigeria 39, 70, 75, 89, 108, 115
  130, 164
Nissanke, Machiko 17, 18, 46, 116
Nixon-Kissinger's initiatives 154
NORAD 139
North Korea 124, 126
Norway 9, 19, 53, 75, 78, 79, 80,
  82, 129-144
Nyerere, Julius 59

Obasanjo, Olusegun 157
Occam's razor 44
ODA 7, 13, 37, 38, 47, 57, 60, 62,
  63, 64, 65, 66, 67, 75, 76, 78,
  91, 94, 95, 104, 106, 109,
  111, 115, 122, 130, 148, 160
  Charter 106, 113
ODA/GNP ratio 67, 70, 80, 93, 97
  104, 109, 110, 111, 133, 140,
  147, 149, 155, 159, 161
  target 67
OECD 17, 44, 49, 106
OEEC 49
Ogaden 151
Olsen, Gorm-Rye 20, 21
ordinary least square (OLS) 46
Ostrom, Charles 46

Packenham, Robert 23
Pakistan 61, 124
Palestinians 134
Pearson, Lester 32, 56
Pincus, J. A. 14
Poland 78, 79
political support for aid 176

Pompidou, Georges 91
pooled time series 47
Portugal 136
Powell, Colin 158
public goods 122
Public Law 99, 63, 177

Radical Party 63
Reagan, Ronald 148
realism/neorealism 1, 23, 32
Reform Bill 65
regime 49, 77
relative gains 77
reparations 107
Results of Pooled Time-Series Regression 51
Romania 78
Russia 1, 140
Rwanda 12, 39, 75, 91, 146, 149, 153, 158, 171, 186

SAREC 67
SAS 47
Schraeder, Peter 17, 19, 20, 21, 43
Selassie, Haile 154
Senegal 39, 69, 94, 101, 114, 117, 130, 147, 183
SIDA 67, 68
Sierra Leone 39, 63, 70, 115
Singapore 23, 184
small donors hypothesis 135
socialism 24
socialization 76
Somalia 12, 39, 63, 64, 75, 115, 149, 153, 154, 171
sources of threats to the continuation of aid 176
South Africa 155
South Korea 23, 184
SPSS 47
Storting Report 130
strategic 2, 39
    importance 19, 39

mineral index (SMI) 9, 41, 47, 60, 75, 116
minerals 17, 18, 40, 75
Sudan 39, 61, 114, 153, 171
Summit on Africa 186
Sweden 9, 19, 48, 53, 65, 75, 76, 78, 79, 80
SYSTAT 47

t Scores 50, 53, 54
Taiwan 23, 184
Tanzania 39, 59, 61, 64, 71, 109, 117, 140, 164, 171, 183
the impact of the end of the Cold War on aid 182-183
theoretical perspective 32
Thucydides 30
Togo 39, 89
Tokyo agenda 112
Tokyo International Conference on African Development 112
Top Ten Recipients of France's Aid 97
Top Ten Recipients of Japan's Aid 118
Top Ten Recipients of Norway's Aid 140
Top Ten Recipients of US Aid 155
trading interest 42
Truman, Harry 91
Tsousoplides, Constantine 17, 18, 46
Tunisia 90
Turkey 61

Uganda 39, 71, 109, 140
Ukraine 79
underdevelopment 23
United Kingdom 38, 41, 48, 53, 69, 76, 172
United Nations Charter 58
United Nations Development Program (UNDP) 58, 189

United Nations recommendation 80
United States 2, 7, 8, 9, 14, 15, 38, 54, 75, 82, 145-159
USSR 1, 107, 122

Van Evera, Stephen 32
variables 12, 62
Vasquez, John 33, 34, 35
Vengroff, Richard 16, 17, 42, 146

Wallerstein, Immanuel 24
Waltz, Kenneth 5, 7, 29, 30, 45, 77, 82, 117, 120, 125
WID 66

Wittkopf, Eugene 13, 14, 15
Wolfson, D.J. 32
World Bank 92, 104

Yeltsin, Boris 121

Zacher, Mark 30, 33
Zaire 39, 60, 61, 63, 64, 89, 91, 171
Zakaria, Fareed 27
Zambia 39, 61, 71, 109, 114, 130, 171, 183
Zedong, Mao 107
Zimbabwe 39, 60, 130